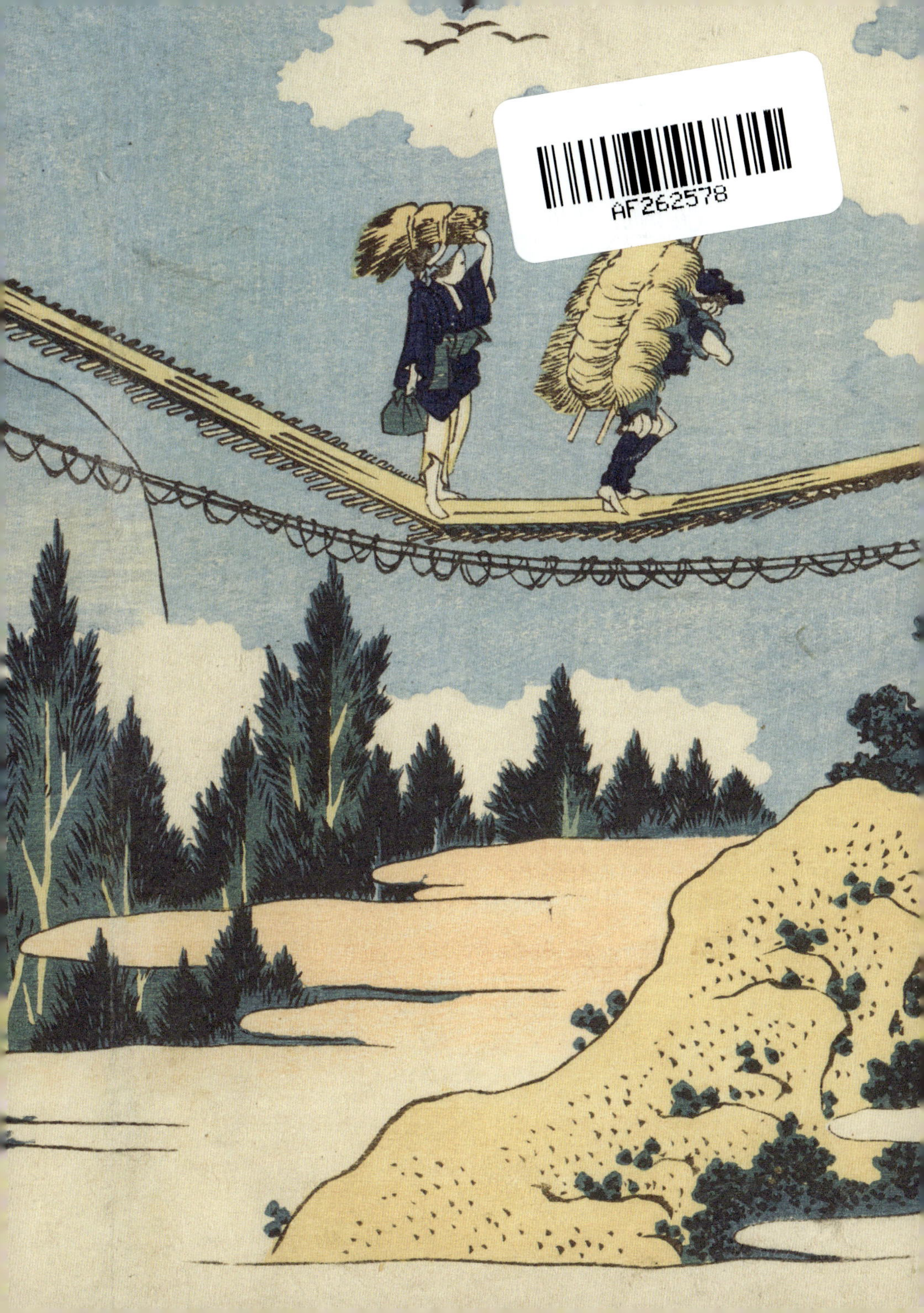
AF262578

KATSUSHIKA HOKUSAI

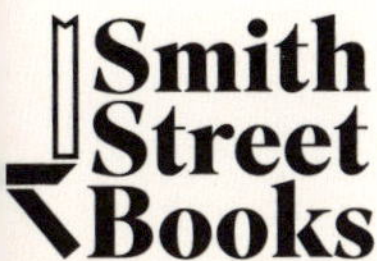

Smith Street Books

The essential masterpieces
by Sally Grant

Introduction

Katsushika Hokusai was born in Edo (now Tokyo) in October 1760. He lived most of his life in that bustling city during a period of incredible cultural and artistic vibrancy. When he was a teenager Hokusai entered the studio of Katsukawa Shunshō, where he was schooled in the creation of *ukiyo-e*, or 'pictures of the floating world'. His depictions of kabuki actors, sumo wrestlers and beautiful women were later joined by masterful prints and paintings of landscapes and nature motifs. A hard-working and highly productive artist, Hokusai also made illustrations for over 250 books, and his total artistic output over the course of his seventy-year career was in the thousands.

Hokusai is most famous for the woodblock print series *Thirty-six views of Mount Fuji*, which includes the iconic *The Great Wave*. With its new focus on the landscape and its technical synthesis of Japanese and European art making, the series was ground-breaking, and a roaring success. Hokusai was then in his seventies, but his insatiable curiosity and verve for life meant many more exceptional artworks were to come before his death, at age eighty-eight, in May 1849. What characterises Hokusai's pictures is a sensitivity to nature and to the lives of ordinary people, which he captures with warm humour and a sense of the divine in the everyday.

The Sumo Wrestlers Uzugafuchi Kandayu and Takasaki Ichijuro

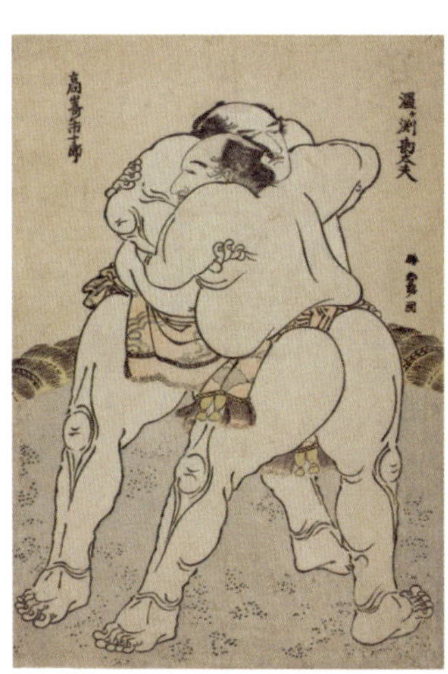

Woodblock print,   1783-1784
ink and colour
on paper
32.7 cm × 22.5 cm
(12⅞ in × 8⅞ in)

Hokusai said that he began drawing at the age of six. Otherwise, we know little of the artist's early years. He was born in the Year of the Dragon, 1760, in Edo, present-day Tokyo, on the 23rd day of the ninth lunar month (31 October in the Gregorian calendar). Who his parents were is unclear. It seems he was adopted by a family of mirror polishers and he may have been the son of Nakajima Ise, the *iemoto*, or family head, and a concubine. When Hokusai was a teenager, he worked as a delivery person for a lending bookstore, and he became an apprentice to a woodblock-cutter. Both roles gave him firsthand experience of an art form for which he would become world renowned.

In 1778 Hokusai became a student of Katsukawa Shunshō (1726–1792). An acclaimed *ukiyo* (floating world) artist, Shunshō was known for innovative woodblock prints of kabuki actors and paintings of beautiful women. For the next fifteen years, Hokusai learnt the skill of his craft in this studio.

Sumo wrestling, like kabuki theatre, was a hugely popular entertainment during the Edo period (1603–1868). This early work already demonstrates Hokusai's skilful means of expression by way of a series of concise, bold lines.

The Sumo Wrestlers Uzugafuchi Kandayu
and Takasaki Ichijuro

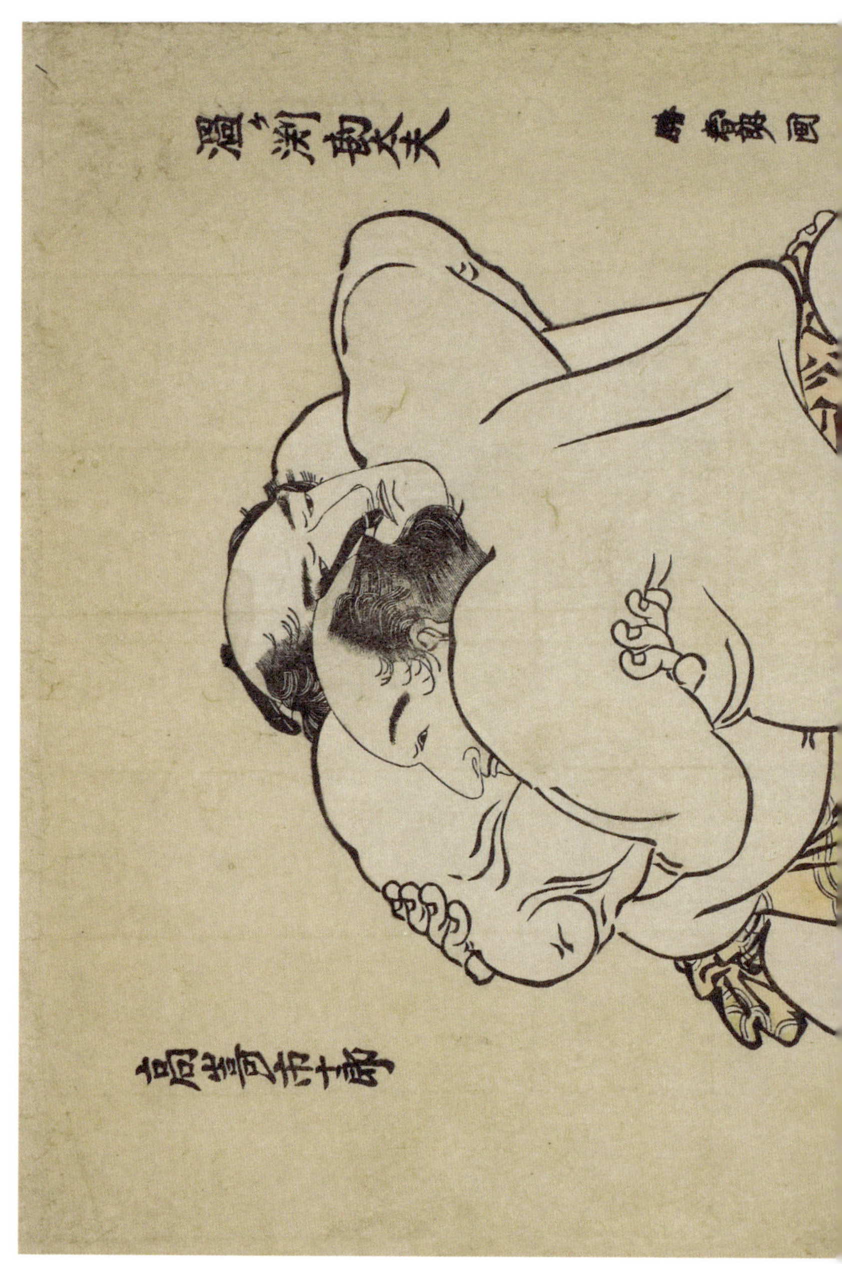

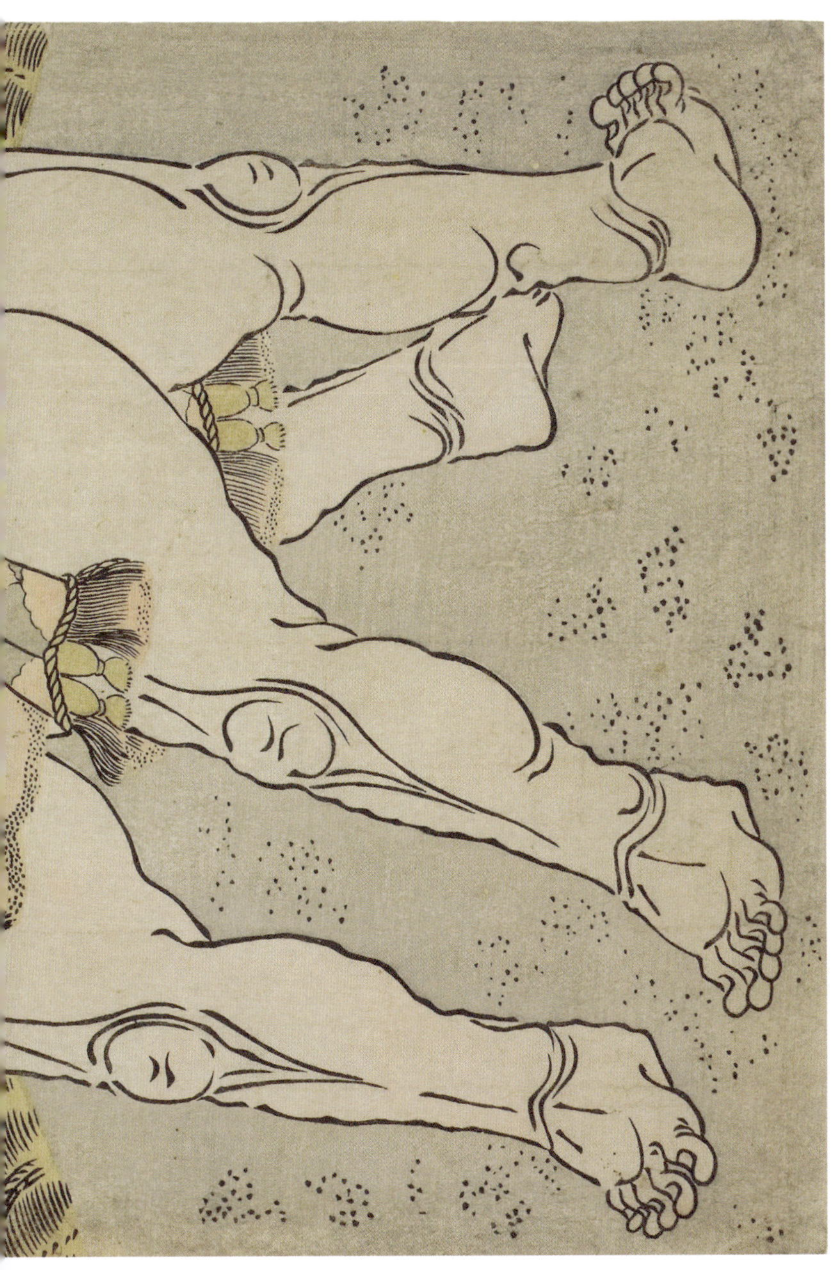

The Day Before the Beginning of Spring

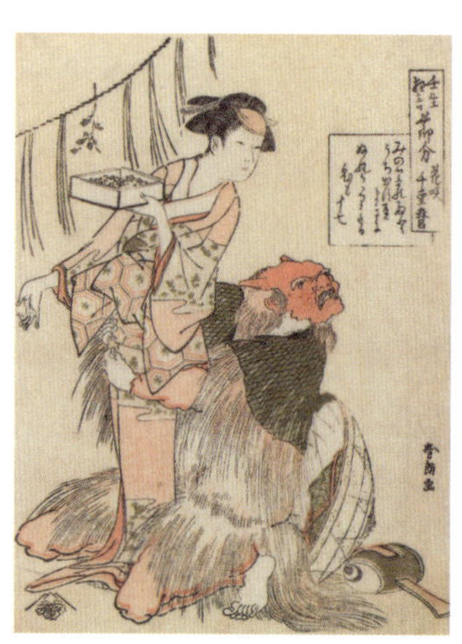

Woodblock print,   c. 1790
ink and colour
on paper
21.2 cm × 15.3 cm
(8¾ in × 6 in)

Towards the end of his apprenticeship with the Kastukawa school (see *The Sumo Wrestlers Uzugafuchi Kandayu and Takasaki Ichijuro* on page 4), Hokusai received a commission from well-known Edo publisher Tsutaya Jūzaburō. The artist's task was to illustrate a selection of contemporary poems on the subject of comic religious plays called *Mibu kyōgen*. *The Day Before the Beginning of Spring* is one example from the collection and it's signed Shunrō, a name Hokusai was given in traditional deference to his teacher, Katsukawa Shunshō.

The play depicted takes as its subject matter a Japanese ritual performed on the eve of spring (*setsubun*), when people throw roasted soybeans around their homes to ward off evil spirits. In this deftly drawn print, freshly coloured in pink and green, a demon clings to an elegantly dressed woman. Yet, as indicated by the box of beans she holds and his angry mask, the demon's entreaties are in vain.

Mibu kyōgen, which presents Buddhist teachings in pantomime form, is now designated an Important Intangible Folk Cultural Property. Performances can still be seen at Mibu-dera Temple in Kyoto (see also *The Bucket Bearer* on page 12).

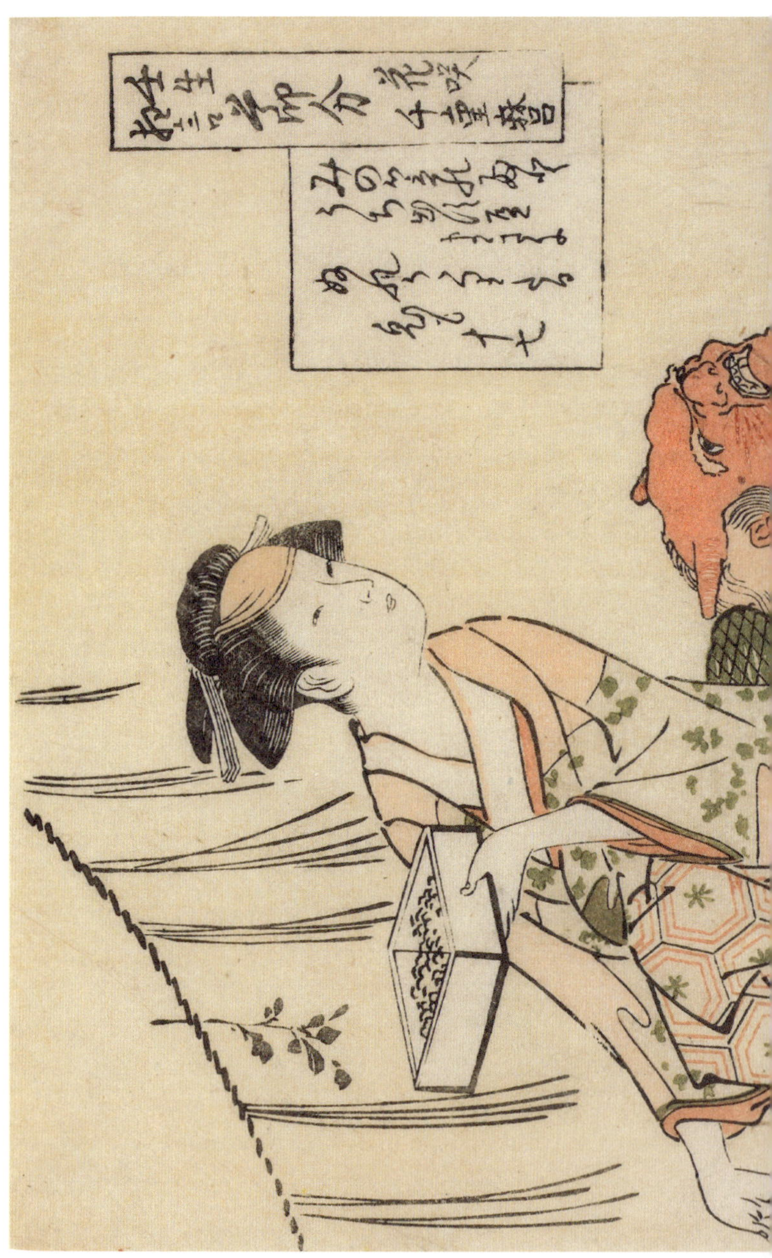

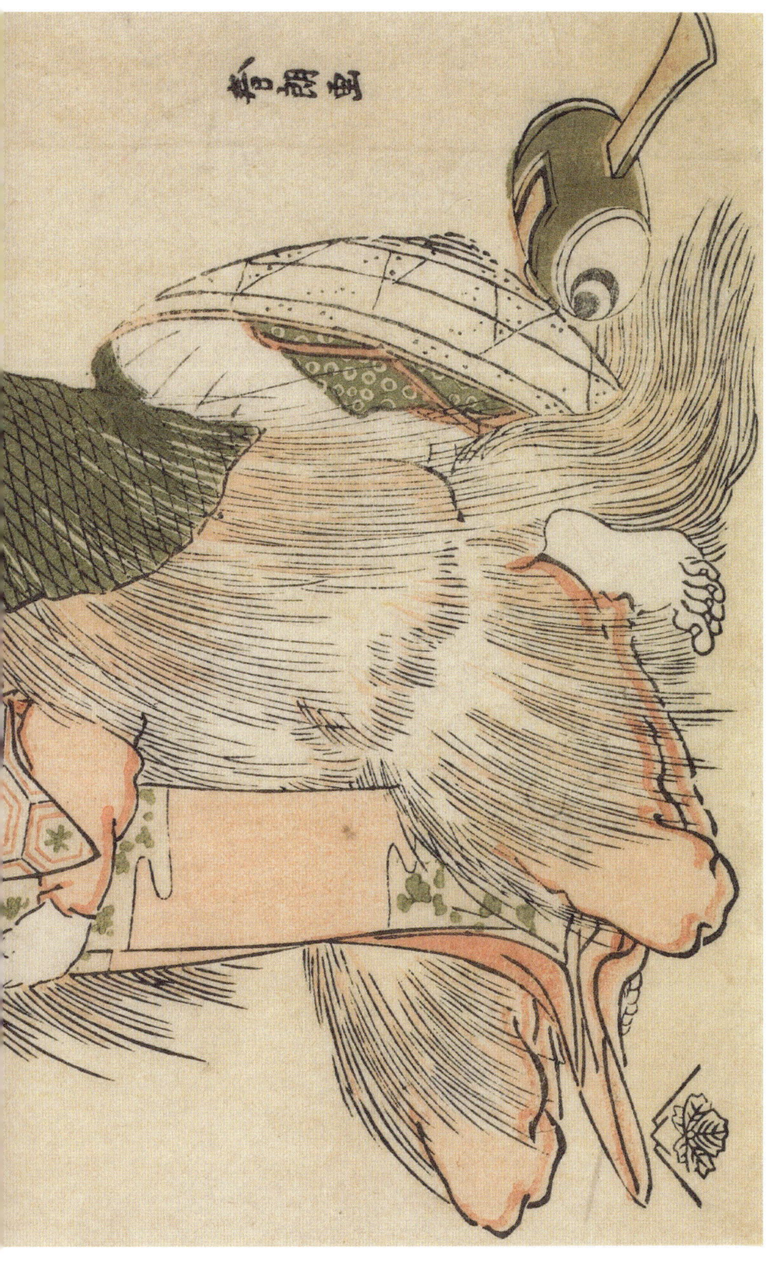

The Bucket Bearer

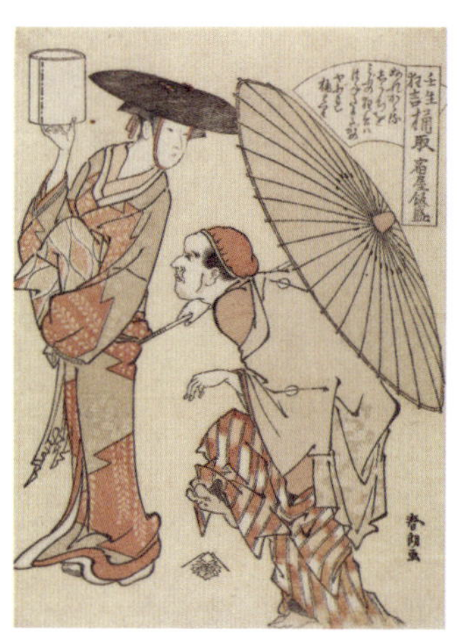

Woodblock print,
ink and colour
on paper
21.1 cm × 15.3 cm
(8¼ in × 6 in)

c. 1790

Adopting a similar compositional arrangement as *The Day Before the Beginning of Spring* (page 8), this illustrated poem from the same collection indicates the Edo period's vibrant literary, artistic and theatrical culture. It also reveals Hokusai's spirited humour.

Like the aforementioned print, *The Bucket Bearer* combines the expressive actor portraits and images of beautiful women that were so popular in early-modern Japan. The inclusion of a poem that is a riff on a key performance at Kyoto's Mibu-dera Temple furthers the print's intellectual sophistication. The play *Oketori* tells of a dancer who brings water to Buddha as an offering. She is spotted by an elderly married man who attempts to seduce her, as the poem by Yadoya no Meshimori (also known as Rokujuen; 1754–1830) in the top right describes.

What is so comical is that Hokusai has portrayed the elderly man fawning over the dancer as the poet, Meshimori. The acclaimed scholar and creator of *kyōka* (mad verse) poetry clearly didn't take offence by the artist's witticism as they collaborated in the future. Hokusai illustrated Meshimori's novel *The Story of a Hida Craftsman* in 1808, and Meshimori later contributed three of the prefaces to Hokusai's famous multi-volume *Manga* (see pages 68 and 72).

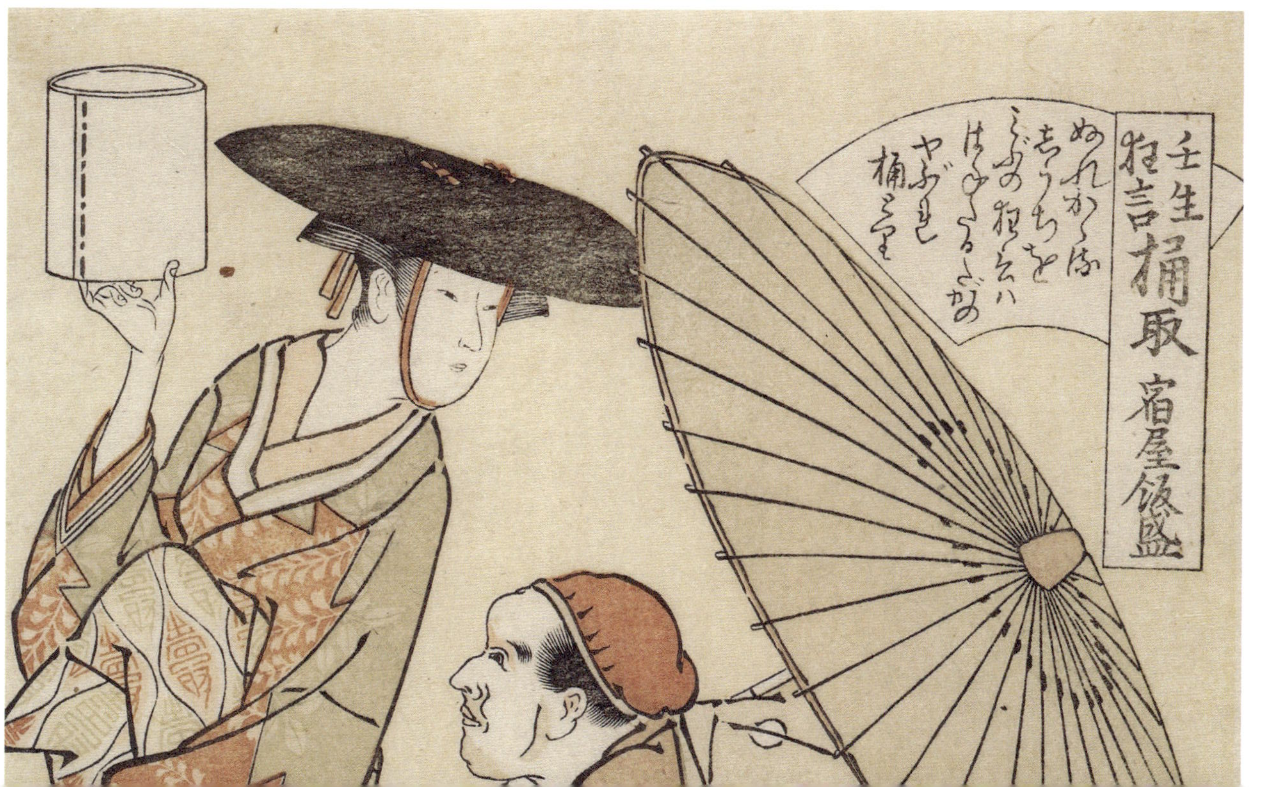

壬生狂言桶取　宿屋飯盛
ぬれかくほ
もうちを
ふぶの狙をハ
はつくるさが
やぶき
桶とて

c. 1790

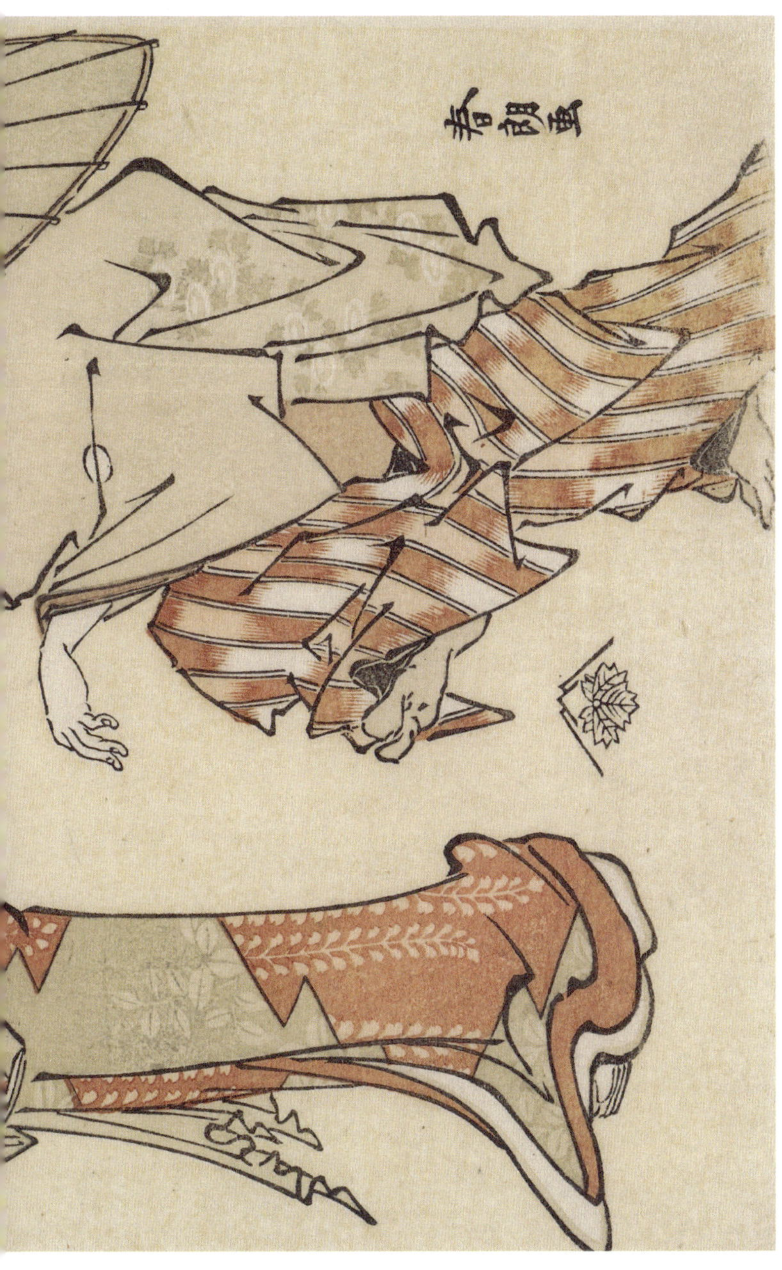

Ichikawa Ebizō (Danjūrō V)

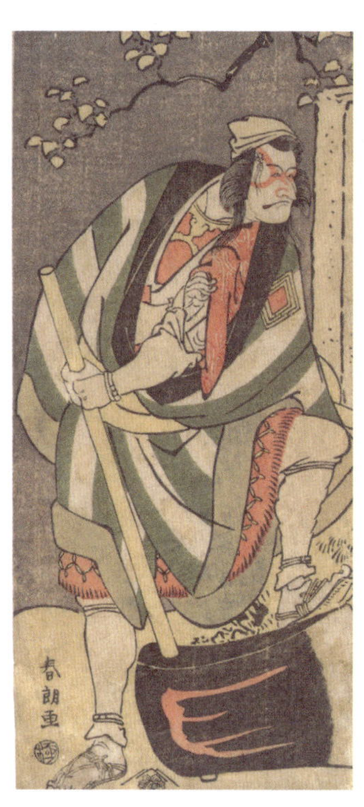

Woodblock print,   1791
ink and colour
on paper
29.8 cm × 13.3 cm
(11¾ in × 5¼ in)

Throughout the largely peaceful and politically stable
Tokugawa or Edo period (1603–1868), Japan was ruled
by the shogun of the Tokugawa family, which governed
from Edo (now Tokyo). As a means of social control, the
shogunate divided society into four classes: warriors,
farmers, artisans and, finally, merchants. Mobility
between the classes was forbidden. Yet, while merchants
were on the lowest rung of the social ladder they were
growing in financial power.

These affluent urbanites frequently sought to spend their
money on entertainment. Cities soon accommodated
this demand with dedicated, government-controlled,
pleasure quarters – in Edo, the area was called Yoshiwara
– as well as restaurants, wrestling venues and theatres.
Kabuki theatre, which emerged in the early seventeenth
century, was hugely popular with the rising bourgeoisie,
and the actors, akin to present-day film or musical stars,
had fervent fans.

Artists and publishing houses responded to this clamour
with affordable portrait prints. Danjūrō V was one of the
most loved kabuki actors, and Hokusai has portrayed
him in a characteristically dramatic moment, with his
foot on a huge axe, and his face suitably expressive.

'From the age of five, I have
had a mania for sketching the
forms of things.'

- Katsushika Hokusai

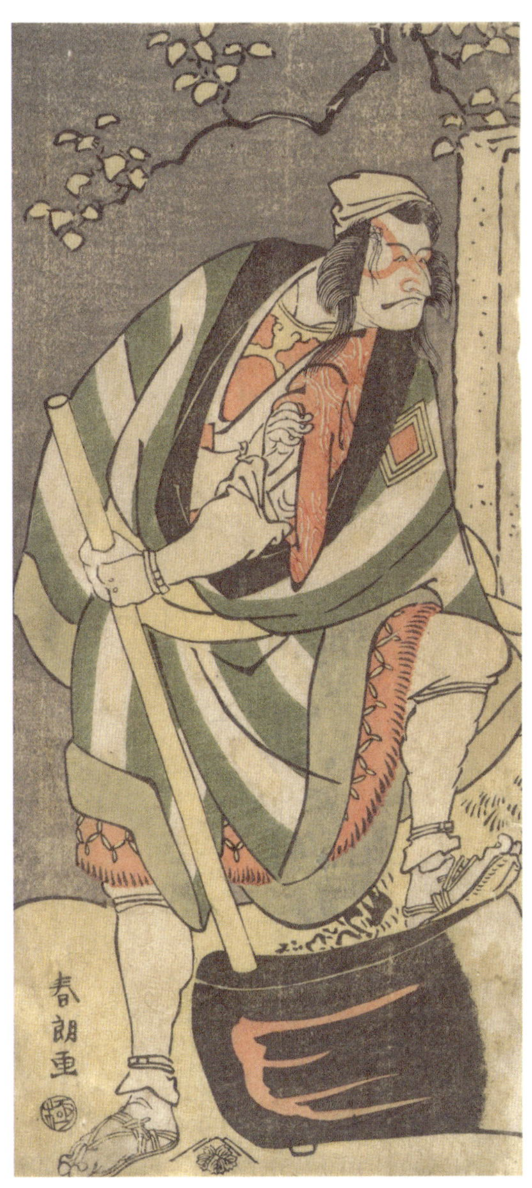

Two Flatfish and
a Plum Branch

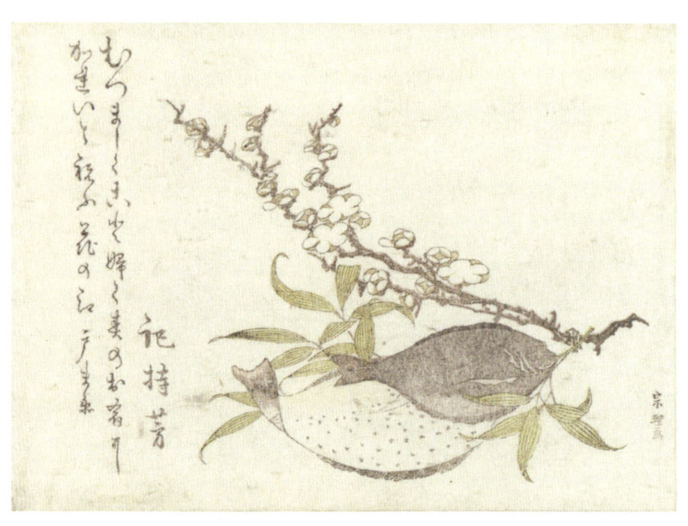

Woodblock print,   c. 1795-1800
ink and colour
on paper
12.4 cm × 16.7 cm
(4⅞ in × 6⅝ in)

Hokusai's master, Shunshō, died in 1793 and Hokusai subsequently left the Kutsukawa school (see *The Sumo Wrestlers Uzugafuchi Kandayu and Takasaki Ichijuro* on page 4). It's unclear why this break occurred, though it's been suggested that his desire to explore other artistic styles was the cause. Certainly, Hokusai's influences ranged widely, from classical Japanese and Chinese art, to modern European painting. The assimilation of various traditions, combined with his irrepressible curiosity and wit, would lead to a masterful style all his own.

From the mid-1790s, when Hokusai was in his thirties, he became immersed in the dazzling literary world of Edo, where there was a flourishing demand for sophisticated works that combined word and image. These included surimono (printed things) and poetry books of lively, sardonic kyōka (mad verse). Hokusai soon became one of the leading illustrators of these genres.

This arresting still life print of two flatfish and a plum (*ume*) branch is an example of *surimono*. These were privately commissioned prints that, like opulent greeting cards, marked special occasions such as the New Year. Thousands of these high-quality prints were made for a cultured literati who delighted in the often complex link between verse and image.

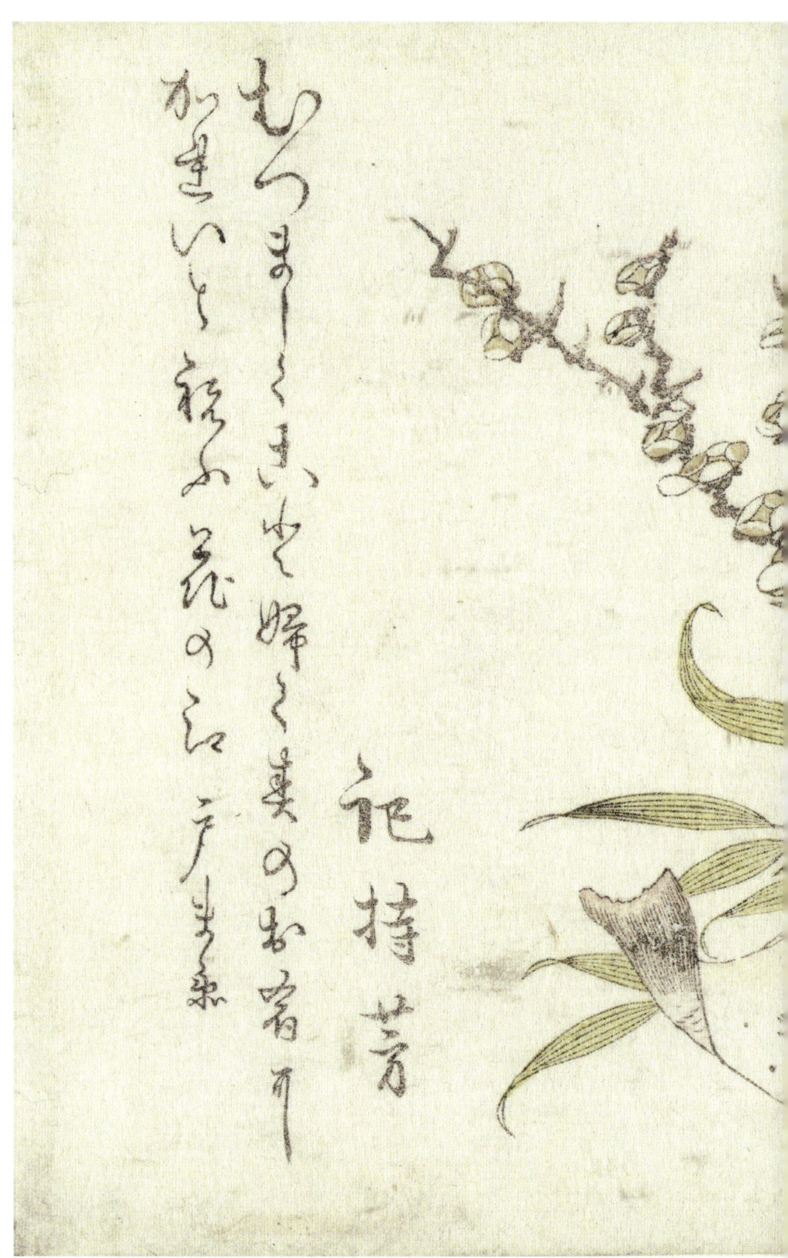

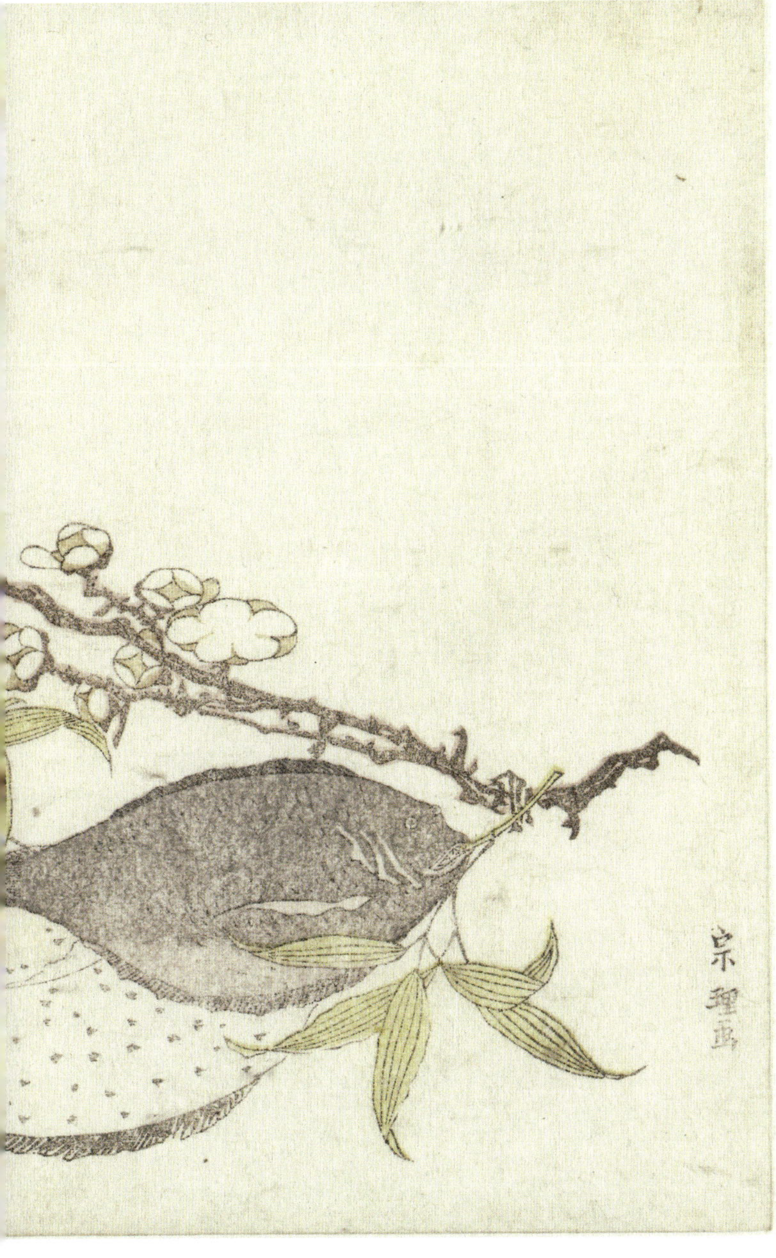

Woman Spinning
Silk

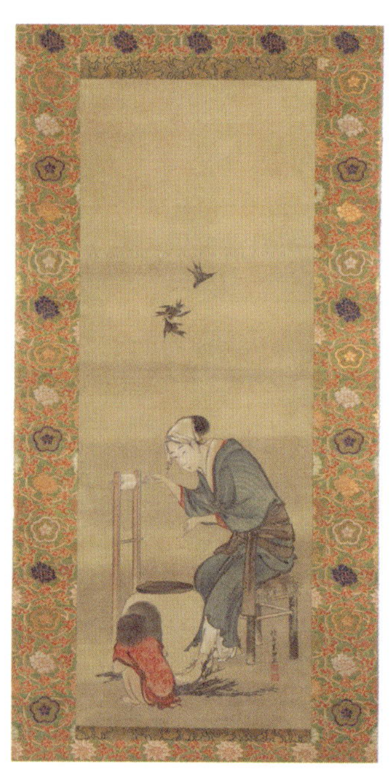

Hanging scroll, ink   1797-1798
and colour on silk
85.8 cm × 31.3 cm
(33¾ in × 12⅜ in)

As well as finding entertainment in the cities' pleasure districts (see *Ichikawa Ebizō* on page 16), the well-to-do working classes sought out painted and printed images of this *ukiyo*, or 'floating world'. The term *ukiyo* is Buddhist in origin and refers to life's ephemeral nature, but the notion that this was a cause of suffering was inverted in the Edo period. Instead, *ukiyo* came to represent a floating world of pleasure.

Ukiyo-e, 'pictures of the floating world', extended Japan's tradition of genre painting – depicting scenes of everyday life – which emerged in the sixteenth century. Responding to their urban clients' desires, artists created pictures of city life and its *demi-monde*, including portraits of actors and courtesans as well as scenes of erotica. *Bijin-ga*, representations of beautiful women, were especially sought after.

Hokusai's fame is largely owed to his woodblock prints, but *Woman Spinning Silk* reveals his exquisite painting ability at this early stage in his career. Rendered on silk, it is a tender depiction of a woman spinning while a child crouches by the stove at her feet. The four swallows represented in the large expanse of negative space above is a delightful foretaste of Hokusai's keenly observed studies of the natural world that were to come.

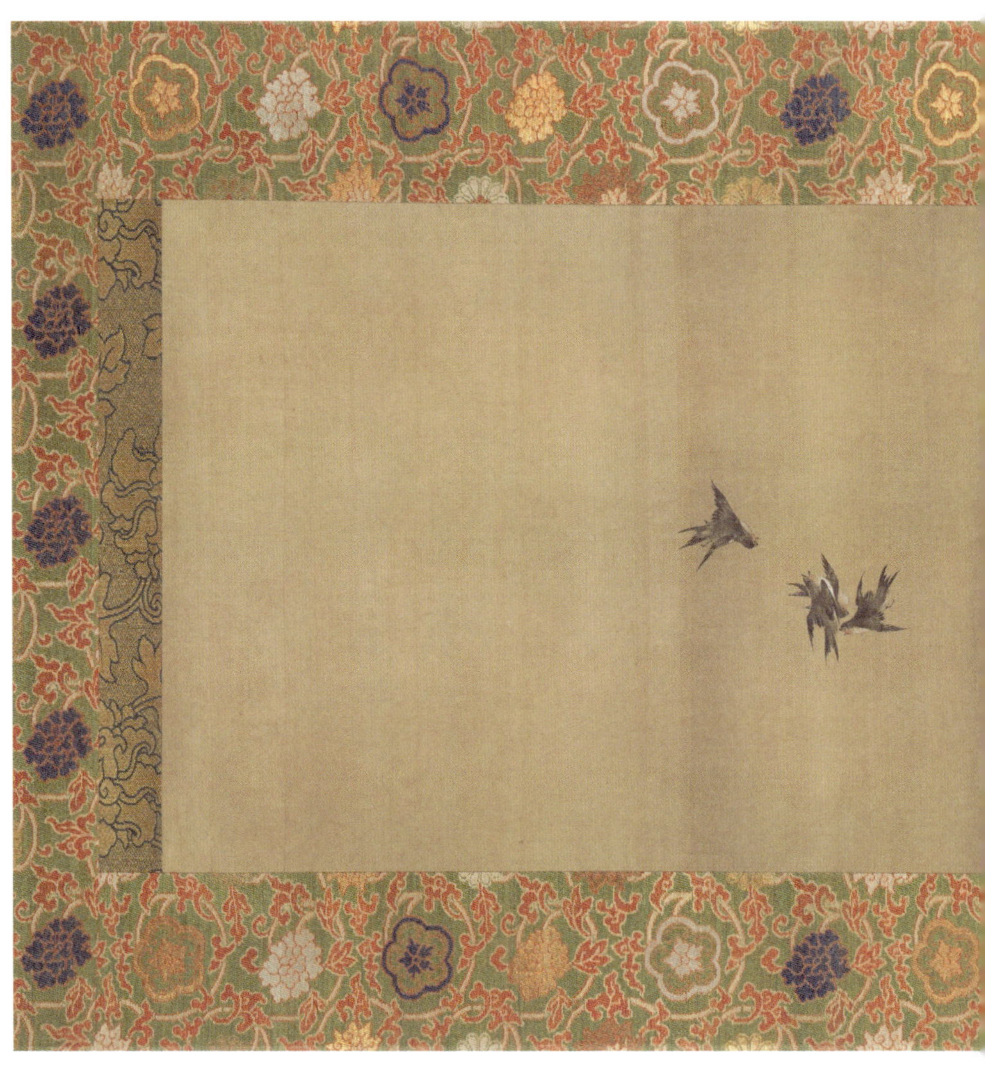

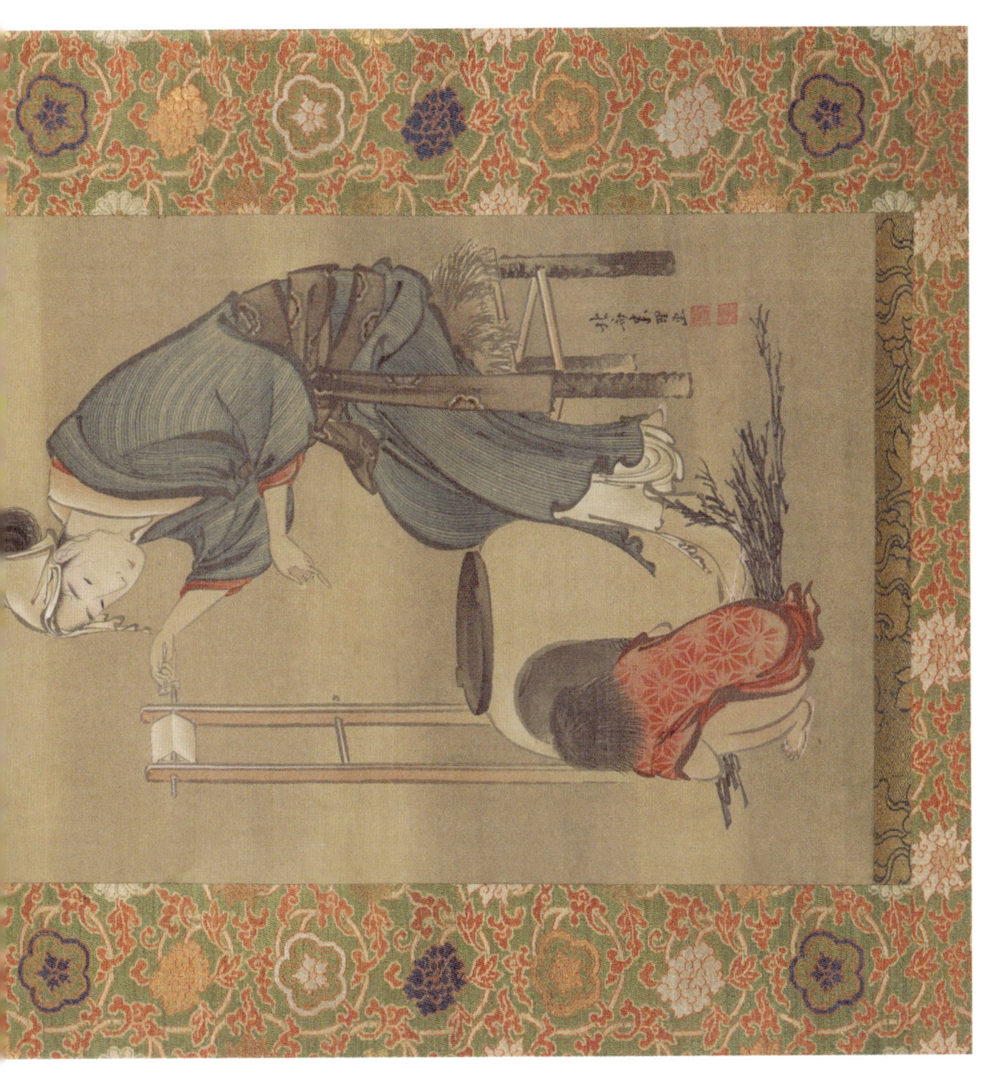

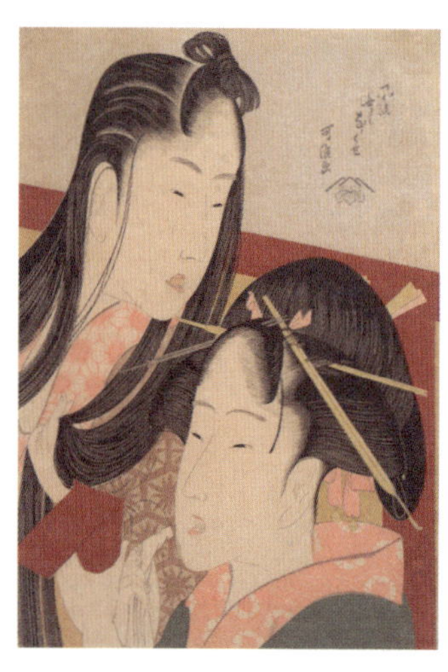

Squeaking a Ground Cherry from the series *Seven fashionable foibles*

Woodblock print,
ink and colour
on paper
36.4 cm × 24.8 cm
(14⅜ in × 9¾ in)

c. 1798

This remarkable composition is a highlight among Hokusai's *bijin-ga* (pictures of female beauties) that he made around the turn of the century. It depicts two courtesans of the Yoshiwara pleasure district getting ready for the day. The woman on the right already has her hair up in the fashionable *shimada* style and she looks in a hand-held mirror to apply her make-up. The figure on the left, whose act of sucking on a ground cherry provides the print's title, is currently less prepared.

Aside from the theatre and other forms of popular entertainment, like boat trips, festivals, and outings to scenic sites and teahouses, the citizens of Edo had access to a separate, licensed red-light area. Regulated by the shogunate, the Yoshiwara pleasure quarters were surrounded by a fence and a moat, with access via a fabled entrance gate. It was a bustling neighbourhood of restaurants, shops and, primarily, brothels, where courtesans and customers, and artists and writers, met.

It seems that this series was one of the last works of the acclaimed publisher Tsutaya Jūzaburō (see also *Shop of the Edo Publisher Tsutaya* on page 32). Sadly, his death in 1797 meant that this design was one of only two published in the intended series.

Squeaking a Ground Cherry from the series
Seven fashionable foibles

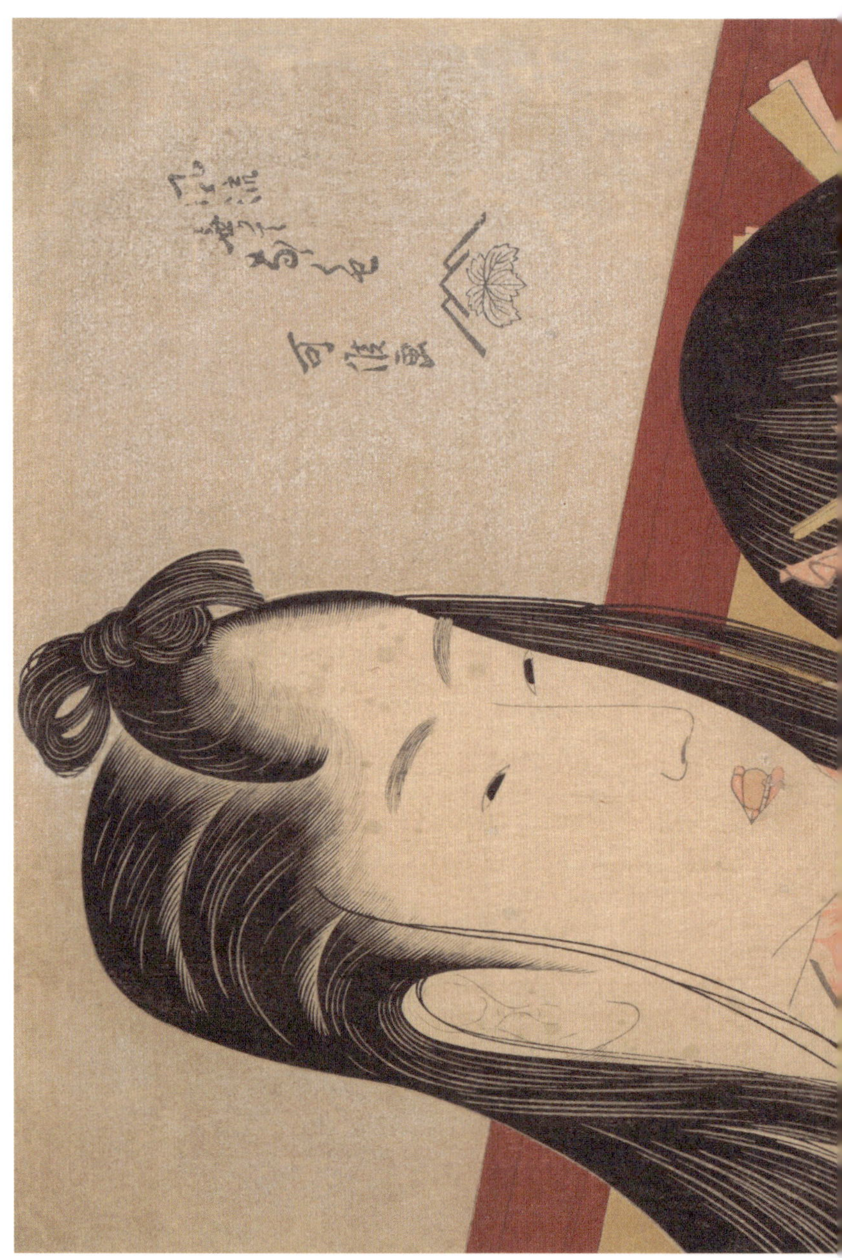

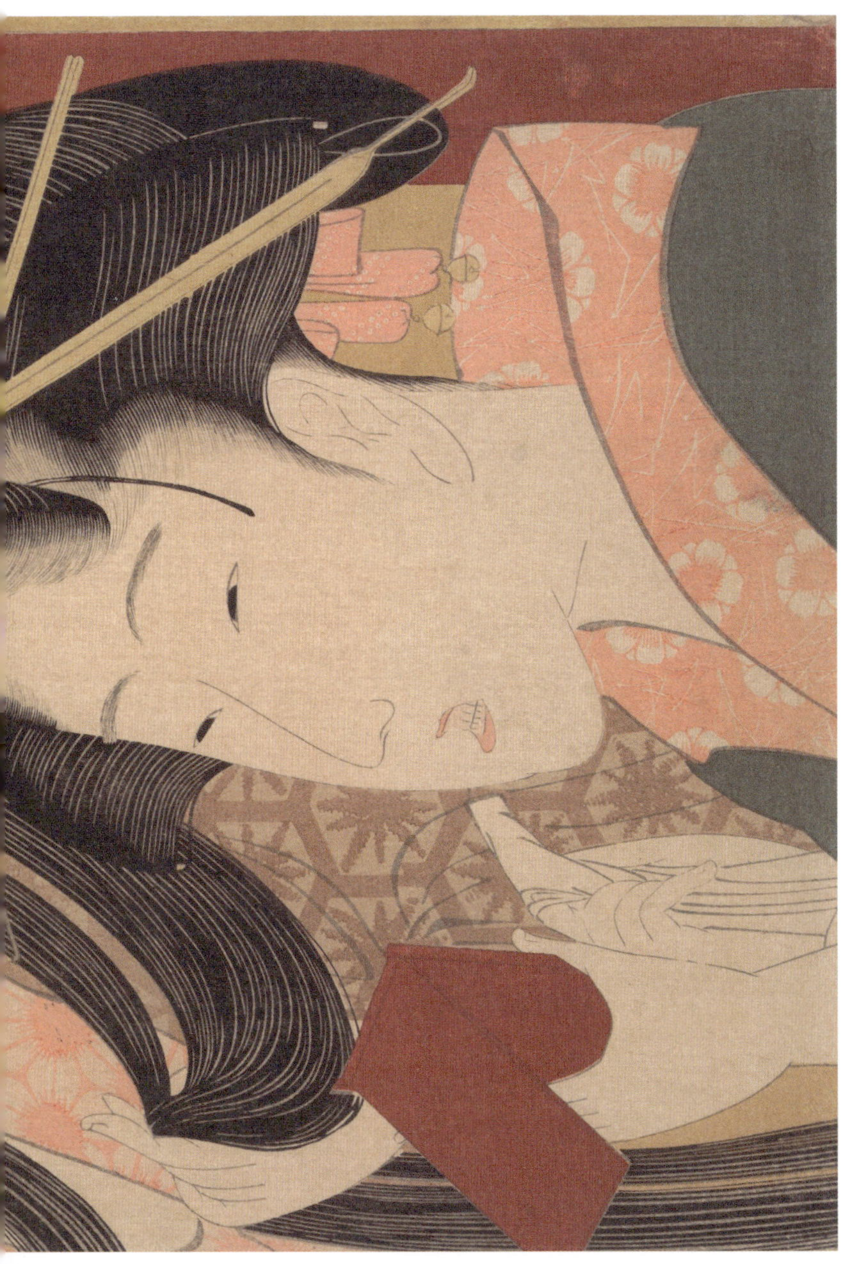

*Shop of the Edo
Publisher Tsutaya*
from the book
*Amusements
of the East*

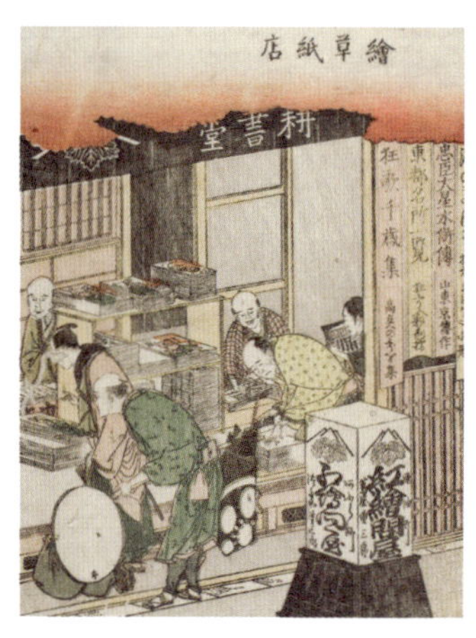

Woodblock print,
ink and colour
on paper
20 cm × 15.1 cm
(7⅞ in × 6 in)

1799–1802

The column in the foreground of this image identifies the owner of this bookshop as the celebrated Edo publisher Tsutaya Jūzaburō. Alongside his name and address is the publisher's symbol comprising Mount Fuji and an ivy-leaf – *tsuta* meaning 'ivy' (the symbol can be found in several other images in this book). The print offers a fascinating glimpse of life in late-eighteenth-century Edo, for Tsutaya's publishing house was at the heart of its floating world.

Tsutaya published semi-annual guides to the licensed quarters, listing all the brothels and their courtesans, and his house was a gathering place for artists and writers. He also created many high-quality *ukiyo-e* books and prints, including several illustrated by Hokusai. A gentleman peruses a stack of such works on the right while a samurai, accompanied by a servant, asks a question of the bookseller on the left.

As Tsutaya died in 1797, it has been suggested that this figure is a memorial portrait of the esteemed publisher. Created a year after Hokusai announced his artistic independence (see *Walking Courtesan* on page 48), this print does indeed read as a warm tribute to an ally who helped him reach this significant stage in his career.

Shop of the Edo Publisher Tsutaya
from the book *Amusements of the East*

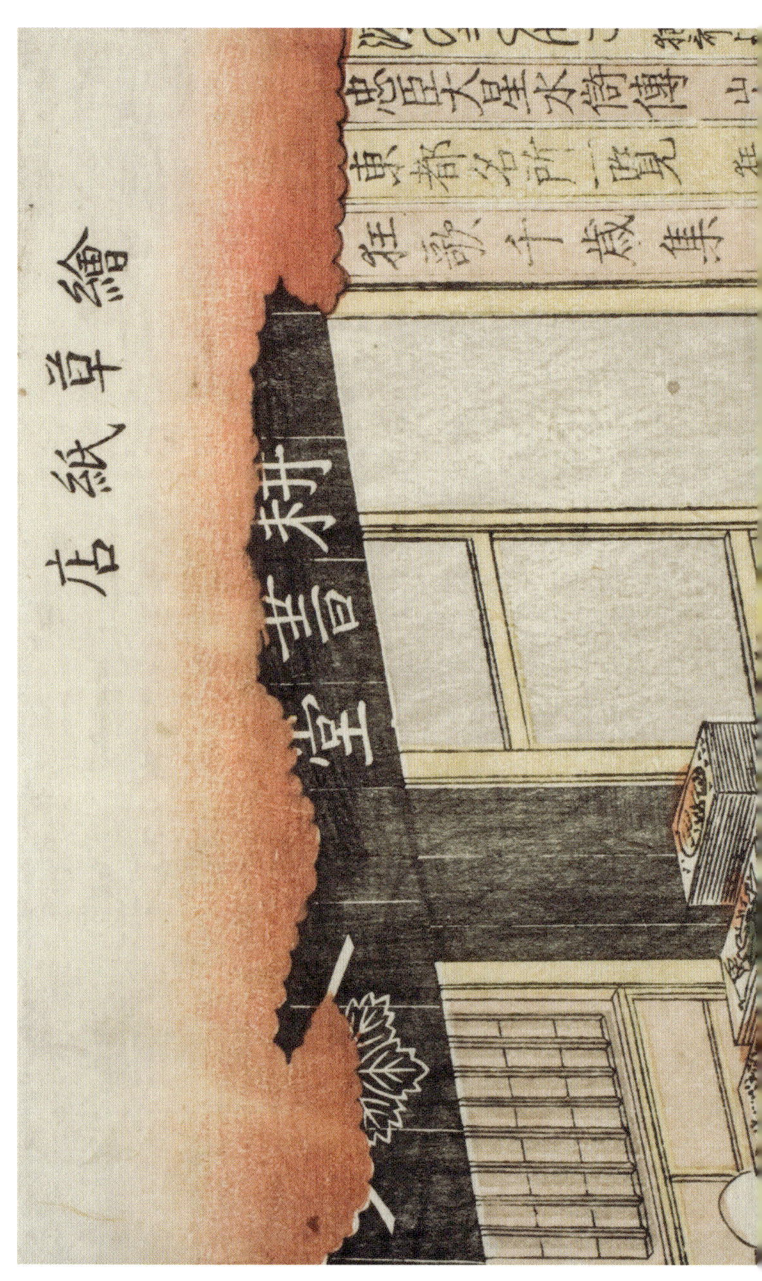

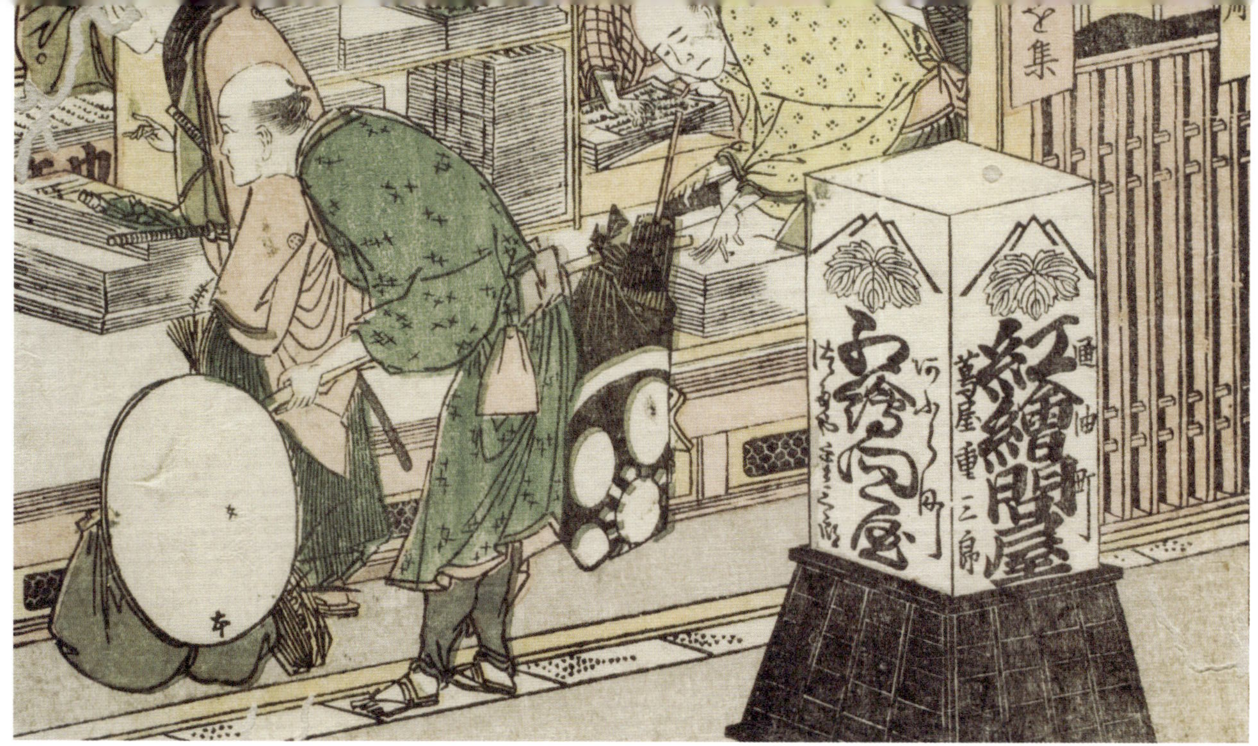
紅繪問屋
蔦屋重三郎
通油町

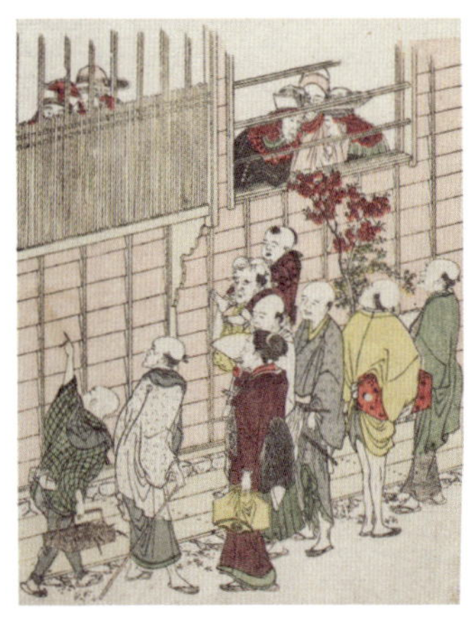

Woodblock print,   1799-1802
ink and colour
on paper
20.3 cm × 15.4 cm
(8 in × 6 in)

House of Nagasaki depicts the housing quarters of the Dutch trading envoys in the centre of Edo, where the exotic visitors are viewed with intense fascination. Like *Shop of the Edo Publisher Tsutaya* (page 32), the print derives from the picture book *Amusements of the East*. The book depicts vignettes of life in Edo, and while it was initially published solely in black ink, its reissue a few years later in colour attests to its popularity, and to Hokusai's growing acclaim.

This also focuses our attention on the production of the *ukiyo-e* woodblock print. The earliest of these were black and white, sometimes with colour added by hand. Eventually, the use of more woodblocks allowed for additional colours and, in 1765, the technique of polychrome printing was established. The outcomes were described as *nishiki-e*, or 'brocade pictures'. The creation of such works required not only the artist, who drew the design on paper, but also a carver, who cut directly through the paper onto cherry-wood blocks, creating a relief. It also required a printer, who made an initial 'key block' print on handmade paper, and then used additional woodblocks to add more colours. The publisher oversaw the whole process and marketed the works.

House of Nagasaki from the book
Amusements of the East

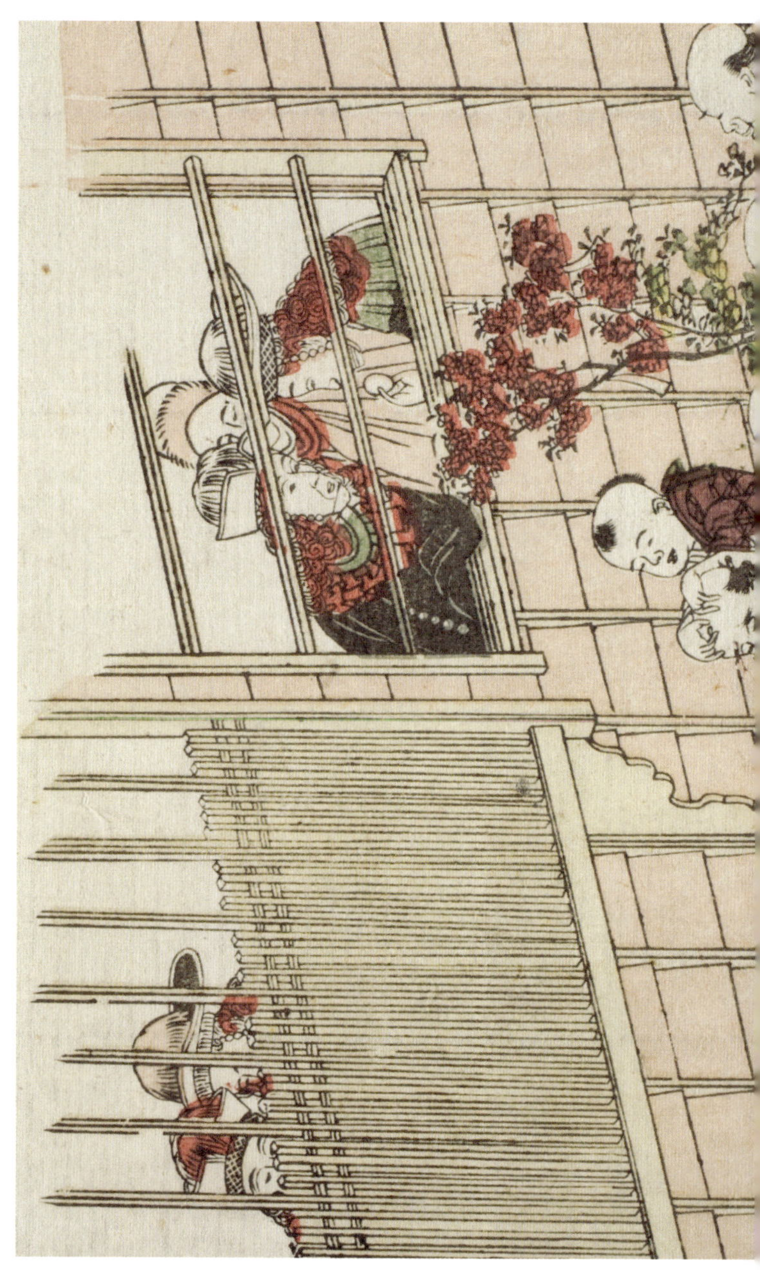

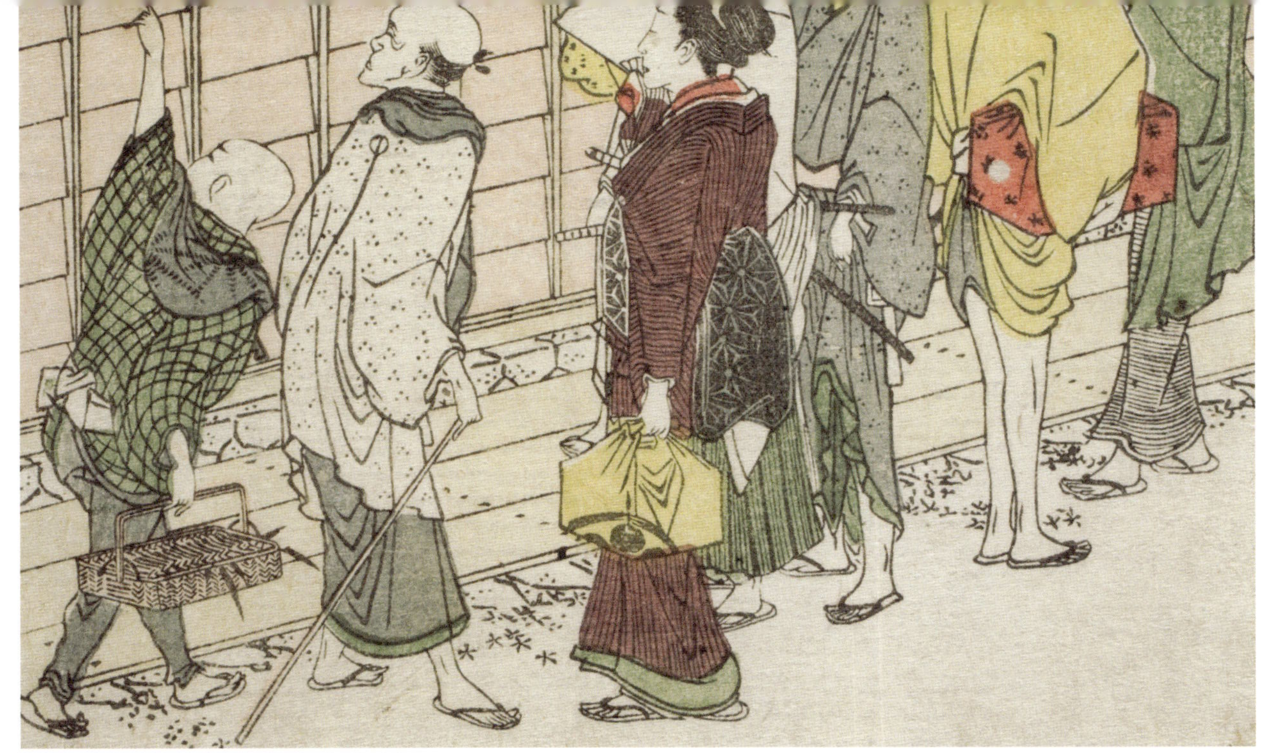

Asukayama (Asuka Hill) from the book Fine views of the Eastern Capital at a glance

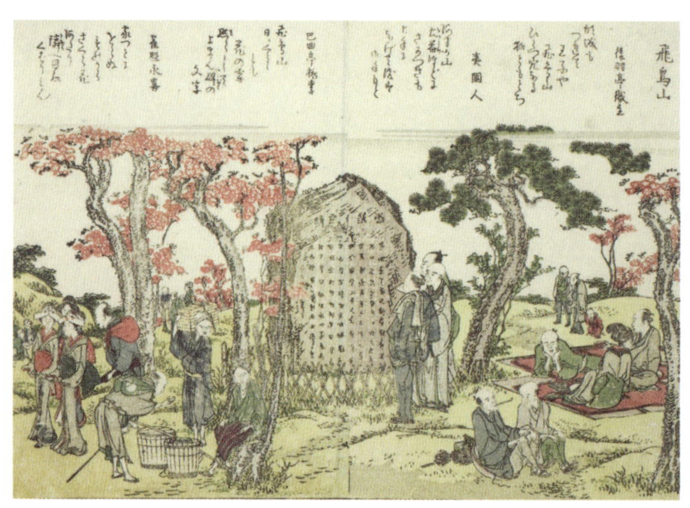

Woodblock print,
ink and colour
on paper
21.1 cm × 29.2 cm
(8¼ in × 11½ in)

1800

The two-volume, extremely popular, picture book from which this print stems was an illustrated travel guide to Edo's best sites. Related *kyōka* poems appear above the scenes, which are portrayed at their ideal visiting times. Asukayama is a hill above the city where Shogun Tokugawa Yoshimune (1684–1751) ordered hundreds of cherry trees to be planted in the early eighteenth century. Thus, it was, and still is, a popular place for *hanami*, the ancient Japanese custom of 'flower viewing' during the short spring blossom season.

Comparing this print with *Two Flatfish and a Plum Branch* (page 20), we see that Hokusai has depicted Asukayama at the height of the season. Nearly every cherry blossom is open, whereas the plum blossoms in the still life vary in stages from tightly closed buds to fully open flowers. This comparison reveals Hokusai's careful observation of nature, while *Asukayama* further demonstrates his evident pleasure in portraying human beings within the natural world.

With its harmonious integration of figure and landscape, *Fine views* was a significant step in Hokusai's career.

Asukayama (Asuka Hill) from the book
Fine views of the Eastern Capital at a glance

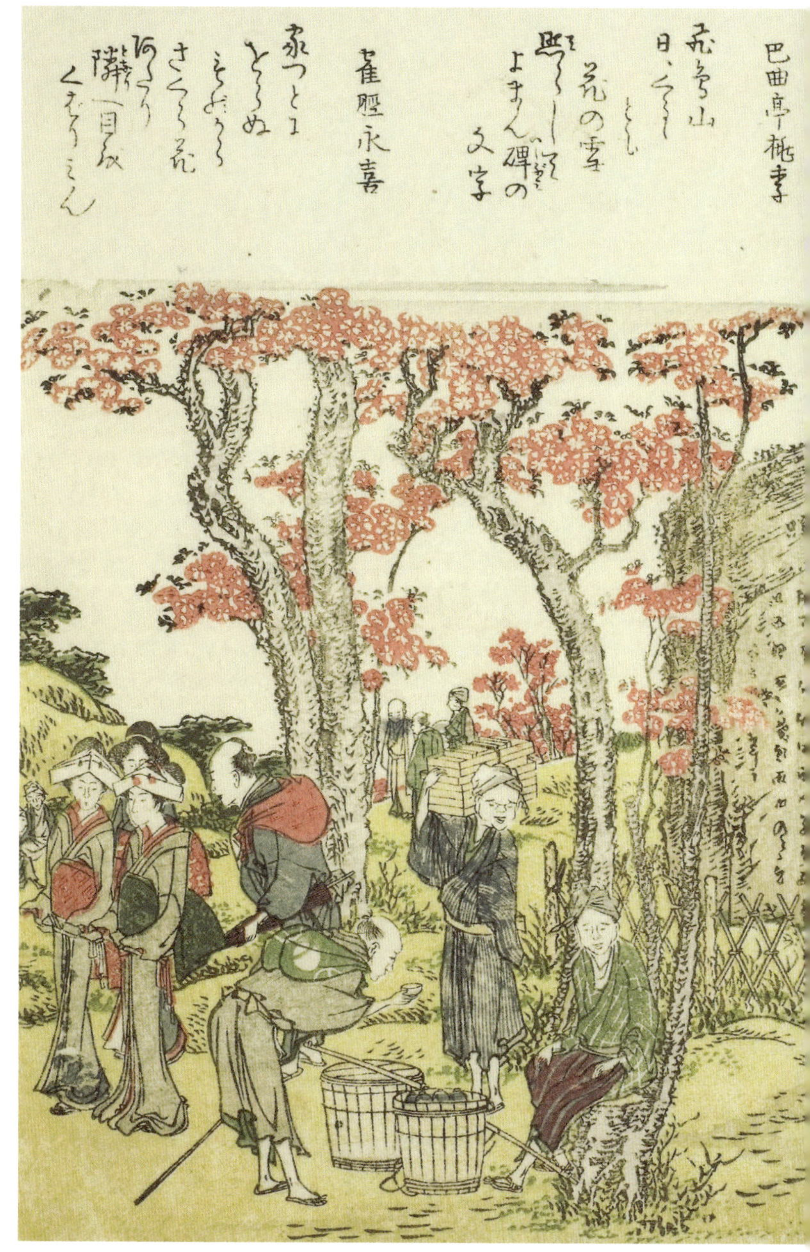

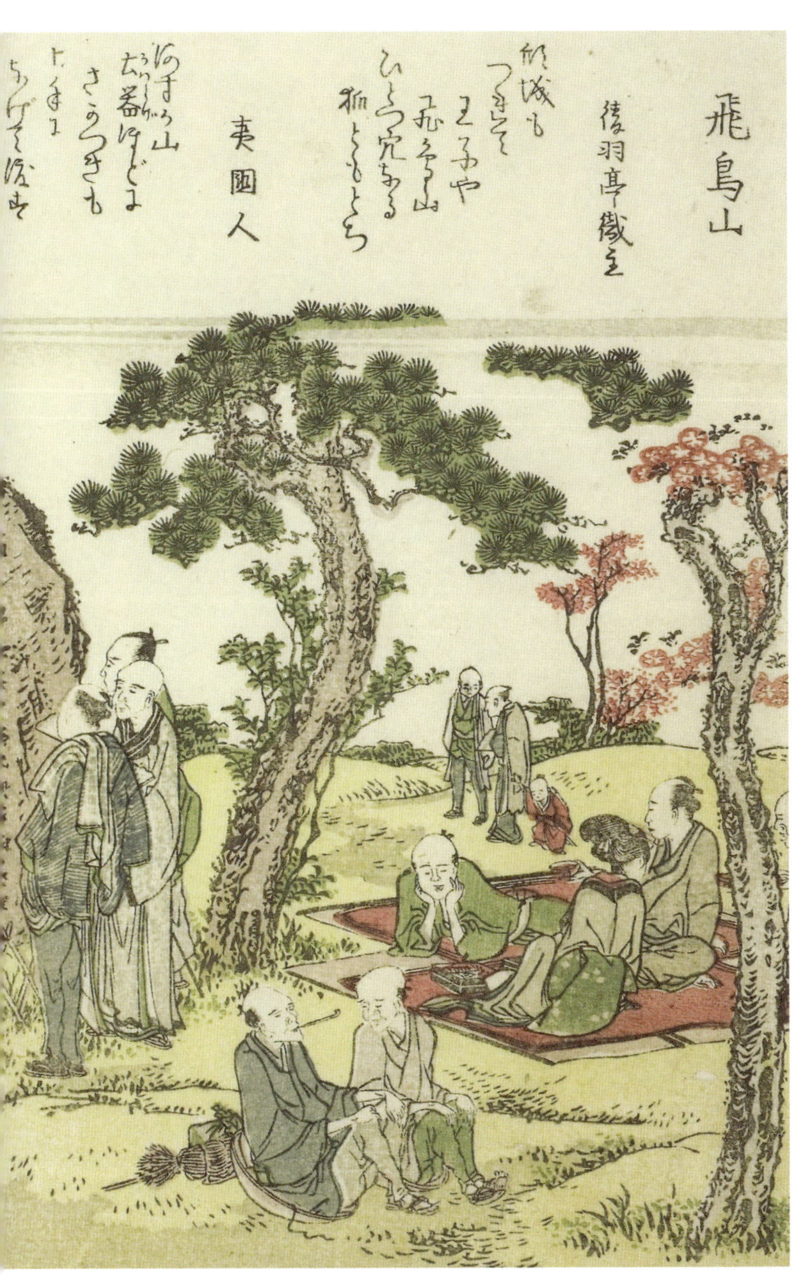
飛鳥山
佐羽亭幾主
飛城も
つきせて
とうや
飛ぶ穴山
ひらつ穴ちる
狐とゝとち
夷圖人
わするゝ山
むりゝ番にどま
さうつきも
トくすⅠ
ちげて涙む

Woman of Ōhara
with Firewood
Bundle and Kite

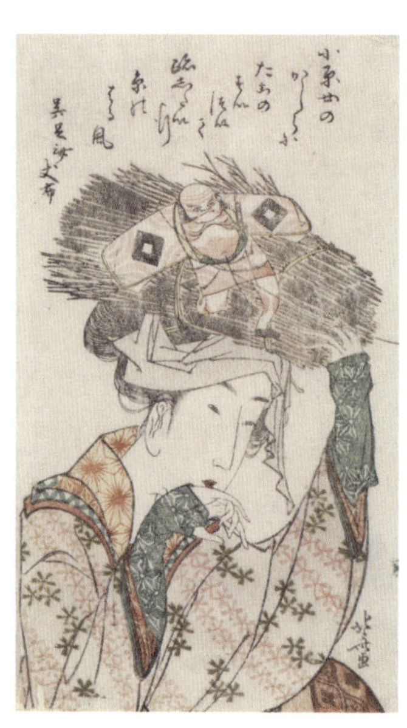

Woodblock print,
ink and colour
on paper
19.3 cm × 10.7 cm
(7⅝ in × 4¼ in)

c. 1800

In this delightful *surimono* (see *Two Flatfish and a Plum Branch* on page 20), an *ōhara-me*, a woman from Ōhara, is depicted carrying a bundle of firewood in which a kite, in the form of the legendary warrior Asahina, has become entangled. She wears the traditional clothing of Ōhara, a mountain village north of Kyoto, where it was customary for women to transport kindling and other goods to market on their heads. The way in which the colours of her outfit are reflected in the kite is particularly charming.

Like *Squeaking a Ground Cherry* (page 28), the portrait is tightly cropped, with the figure's torso filling the pictorial frame. Both works indicate the influence of the masterful *ōkubi*, or 'large headed' portraits of Tōshūsai Sharaku (active c. 1794–1795) and Kitagawa Utamaro (c. 1753/4–1806). The former artist is known for actor prints, the latter for pictures of beautiful women. But here the style and warm humour are distinctly Hokusai's.

Characteristic of this period, Hokusai depicts the women in both these prints with elongated, so-called 'melon-seed', heads. The slender, almost boneless, fingers in the current work are also a distinguishing feature of Hokusai's style.

Woman of Ōhara with Firewood
Bundle and Kite

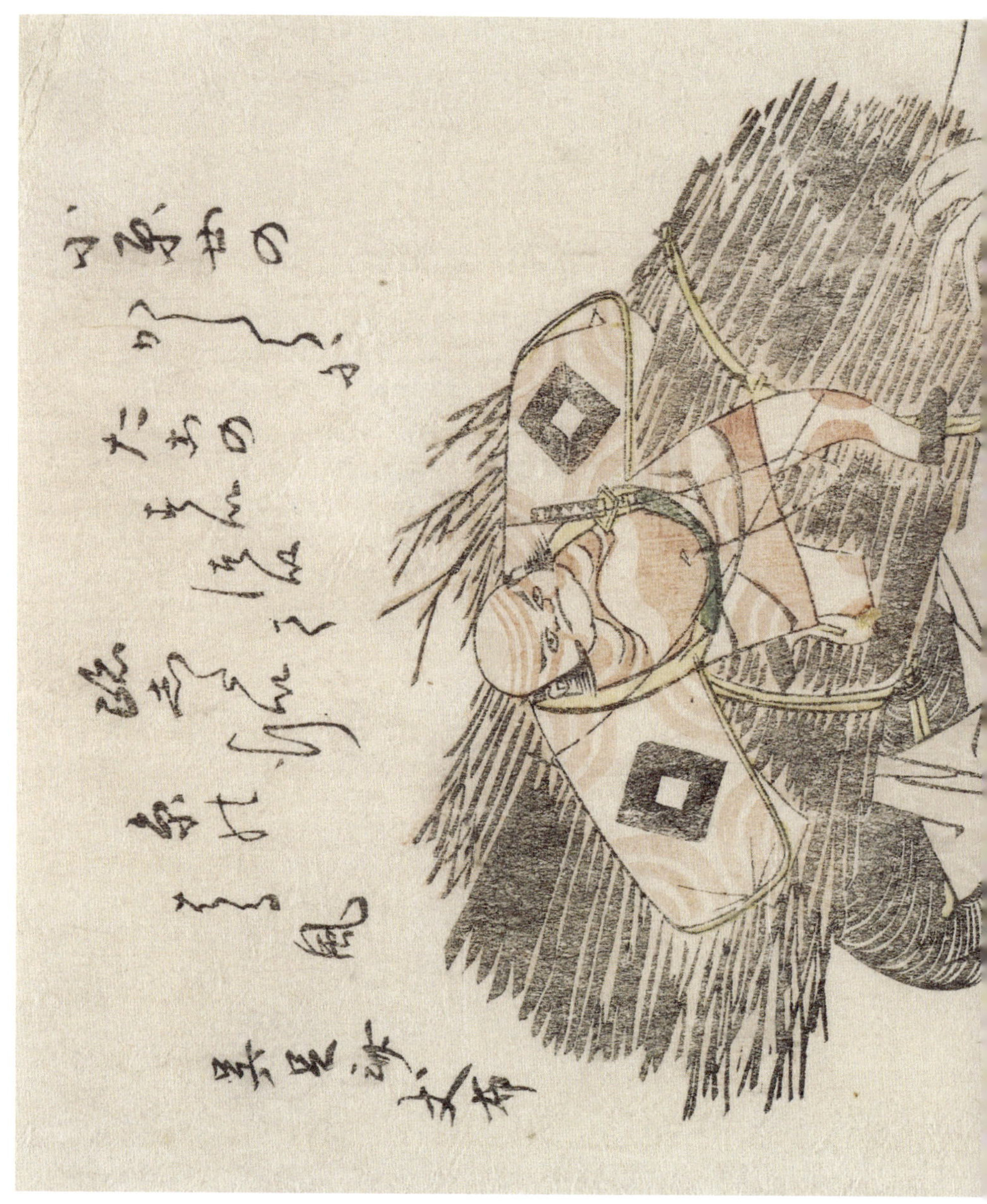

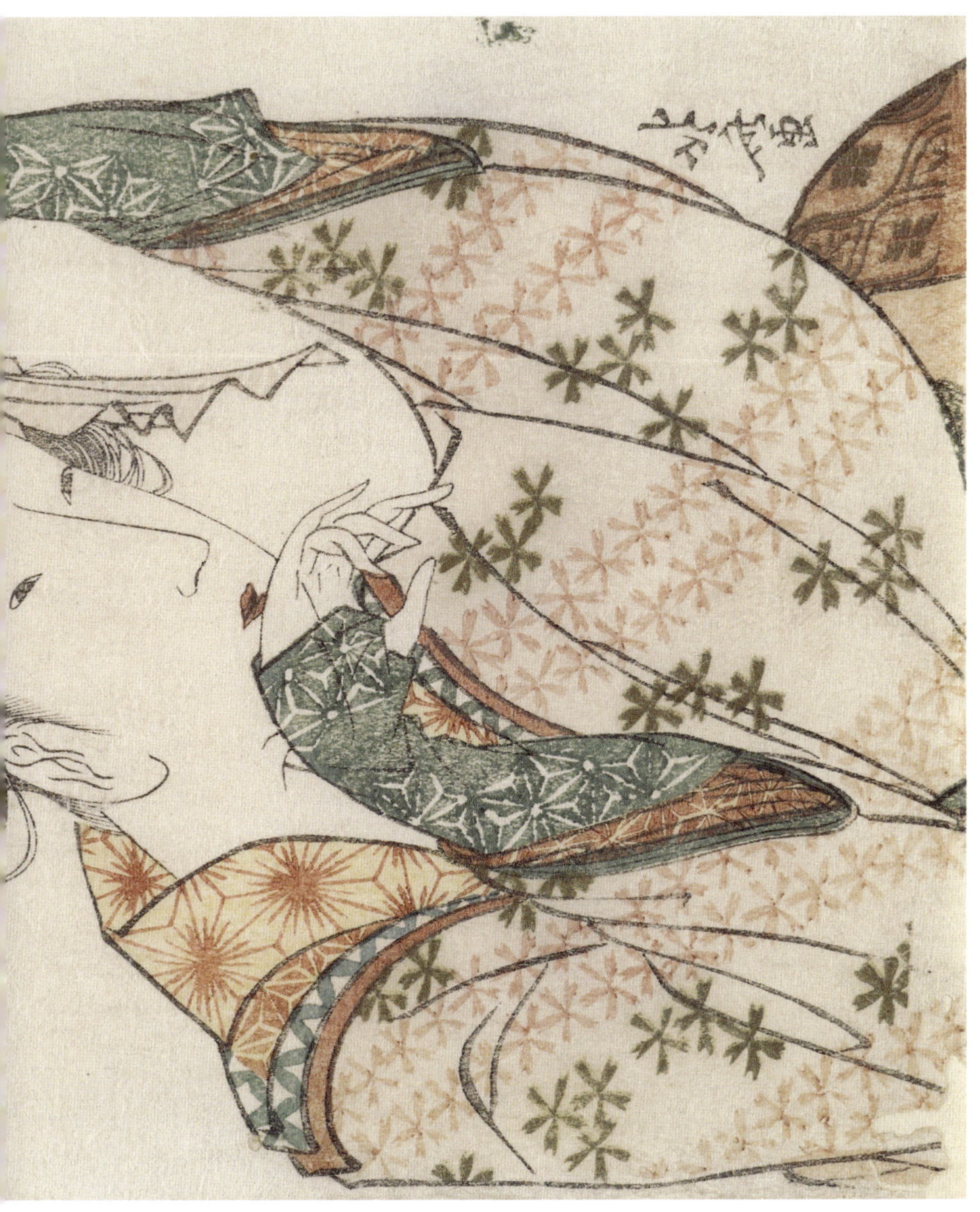

Walking Courtesan

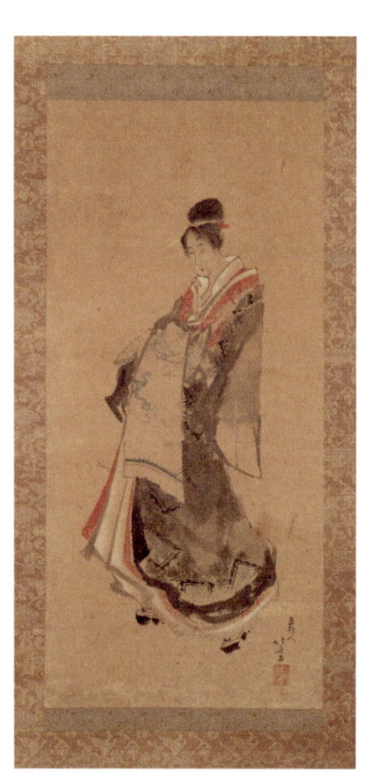

Hanging scroll, ink
and colour on paper
56.5 cm × 26 cm
(22¼ in × 10¼ in)

c. 1803-1804

While the artist discussed in this book is now known as Hokusai, it was not the name he used throughout his life. In childhood he was named Tokitarō, and he went by several other names during his first four decades. He used Hokusai largely from 1796 until 1819, though art historians regard the 'Hokusai period' as dating from 1798 to 1810 (it can get rather confusing!). After this, Hokusai adopted still other names until his death.

This cultural practice of changing names was not unusual in pre-modern Japan, and it tended to mark a transition in a person's life. In 1798, after his years of training, Hokusai was ready to establish his own studio. To announce his independence, he adopted the names Tokimasa and Hokusai, signifying his faith in Myōken, the Buddhist deity of *Hokushin*, the North Star.

The artist's scroll paintings of beautiful women (*bijin-ga*) are particularly notable during his Hokusai period. Comparing this depiction of a courtesan with the earlier *Woman Spinning Silk* (page 24) reveals Hokusai's technical scope. Both are similar in format, with graceful figures appearing to exist in a placeless space. But the latter is painted crisply, while this work is freely executed with summary strokes.

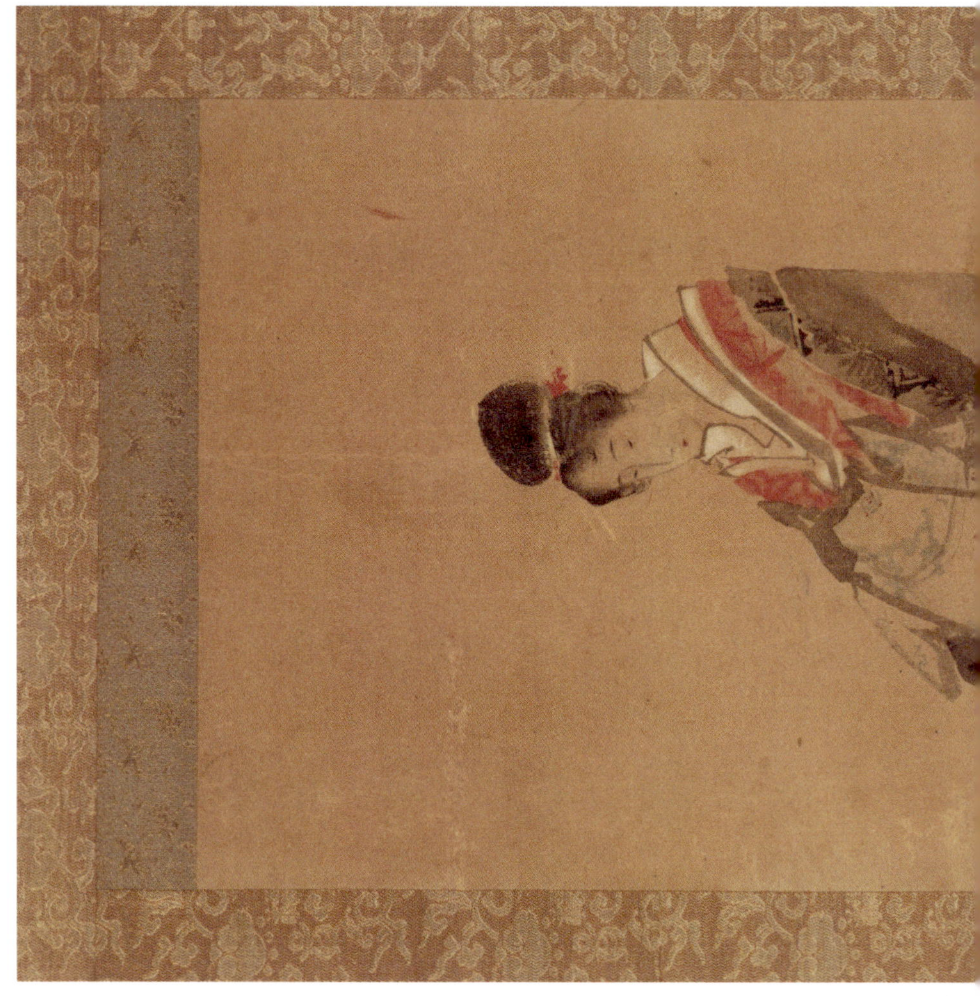

c. 1803-1804

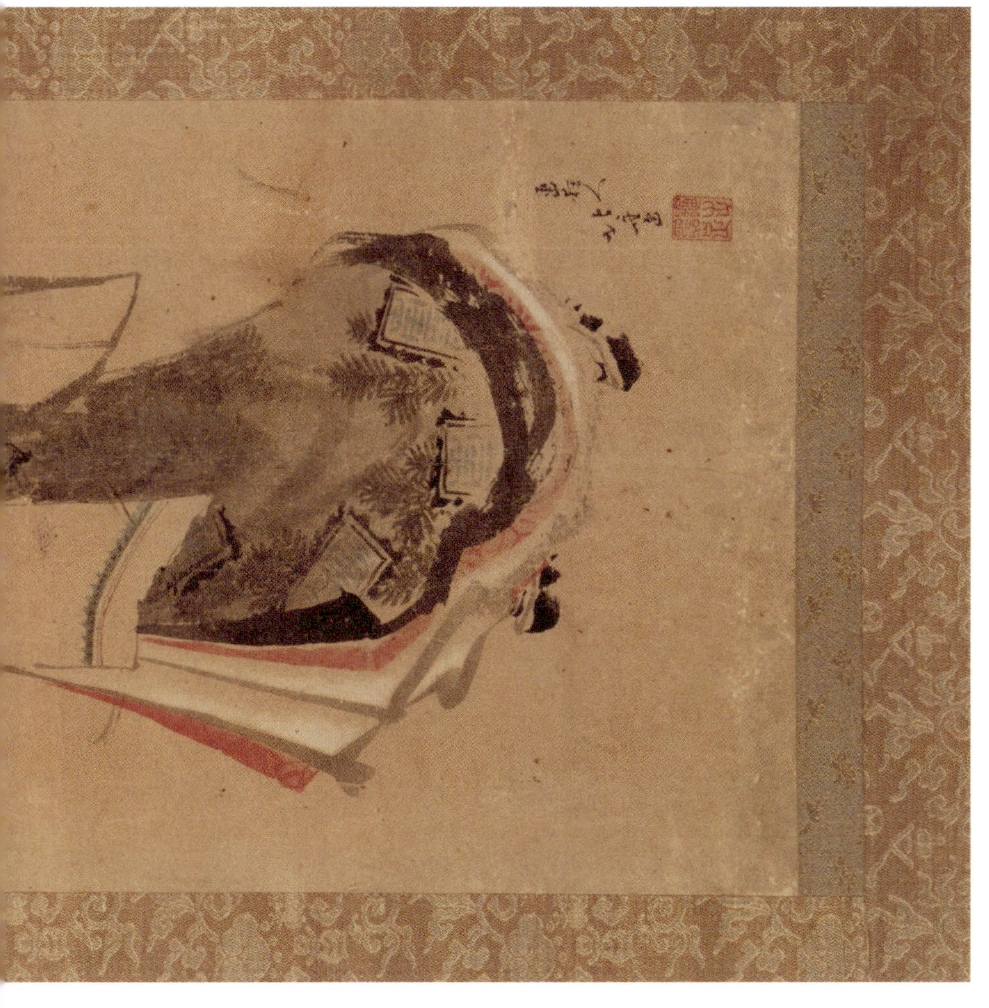

Shower at the New Yanagi Bridge from the book *Panoramic views of both banks of the Sumida River at a glance*

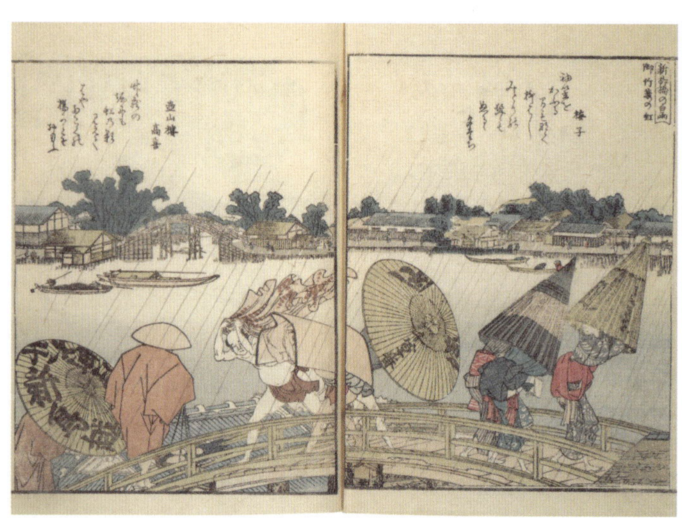

Woodblock print,   1806
ink and colour
on paper
20 cm × 29.8 cm
(7⅞ in × 11¾ in)

Viewing this two-page print alongside the earlier Edo view of *Asukayama* (page 40), we see how much more robust Hokusai's figures became over the course of a few years. They also occupy a much more extensive landscape that, with its sense of perspectival depth, reveals the influence of Western painting.

While Japan was largely isolated from foreign nations during the Edo period, by the late 1700s there was renewed interest in Western science and culture. With Hokusai's limitless curiosity, it wasn't surprising that this intellectual and aesthetic stimulus impacted his work.

This image of figures caught in a sudden shower is part of a picture book of views along Edo's grand Sumida River. While this wry portrayal is marvellous in its own right, the book's overall compilation makes its experience even more delightful. Like a Japanese narrative scroll, each double-page scene connects to the next to form a continual panorama, giving the impression that the viewer also promenades along the river's west bank. The collated images resemble a cinematic montage of passing time.

Shower at the New Yanagi Bridge
from the book *Panoramic views of both
banks of the Sumida River at a glance*

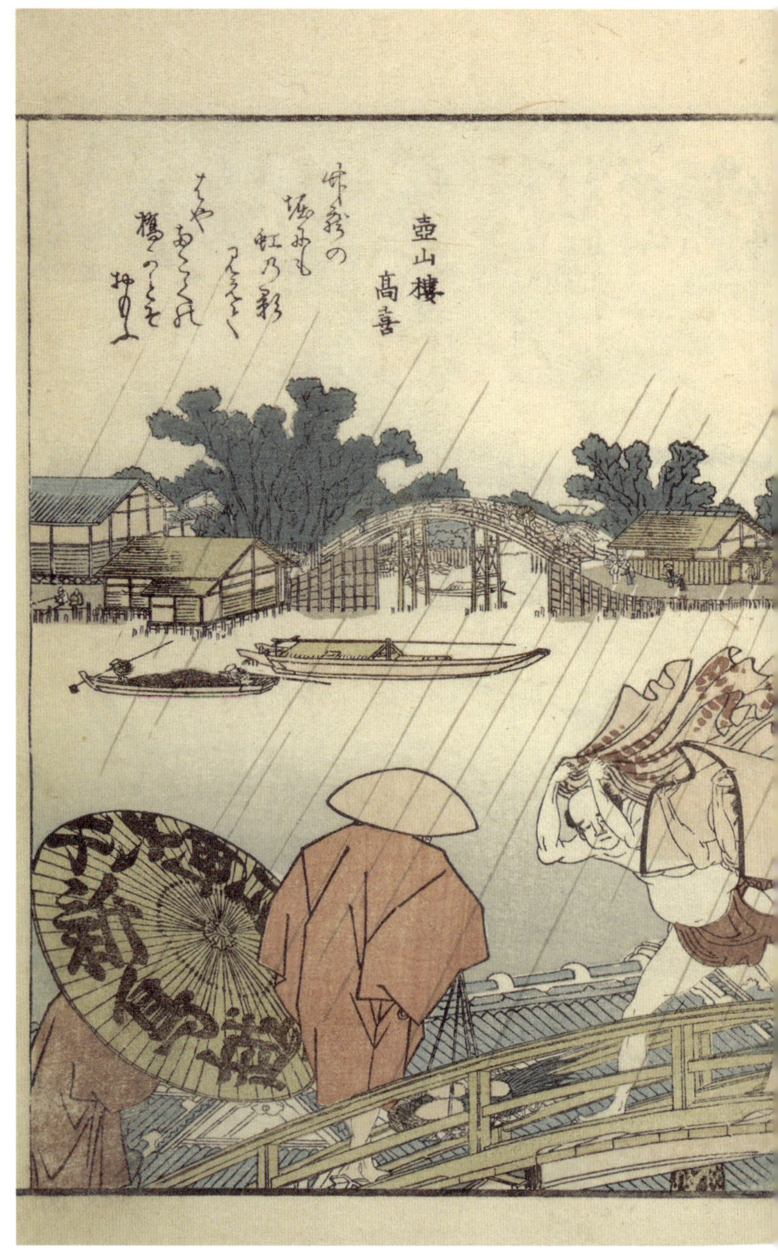

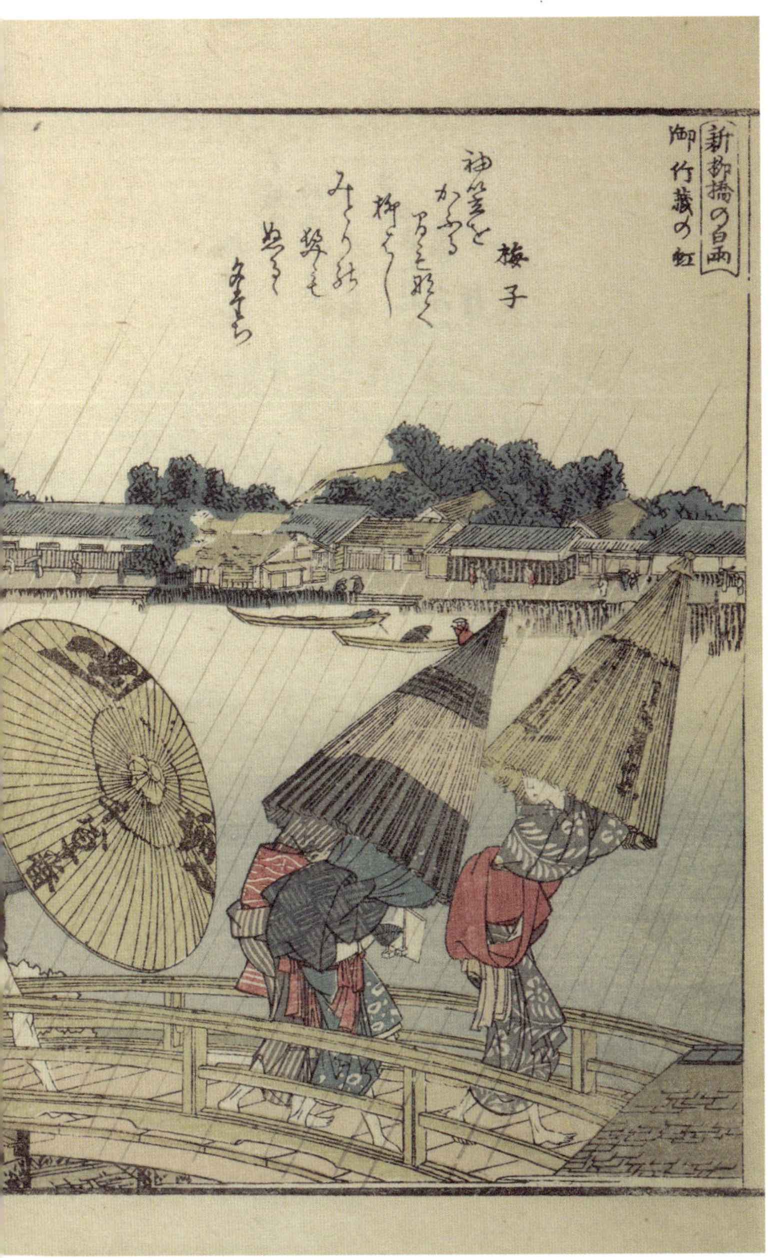
新柳橋の白雨
御竹蔵の虹

梅子

神まつと
かふる
うくと時く
柳そく
みちり舟
袋しも
もくろ
みちち

Hamamatsu
from the series
Fifty-three stations
of the Tōkaidō

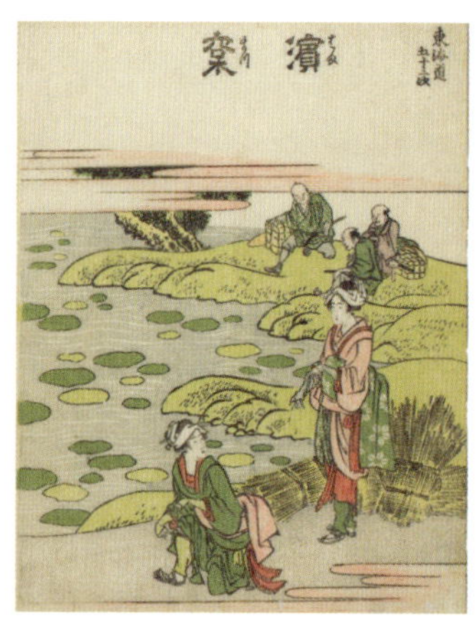

56

Woodblock print, ink
and colour on paper
24 cm × 18.3 cm
(9½ in × 7¼ in)

c. 1806

Travel and tourism grew exponentially in Japan from the late seventeenth century onwards. The quest to see and experience different places resulted in the publication of all kinds of guidebooks, maps and travel literature. Considering the thriving trade in *ukiyo* books and prints, it wasn't surprising that artists added travel images to their views of the floating world.

Most people in the Edo period travelled by foot, and of the country's five major routes, the 515 km Tōkaidō, which linked Edo and Kyoto, was the most famous. In 1833–1834, Utagawa Hiroshige (1797–1858) created what is arguably the finest series of prints of its fifty-three post stations. It was, however, a subject that Hokusai also illustrated in several collections earlier that century.

This print depicts a pause at Hamamatsu (the names of the post stations are included at the top), where three men chatter in the background, and in the foreground two women converse while rearranging their outfits. In its integration of people and setting – the harmonious blending of clothing and landscape colours is particularly pleasing here – Hokusai's Tōkaidō series is a hint of what was to come in *Thirty-six views of Mount Fuji* (see pages 92–119).

Hamamatsu from the series Fifty-three
stations of the Tōkaidō

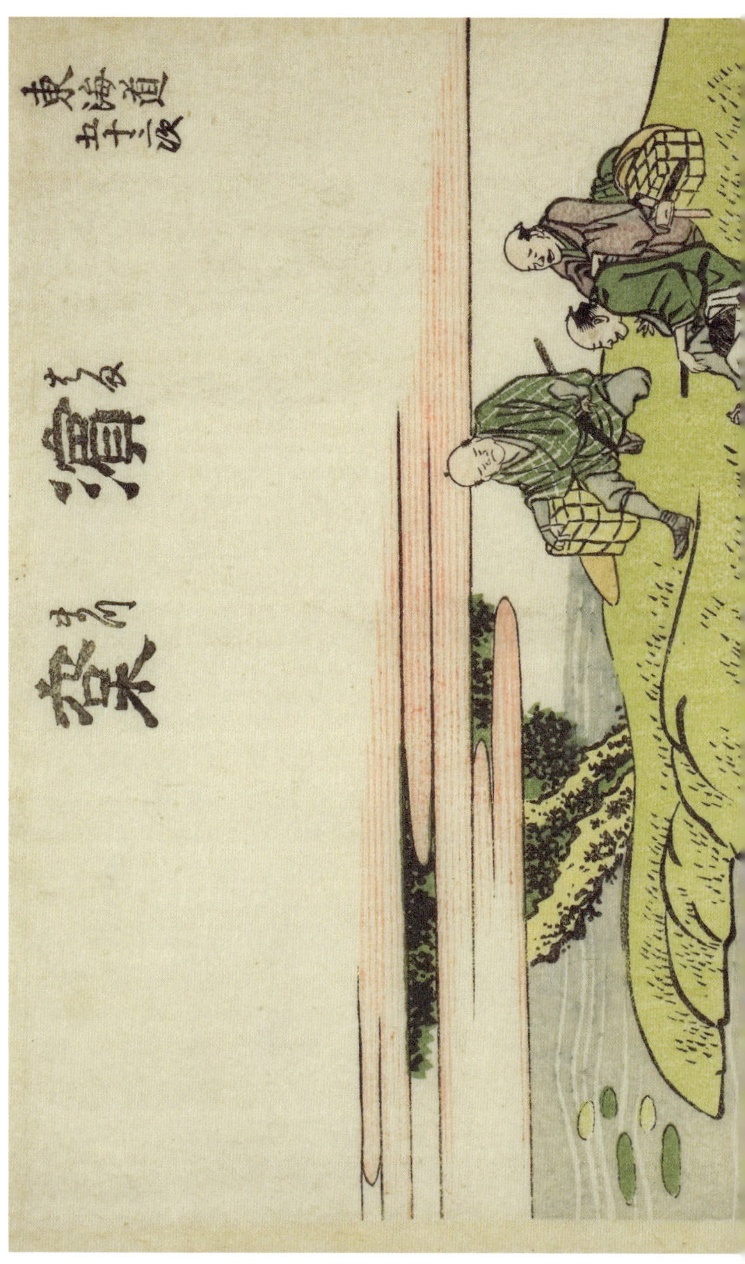
東海道
五十三次
濱
松

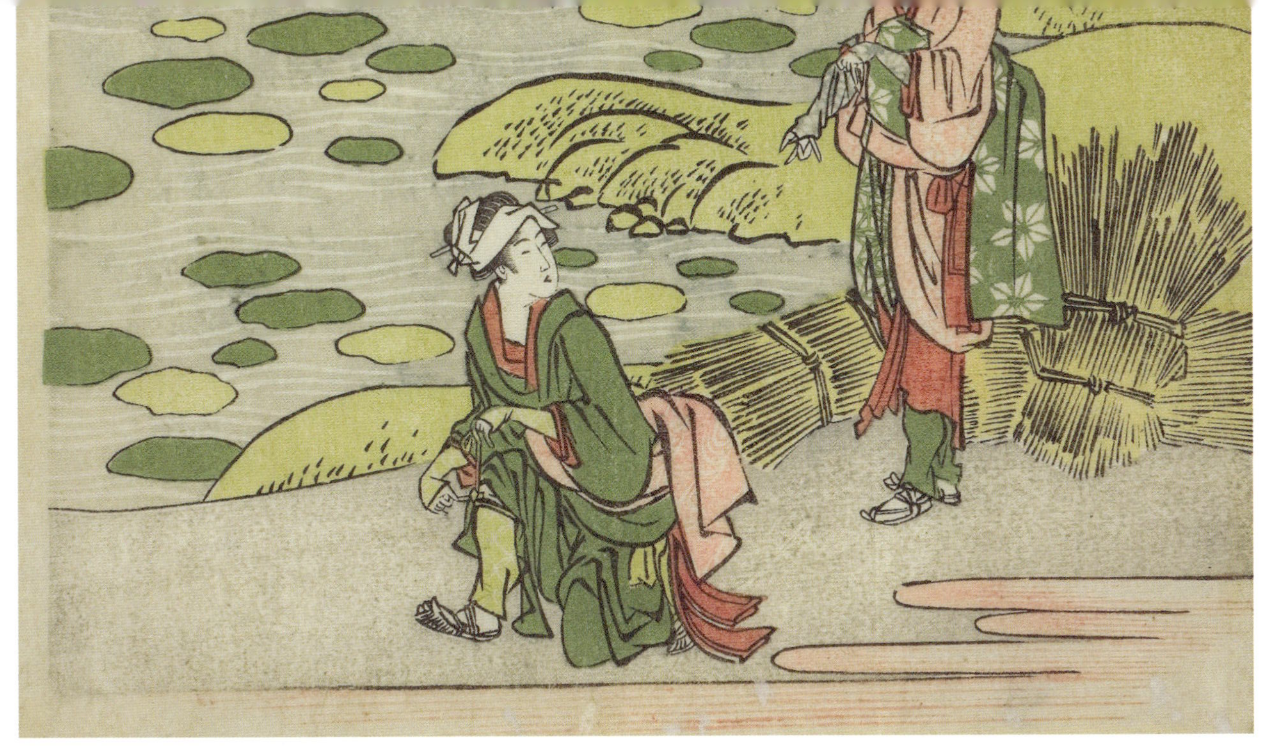

c. 1806

Pages from the new illustrated edition of *Tales of the water margin*

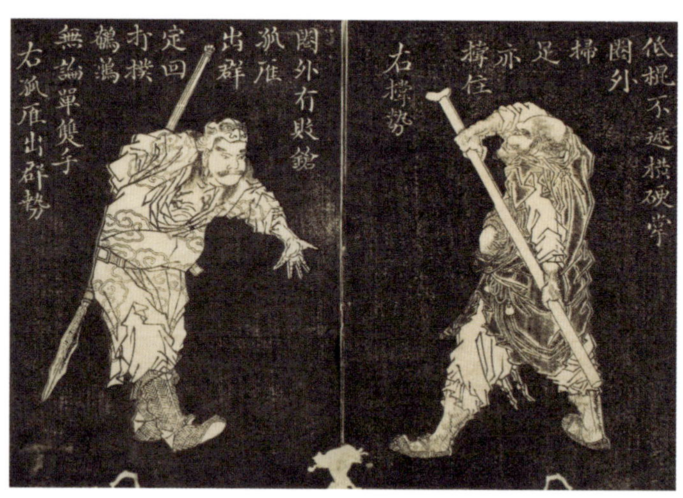

Woodblock print,
black ink on paper
19.2 cm × 27.6 cm
(7½ in × 10⅞ in)

1805–1835

Japan had long been influenced by the older civilisation of China, and this connection frequently guided Hokusai's work. At times this is apparent stylistically, but Hokusai also drew upon Chinese literature and religion as subject matter.

Around 1803 Hokusai began illustrating *yomi-hon* (reading books). These tend to be epic tales of adventure and the supernatural, full of drama and the fantastical, and they frequently adapt stories from China. *Tales of the water margin* (also known as *Outlaws of the marsh*) is an early vernacular masterpiece set in the Song Dynasty (960–1279). The novel recounts the escapades of 108 outlaws who fought against corrupt rulers to help the poor.

Most of the *yomi-hon* illustrations are in black ink on a pale ground, but this double-page image displays the striking effect of a black background. Here the outlaws take up dramatic poses like kabuki actors on stage. Hokusai collaborated with the eminent Japanese novelist Kyokutei Bakin (1767–1848) on over a dozen of these multi-volume picture books. However, the two men's strong personalities meant their relationship could be stormy. Bakin adapted Part I of *Water margin* but Hokusai was joined by a different writer on subsequent volumes.

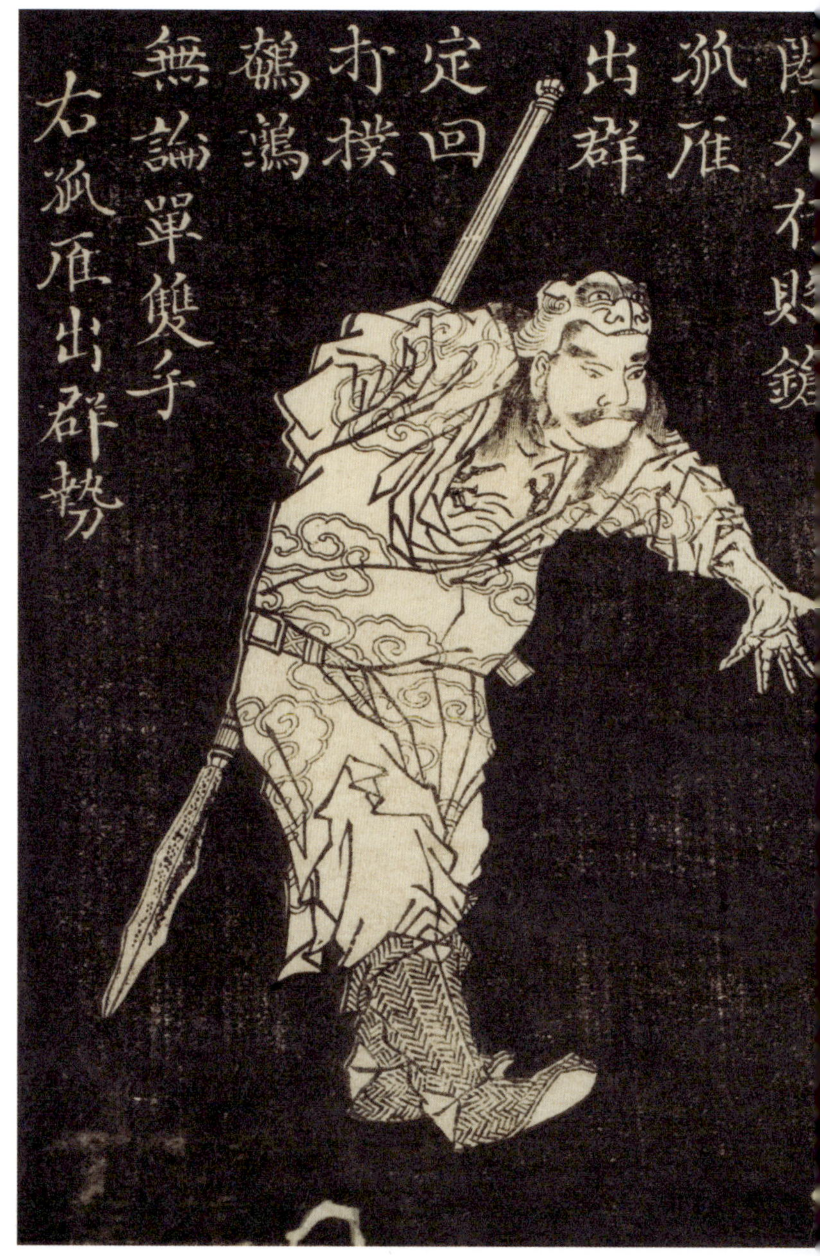
閑夕不貶鍭
孤雁
出群
定回
亦撲
鶴鴒
無論單雙手
右孤雁出群勢

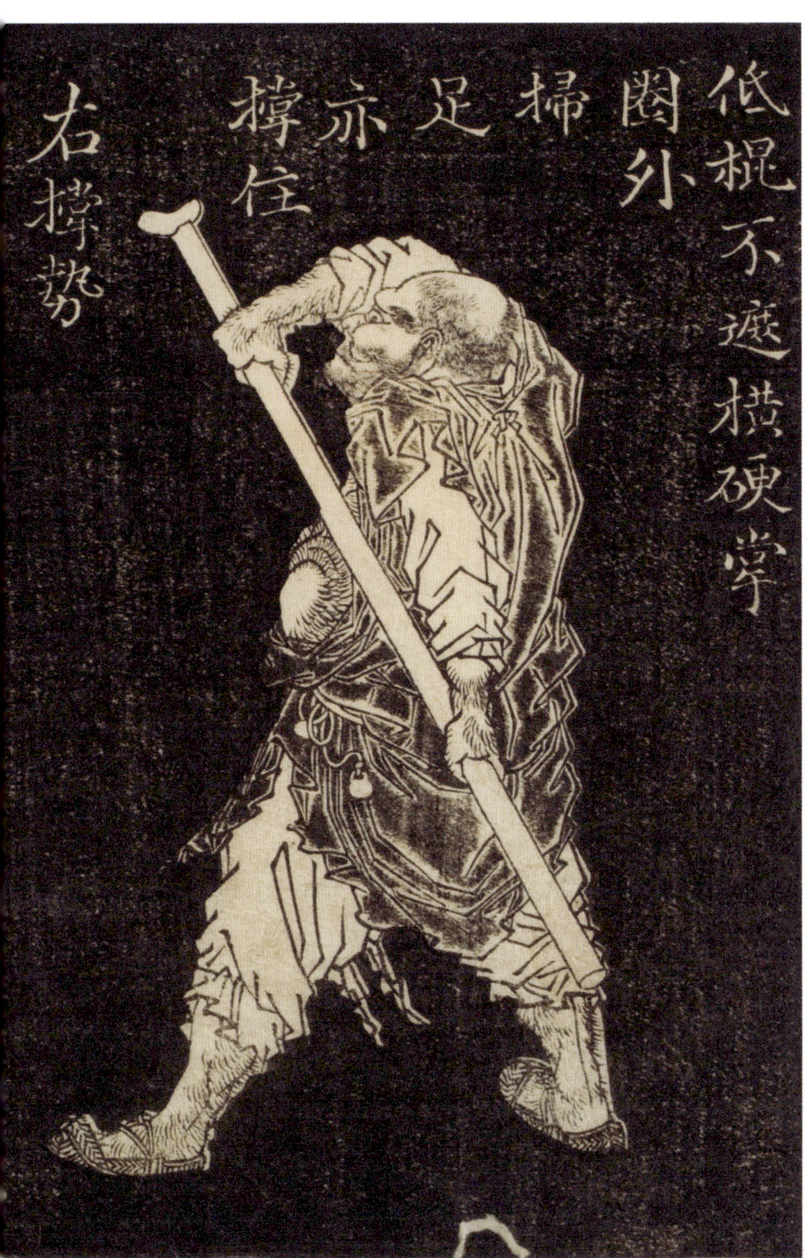
低棍不遮橫硬掌
閔外
掃足
亦住
撐住
右撐勢

Ariwara no Narihira
from the series
The six poets

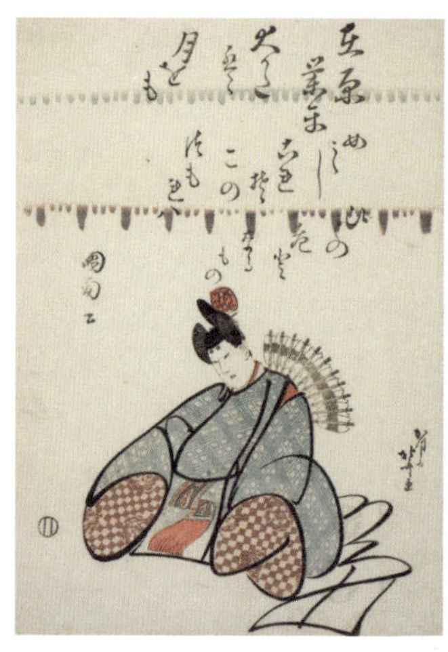

Woodblock print,   c. 1810
ink and colour
on paper
38 cm × 26 cm
(15 in × 10¼ in)

This portrait of *Ariwara no Narihira* (825–880) is one in a series of six large prints of revered Japanese poets. Ingeniously, Hokusai has used the shape of the Japanese characters that spell each poet's name to also form their bodies. These thick black lines, created with a fluid flourish, are then filled in with exquisite patterns in vivid colours. This inventive technique points to Hokusai's playfulness, and to the use of performance in his work.

In 1804, for instance, Hokusai staged an event at Gokoku Temple on the outskirts of Edo. On roughly 200 square metres of combined sheets of paper, in front of crowds of people, Hokusai used a broom and ink to paint a monumental bust of Daruma, the founder of Zen Buddhism. He repeated the performance in 1817 at a temple in Nagoya, where it was even more of a sensation. So as not to typecast himself, and to further demonstrate his artistic capabilities, Hokusai contrasted these large-scale art performances by drawing two sparrows on a grain of rice.

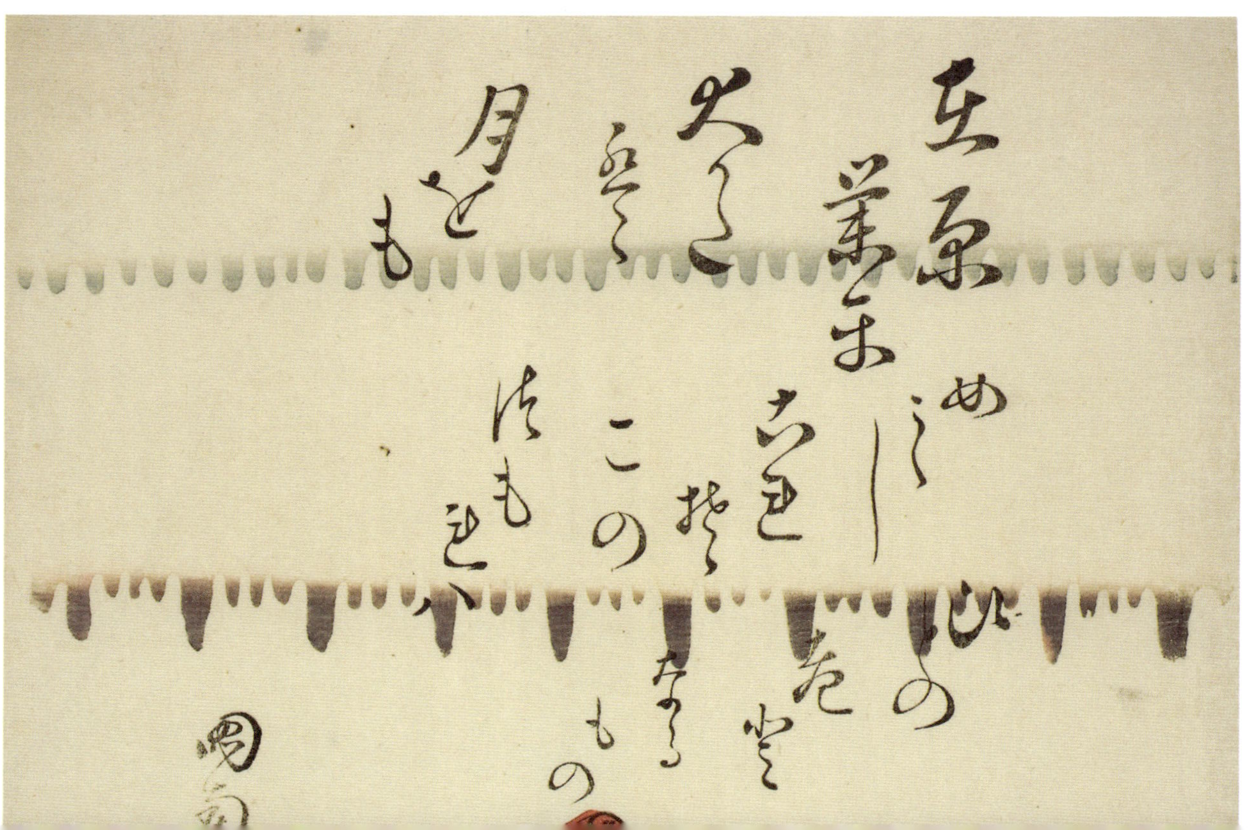

Ariwara no Narihira from the series
The six poets

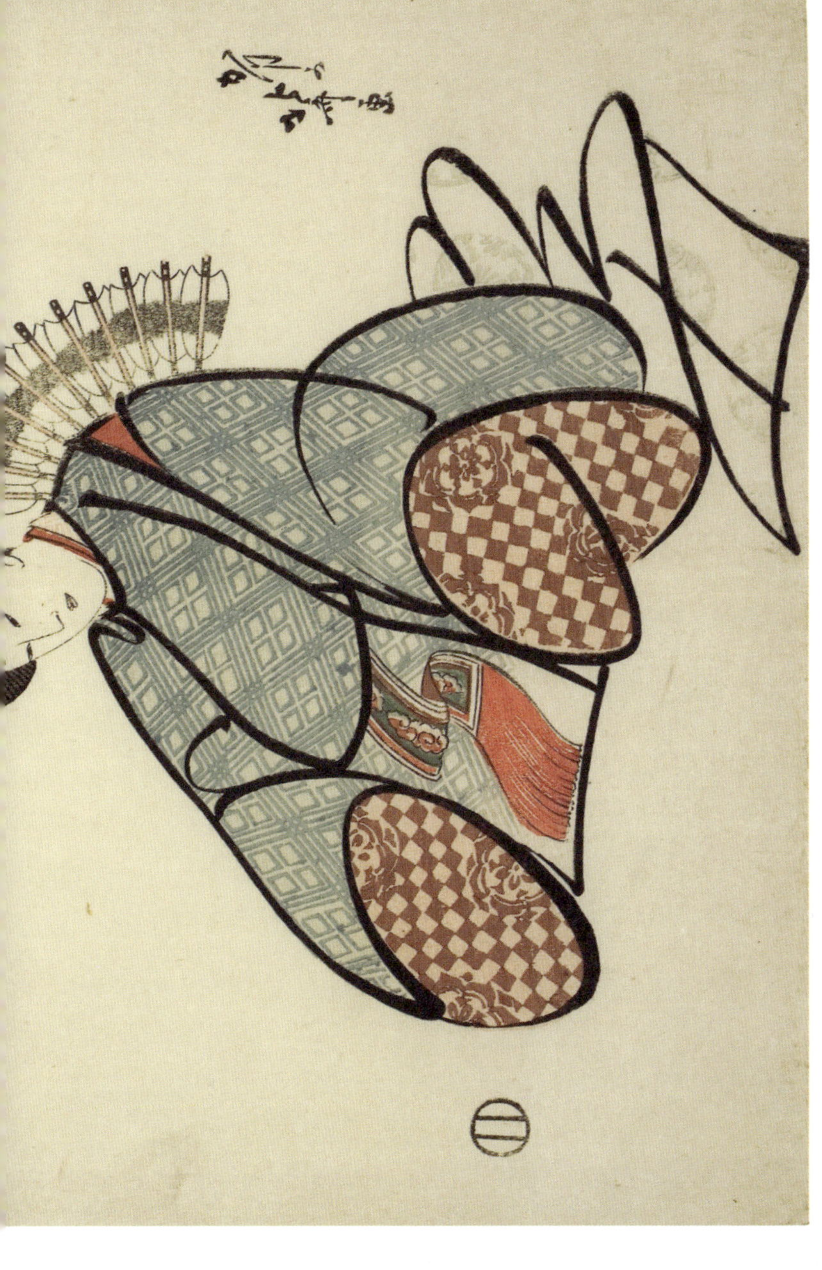

Sumo Wrestlers from *Manga,* volume XI

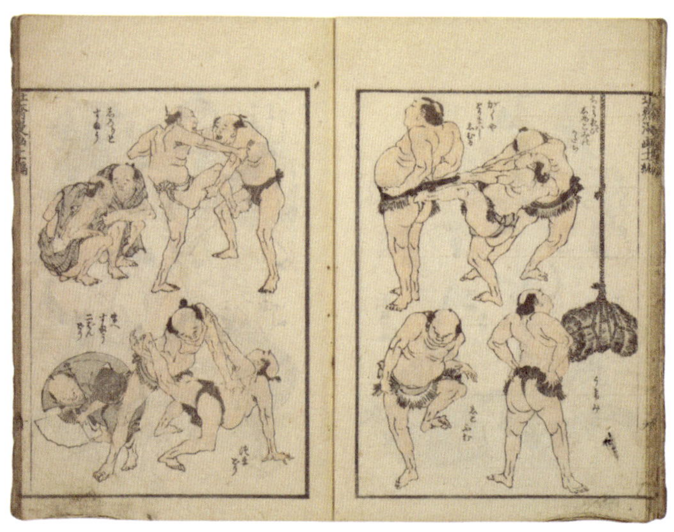

Woodblock print,   1814-1878
ink and colour
on paper
22.7 cm × 15.7 cm
(9 in × 6⅛ in)

By 1810 Hokusai was a celebrated artist in Japan. This was also the year that he began creating picture manuals (*e-dehon*). His most famous of these, the *Hokusai manga*, meant that by the middle of the century Hokusai was also renowned in Europe, most particularly among the avant-garde artists in France.

Manga for Hokusai meant something rather different from the comics of present-day manga, though the two genres are not unrelated. The word *manga* can be translated as 'random sketches' or 'whimsical pictures', and Hokusai drew thousands of these. When, in 1812, he was visiting his samurai pupil Bokusen (1736–1824) in the city of Nagoya, the idea came about that the brush-drawn sketches Hokusai made there be compiled into a book. Published in 1814 in both Nagoya and Edo, this first volume was a huge hit. It was followed by fourteen more, three published posthumously.

Filled with drawings of human activity as well as animals and plants, architecture and landscape, and figures of myth and imagination, the *Manga* is teeming with life. The double-page reproductions included in this book can only hint at the work's kaleidoscopic range, but they certainly indicate its colossal spirit (see also *Yakko-odori* on page 72).

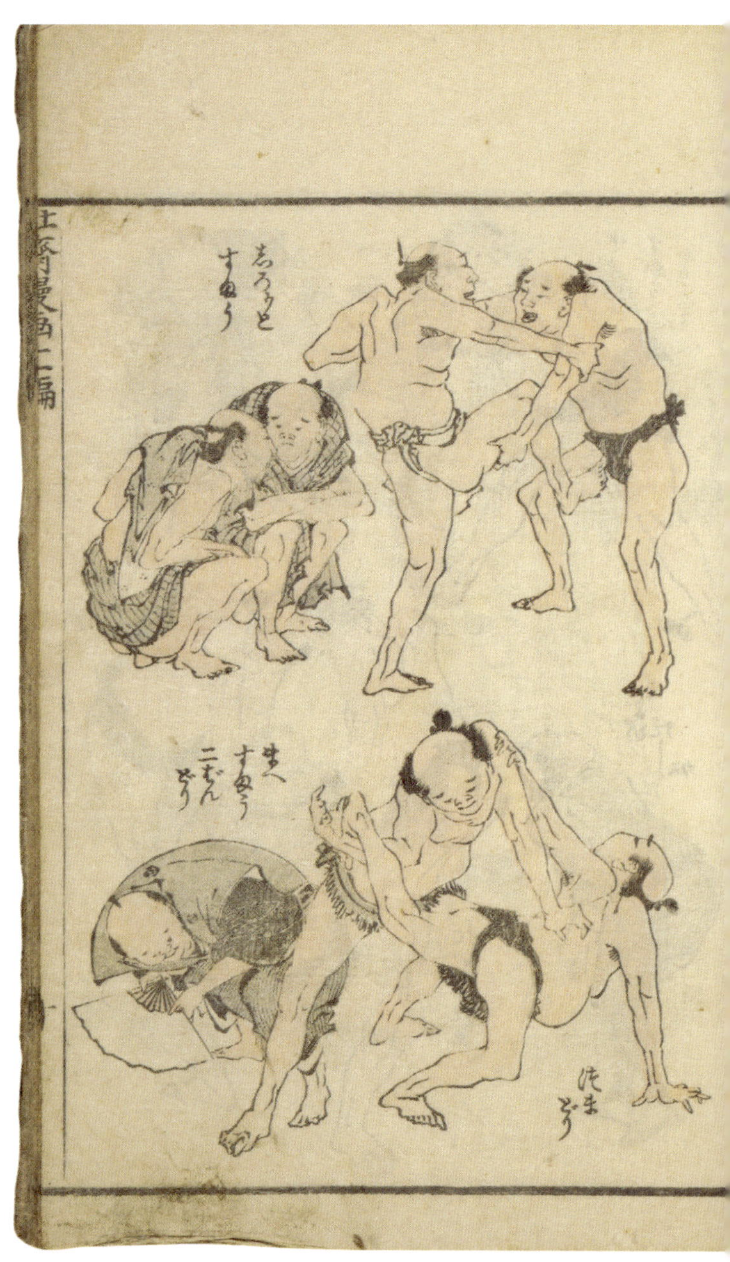

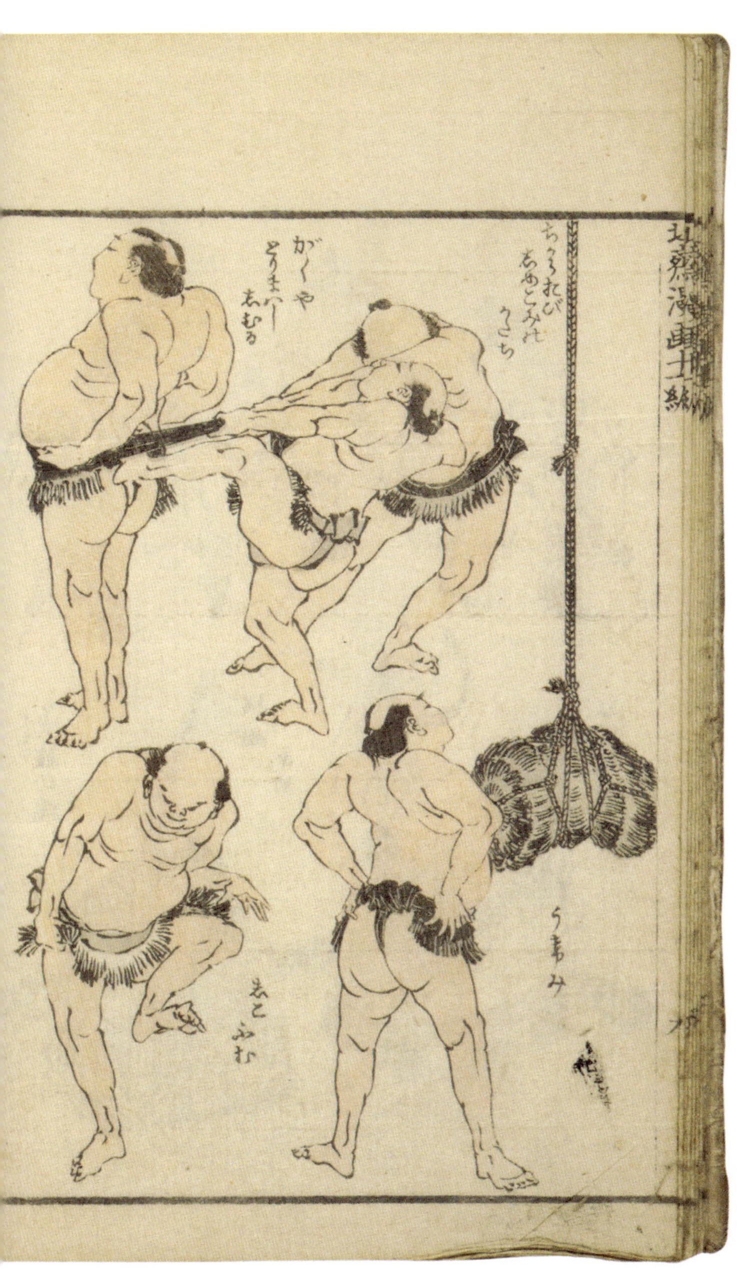

がくや
どりまっ
あむる
ちからむび
あゐとこみゃせ
うこち
うまみ
あとふむ

The Yakko-odori (The Servant's Dance) from Manga, volume III

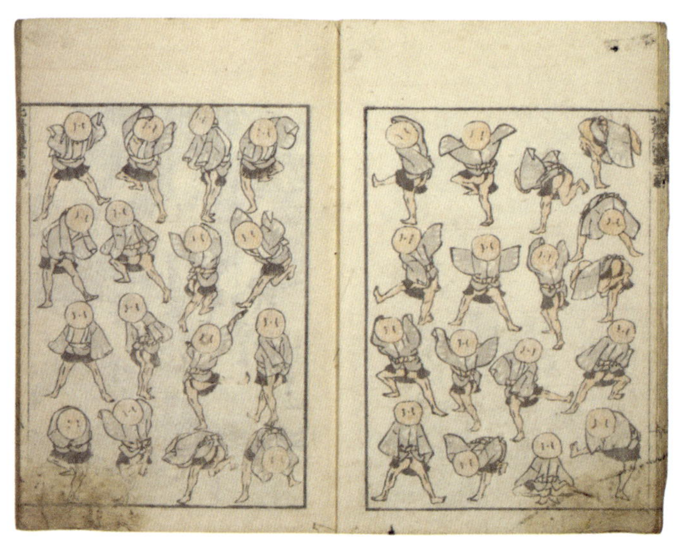

Woodblock print,   1814-1878
ink and colour
on paper
23 cm × 16 cm
(9 in × 6¼ in)

The preface of the first volume of Hokusai's *Manga* opens with the observation that humankind's emotions 'appear readily both on their faces and in their forms'. Like *Sumo Wrestlers* (page 68), this double-page image shows Hokusai's consummate ability to capture human emotion, as well as a person's strengths and vanities, through the body as much as, or in lieu of, facial expression.

The *yakko* was a servant of a *daimyo* (feudal lord). Though lacking in any real power, the *yakko* did not refrain from pushing around others with even less. In his study of Hokusai's *Manga*, James A. Michener writes that the dance depicted here lampoons the servant's airs of grandeur. Yet, even without knowing this background these drawings are captivating and incredibly fun! The servant's round, flat hat both hides and serves as a comic substitute for his face. Our attention is instead brought to the great variety of his energetic dance.

Just as Hokusai's *Manga* was hugely popular among the art-loving public in Japan, when these drawing manuals reached Paris in the mid-1800s, they were equally inspirational to artists like Manet and Degas. The *Manga* volumes helped establish the craze for *Japonisme* in Europe.

The Yakko-odori (The Servant's Dance)
from Manga, volume III

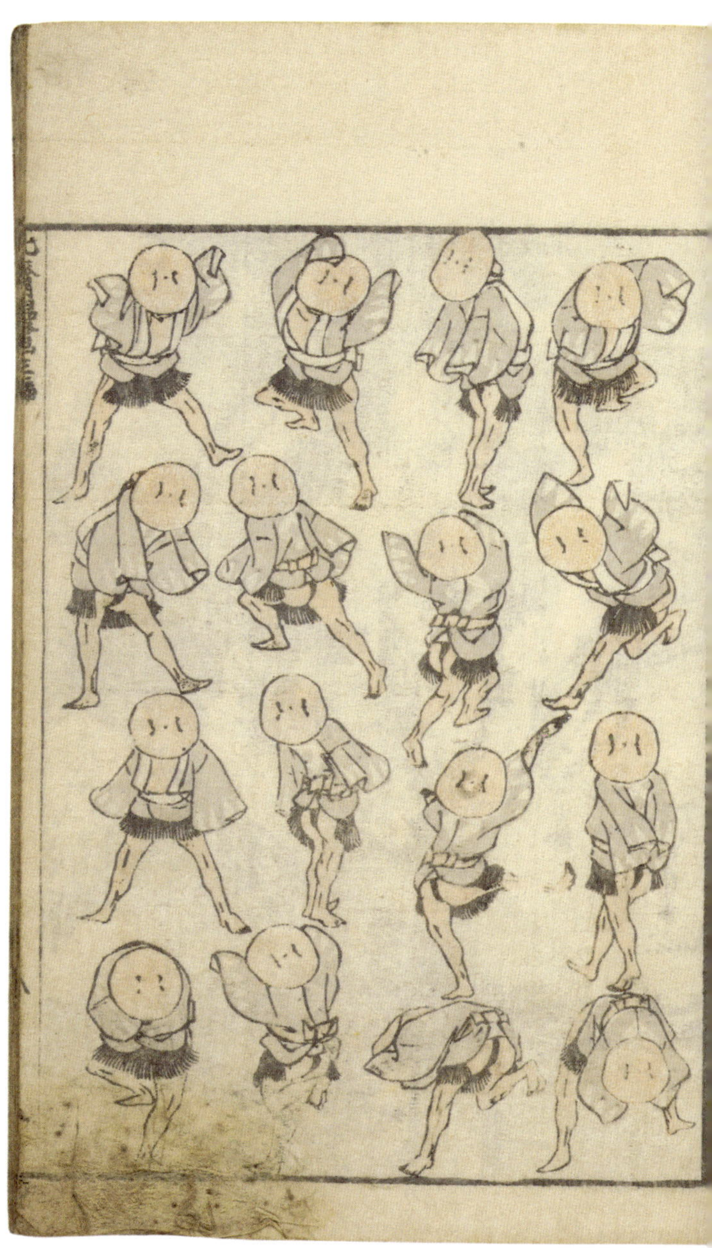

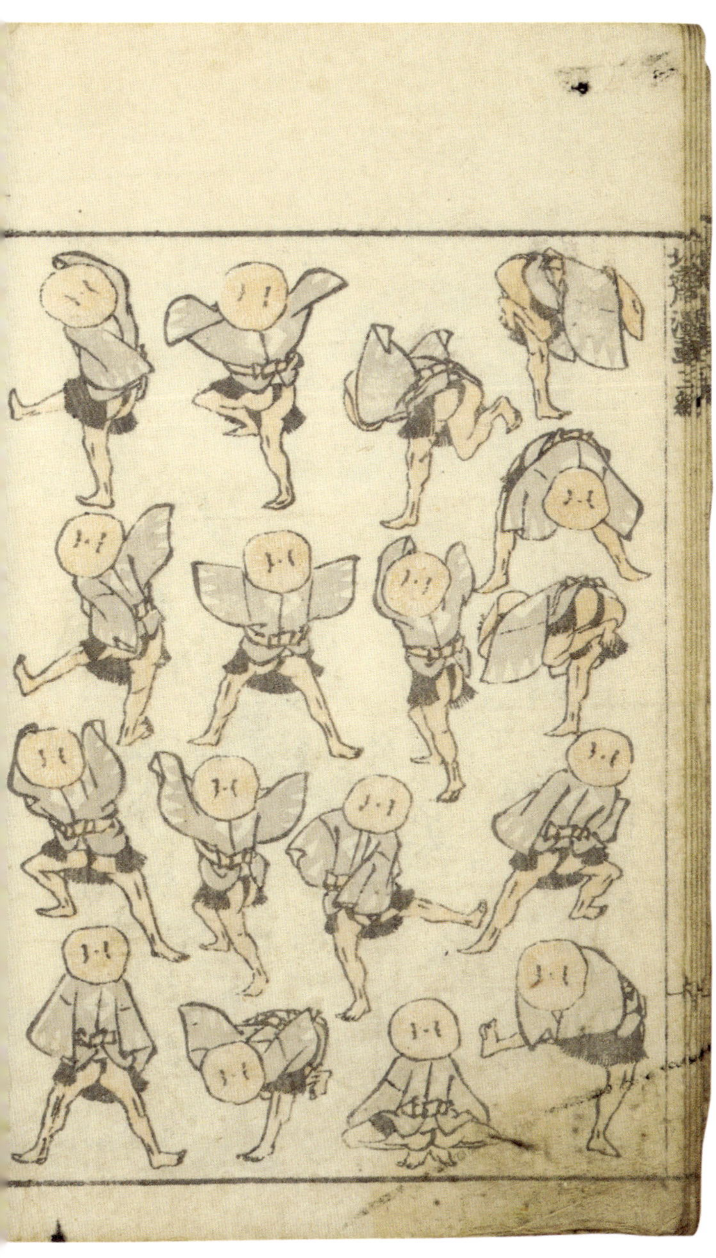

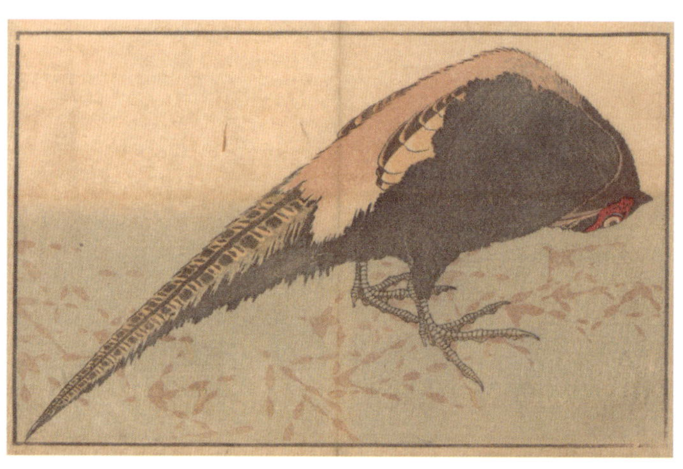

Woodblock print,   c. 1814
ink and colour
on paper
22 cm × 33.8 cm
(8⅝ in × 13¼ in)

During the second decade of the nineteenth century, Hokusai concentrated on the production of erotica and picture manuals. The former was a significant *ukiyo-e* genre, which Hokusai had also depicted earlier in his career. The latter includes the important *Album of drawings from life*, from which this illustration derives. In contrast to the *Manga* sketches, the fifteen double-page images in this work are examples of Hokusai's more finished pictures.

What's unique about these 'drawings from life' is how they convey Hokusai's distinctive approach to the surrounding world. In this print, for instance, we can sense Hokusai's amusement in portraying the pheasant looking down at its own footprints. Their resemblance to autumn maple leaves also recalls an earlier instance of Hokusai's ingenuity.

It's said that in 1804, Hokusai and another artist competed in a painting competition before the Tokugawa shogun Ienari. Hokusai drew some undulating blue lines and then he picked up a chicken, dipped its feet in red ink, and released it over the painting. It was clear to the audience that this was a depiction of maple leaves floating on the Tatsuta River, a spot famous for viewing autumn foliage.

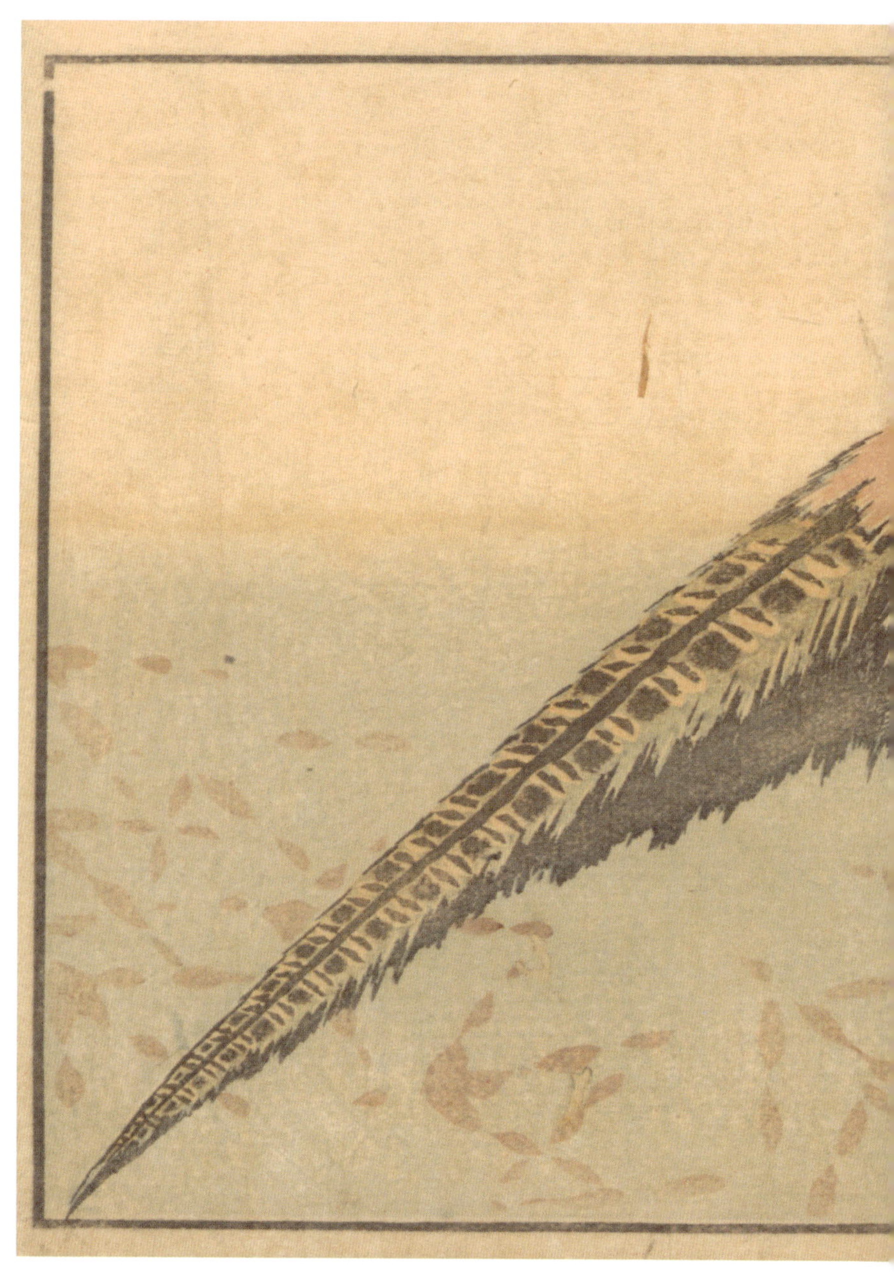

Pheasant in Autumn from the book
Album of drawings from life

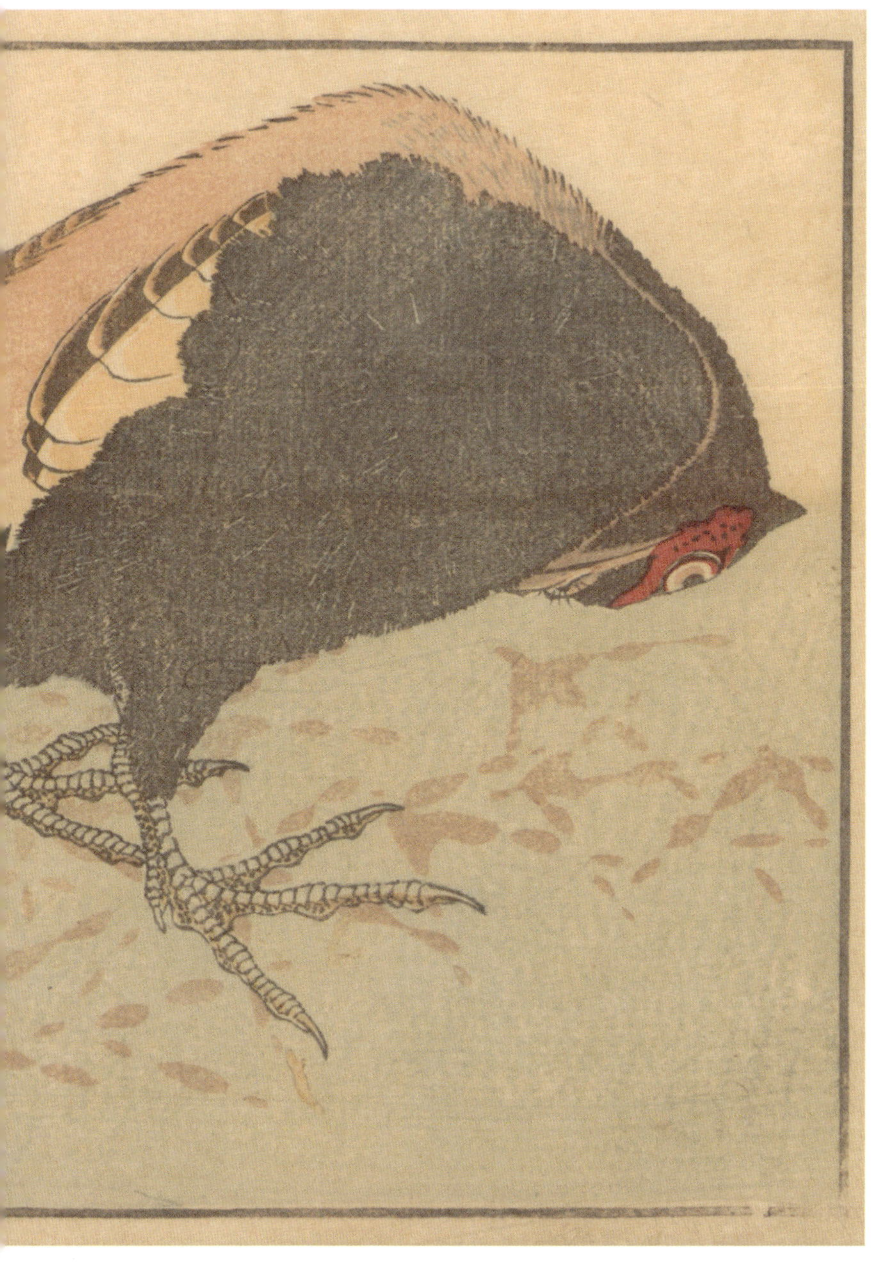

Drawings at One Stroke (Ippitsu gafu)

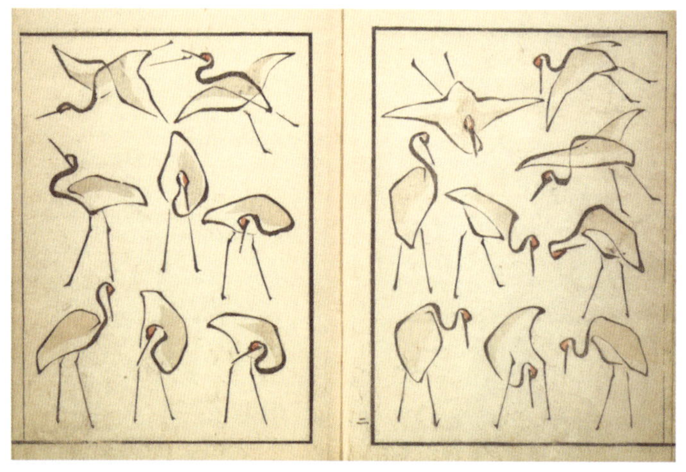

Woodblock print,   c. 1817
ink and colour
on paper
23.8 cm × 16 cm
(9⅜ in × 6¼ in)

When Hokusai began creating drawing manuals in the 1810s – most famously the *Manga* – he once more changed his name. Just as 'Hokusai' referenced the North Star in Ursa Minor, his new name, Taito, derived from the star Taihokuto in that same constellation. During the Taito period, which ended around 1820, Hokusai devoted much of his time to teaching others, including the many pupils he inevitably attracted, through these sketchbooks.

Hokusai's drawing manuals also demonstrate his creative skill, and this is particularly the case in *Drawings at One Stroke*. While this album wasn't published until 1823, Hokusai worked on the drawings around 1817 and the book is signed 'Master Taito, formerly Hokusai'. *Ippitsu* means 'one stroke' and refers to the technique of drawing without lifting the brush. But this is generally a figurative rather than a literal description; instead, as these impeccable drawings of cranes show, a masterful artist can evoke a subject's essence in just a few, spare strokes. The slight use of colour only serves to enhance the exquisite rendering of the tall bird in a variety of thick and thin lines.

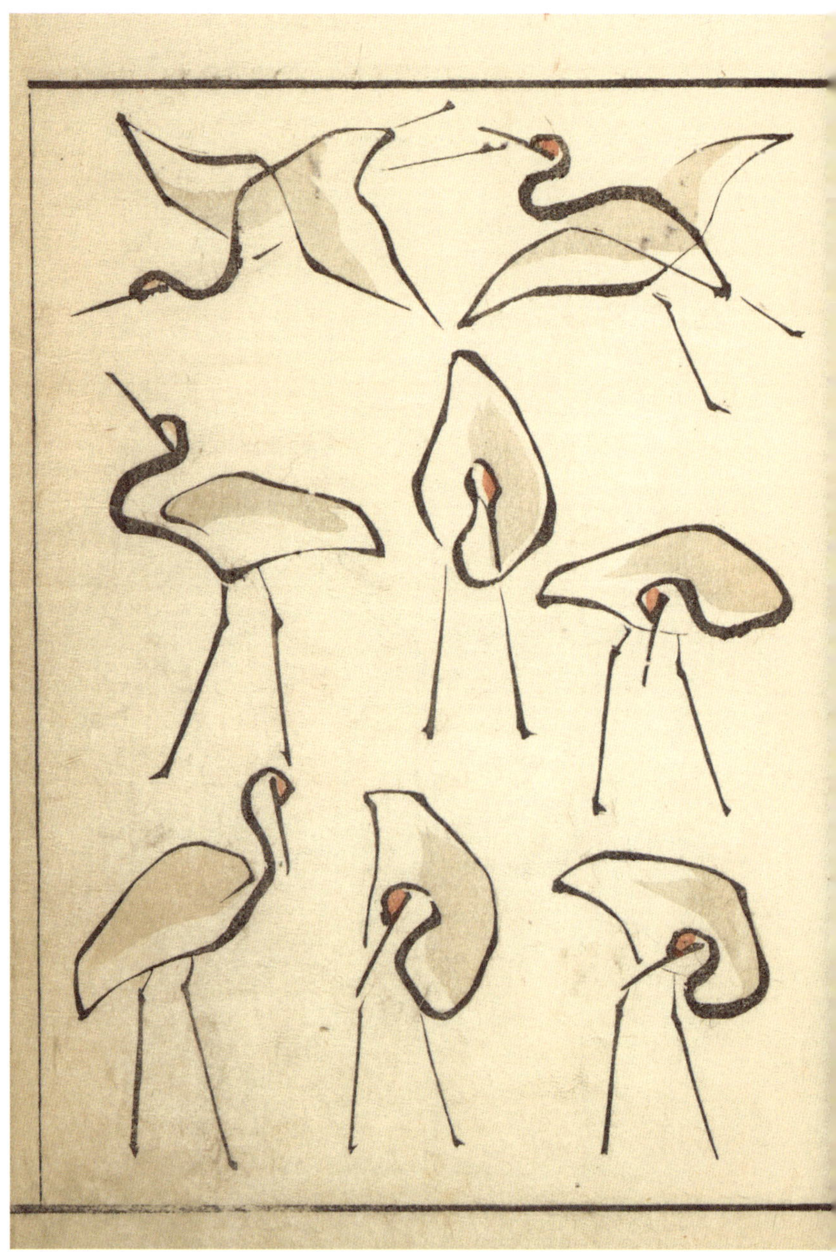

c. 1817

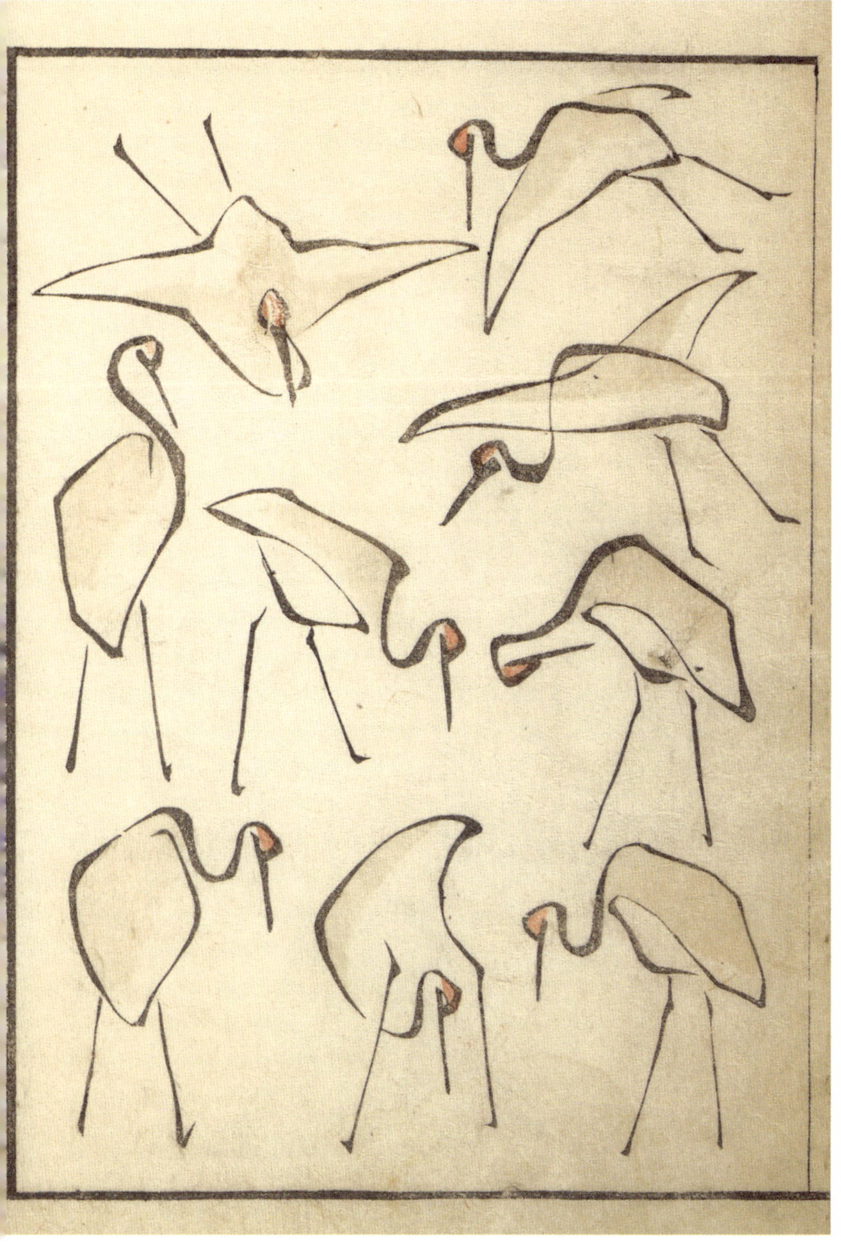

The Bamboo-Blind *Shell* from the series *Genroku poetry shell game*

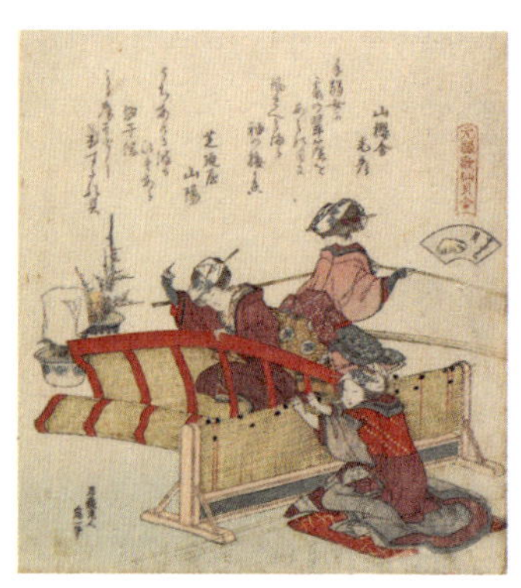

On first glance, this print looks like a captivating depiction of the making of bamboo blinds. The woman with her back to us selects stems; the figure in the foreground attaches them to a frame; and the woman in the middle adds fabric borders. But the red cartouche on the right, and the fan-shaped design below, tell us it is something more.

In the early 1820s Hokusai, who was now in his sixties, once again focused on the production of privately distributed *surimono*. For the year of 1821, a prominent literary club called Yomo commissioned thirty-six such 'printed things'. The title of the series, which appears in the cartouche, refers to a New Year's poetry competition on the subject of shells. The club members supplied the prints' comic verse, which is full of inventive word play. Hokusai contributed to this intellectual playfulness with his own artistic allegories that are frequently difficult to decode.

The audience for these prints was a small group of urbane literati, which explains why the only direct visual reference to a shell is the small representation within the fan motif. The shell's name is alongside. But what's really astounding is how Hokusai accomplished such a detailed, seemingly expansive, composition in such a small print.

The Bamboo-Blind Shell from the
series Genroku poetry shell game

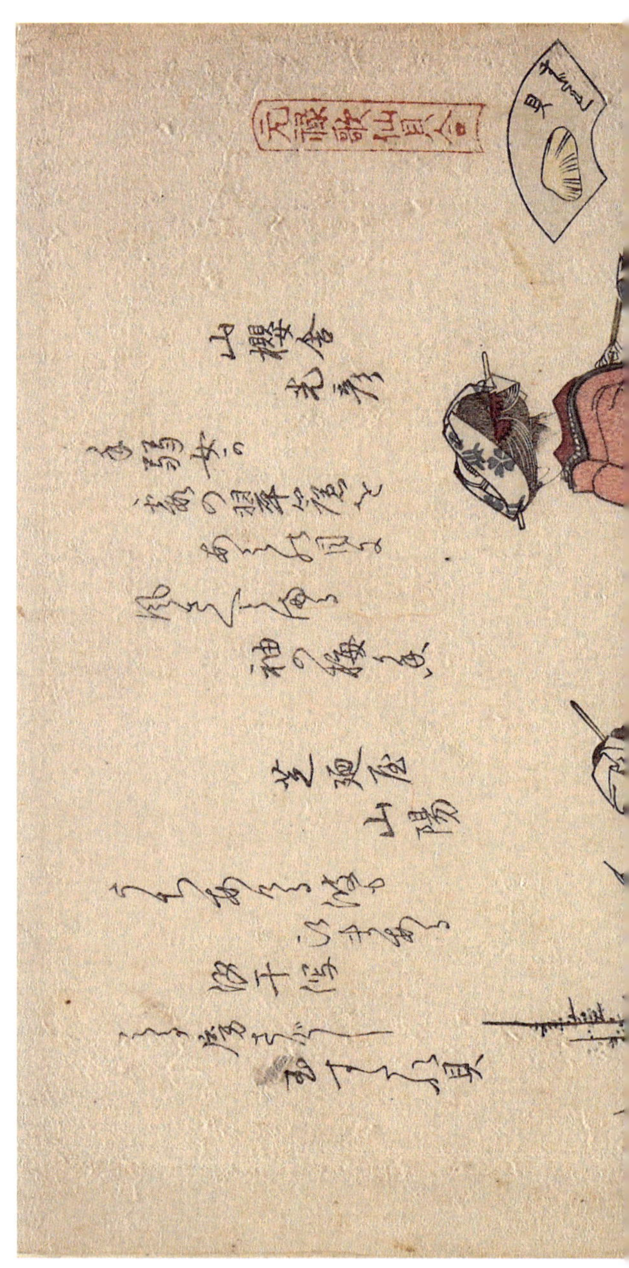

1821

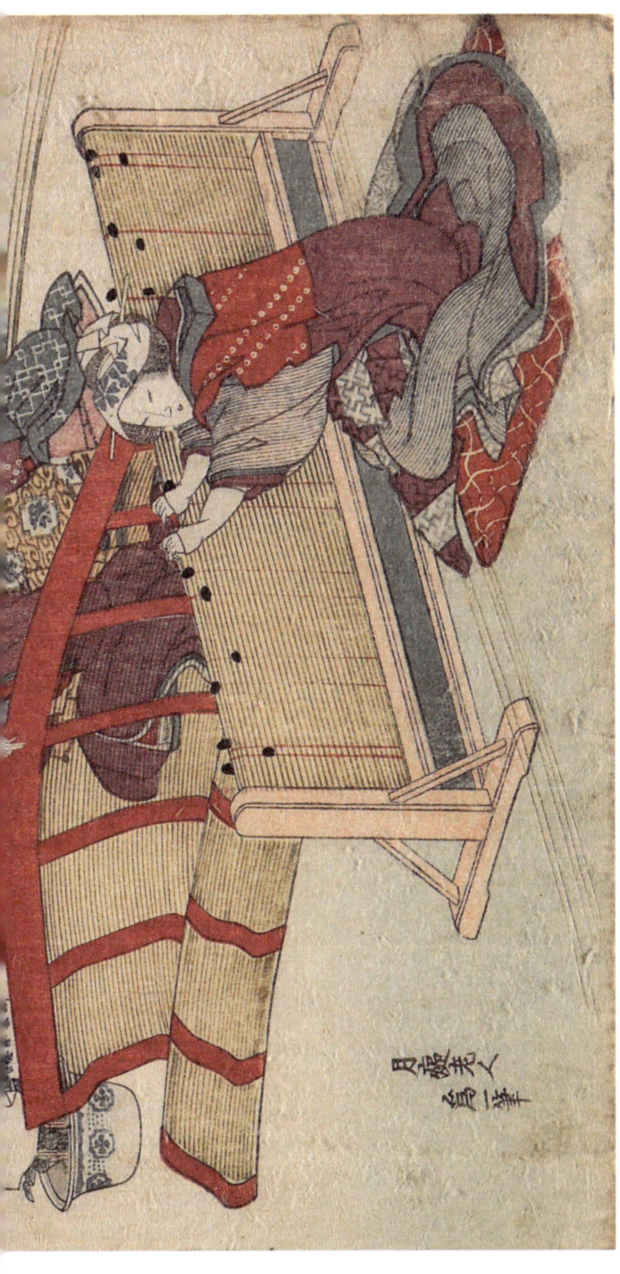

Courtesan Resting with a Copy of 'The Pillow Book'

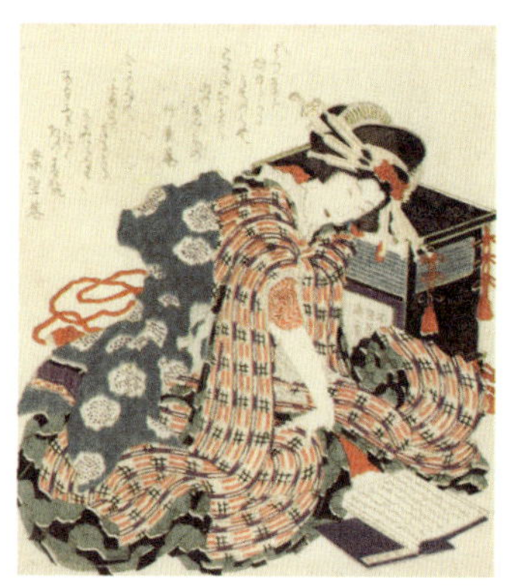

Polychrome woodblock
print with gold and
silver pigment
21.7 cm × 18.9 cm
(8½ in × 7½ in)

c. 1823

The play of patterns and colours in this *surimono* print is exquisite; note that the prominent hues of red and green are even repeated in the woman's lips. She is depicted reading *The pillow book*, a collection of observations and anecdotes from c. 1000 by Sei Shōnagon, a lady of the Heian court. It was customary for high-ranking courtesans of the Edo period to be knowledgeable of classical literature and culture and, with the book open on the floor, this is a fascinating glimpse of a period of quiet study.

The work is signed Iitsu, a new name meaning 'one again' that Hokusai adopted in 1820 to mark his sixtieth year. Hokusai's generally frenetic work pace slowed down from the mid-1820s, perhaps due to family matters. Hokusai had married and had children when he was a trainee artist, but his wife had died young. He remarried a few years later but his second wife and a daughter died in the 1820s. It seems that at this time Hokusai also suffered from occasional paralysis and he had a grandson whose gambling caused financial issues.

And yet, it was only after this difficult period that Hokusai created some of his most famous masterpieces.

Courtesan Resting with a
Copy of 'The Pillow Book'

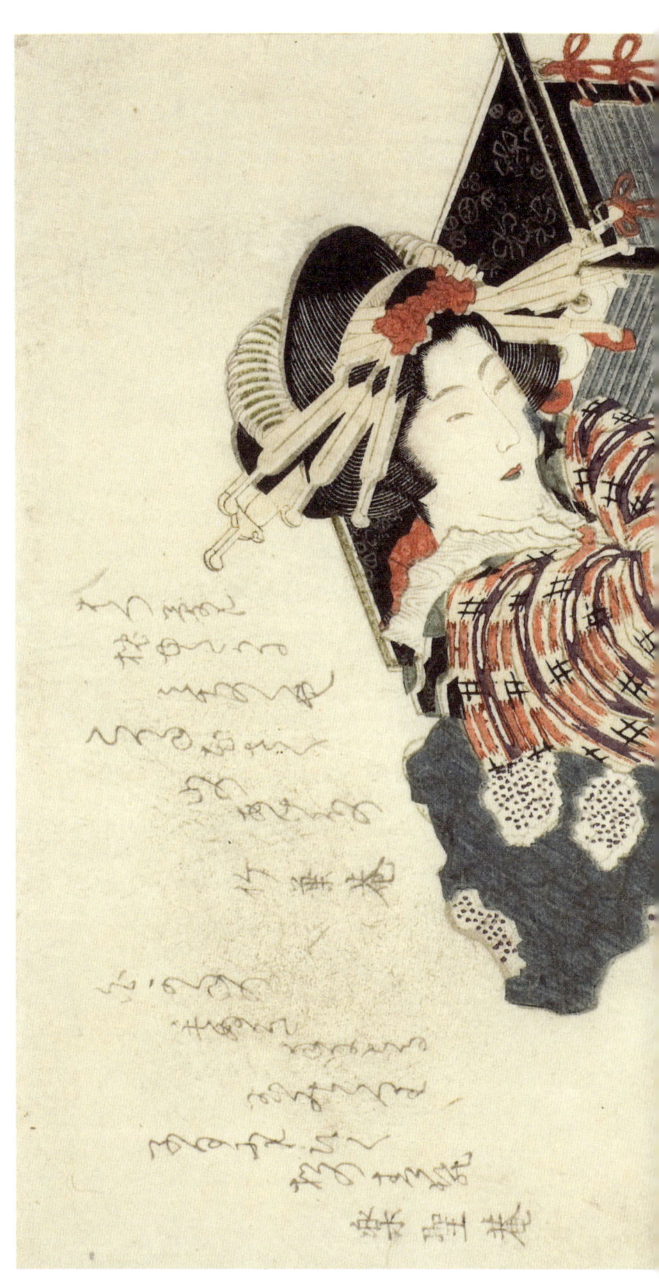

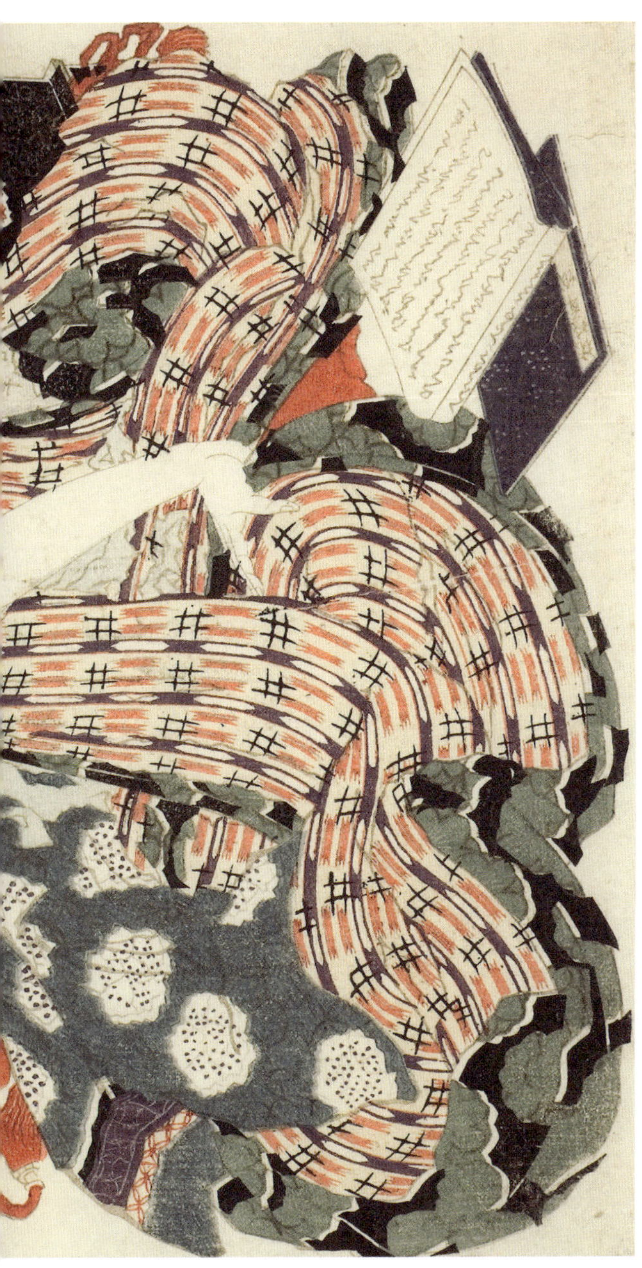

South Wind, Clear Sky from the series Thirty-six views of Mount Fuji

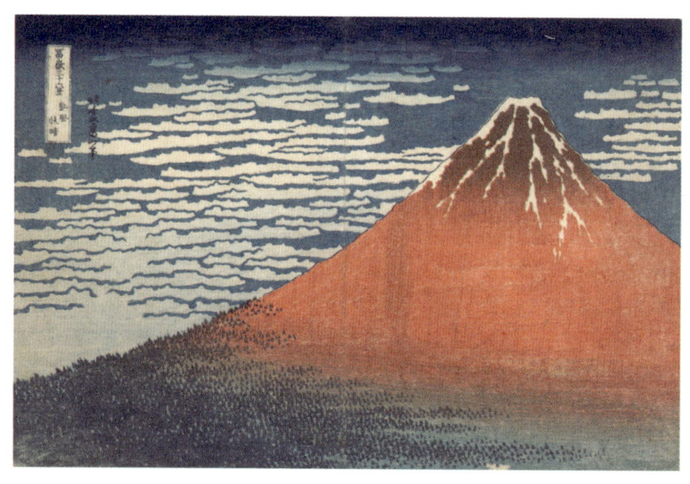

Woodblock print,   c. 1830-1832
ink and colour
on paper
25.4 cm × 37.8 cm
(10 in × 14⅞ in)

When Hokusai began work on his landmark series *Thirty-six views of Mount Fuji*, he was approaching his seventies. Issued in the early 1830s by the acclaimed publisher Eijudō, the prints revolutionised landscape representation in Japan.

While thirty-six views were initially published, ten supplementary ones were later added, though the title of the series has remained the same. The *ōban* (large format) prints depict Mount Fuji from various different viewpoints. People are frequently part of the represented scenes, but at times, as in *South Wind, Clear Sky*, Hokusai presents a pure landscape.

Otherwise known as *Red Fuji*, this work and *Under the Wave off Kanagawa* (page 100) are the series' most celebrated compositions. The mountain's russet colour reflects its appearance at dawn on a fine day in late summer, and the white of the mountaintop's snow streams echo the white of the clouds. These stand out against the deep blue sky, which is mirrored in the blue-green forest at the volcano's base. Among these shapes and hues, the mountain's presence is keenly felt.

South Wind, Clear Sky from the series
Thirty-six views of Mount Fuji

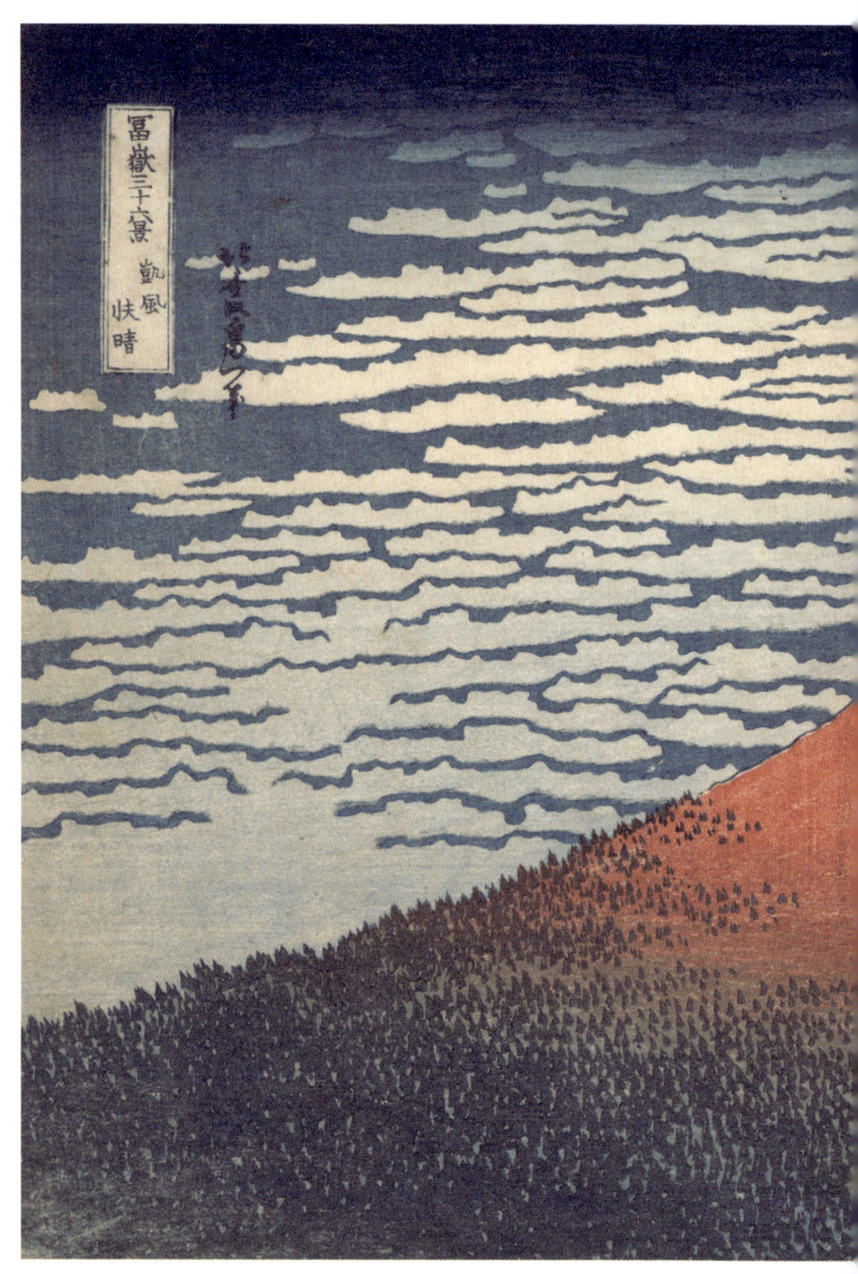

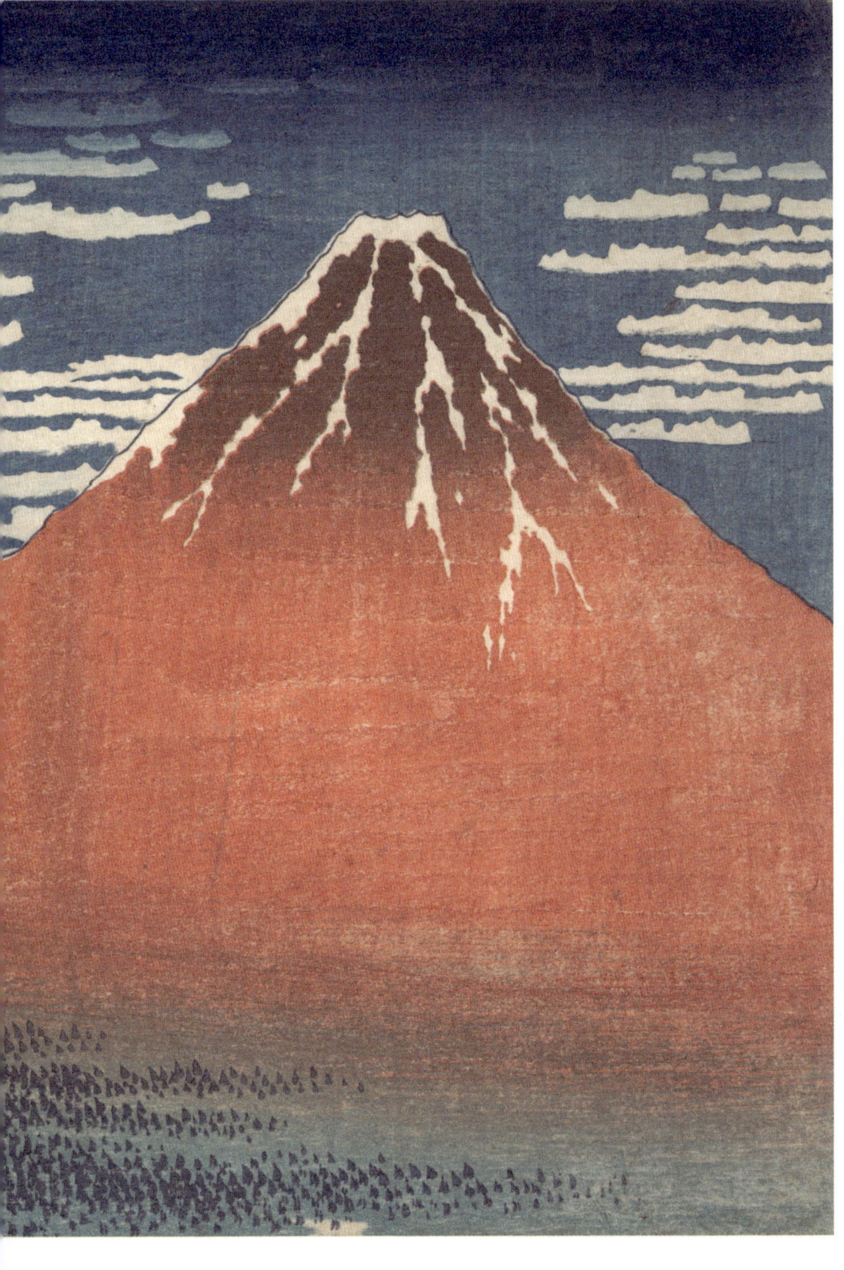

Thunderstorm Beneath the Summit from the series *Thirty-six views of Mount Fuji*

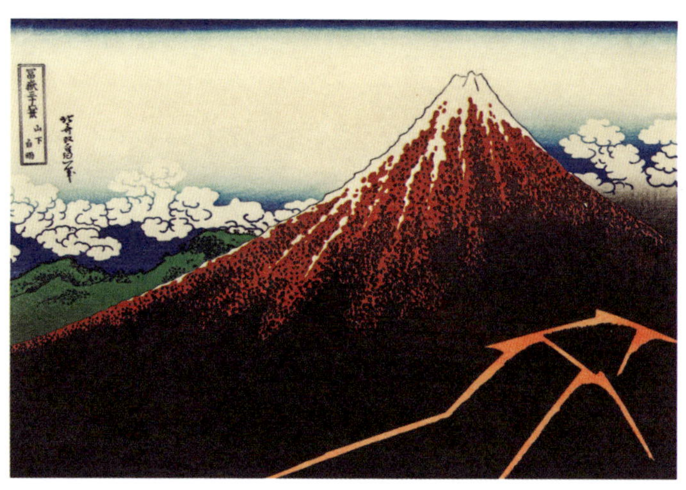

96

Woodblock print,   c. 1830-1832
ink and colour
on paper
25.7 cm × 38 cm
(10⅛ in × 15 in)

Unlike the fresh, breeze-filled morning pictured in *South Wind, Clear Sky* (page 92), this version of *Red Fuji* is a dramatic one at dusk. Mount Fuji is now seen from the other side, and the print's colours are much richer and more vibrant. The mountain's ridges also project more prominently. In the background, Western-style clouds stand out against the bright blue sky and green hills, while the volcano's base is subsumed in darkness. The thunderstorm that rages beneath its summit is marked by a flash of lightning that is strikingly stylised.

Mount Fuji has been regarded as sacred in Japan since ancient times. It is a *kami* (sacred spirit) in the Shintō religion, and the mountain is associated with immortality. Hokusai's *Thirty-Six views* is tied to all these cultural connections. What was novel was how this series in the *ukiyo-e* tradition – affordable prints of the floating world – was devoted to landscape. Certainly, human activity is depicted in many of the scenes; but by assimilating Western-style perspective, classical Chinese and Japanese painting, and contemporary *ukiyo-e*, Hokusai harmoniously merged the natural and the human world in a way that was altogether new.

Thunderstorm Beneath the Summit from the
series Thirty-six views of Mount Fuji

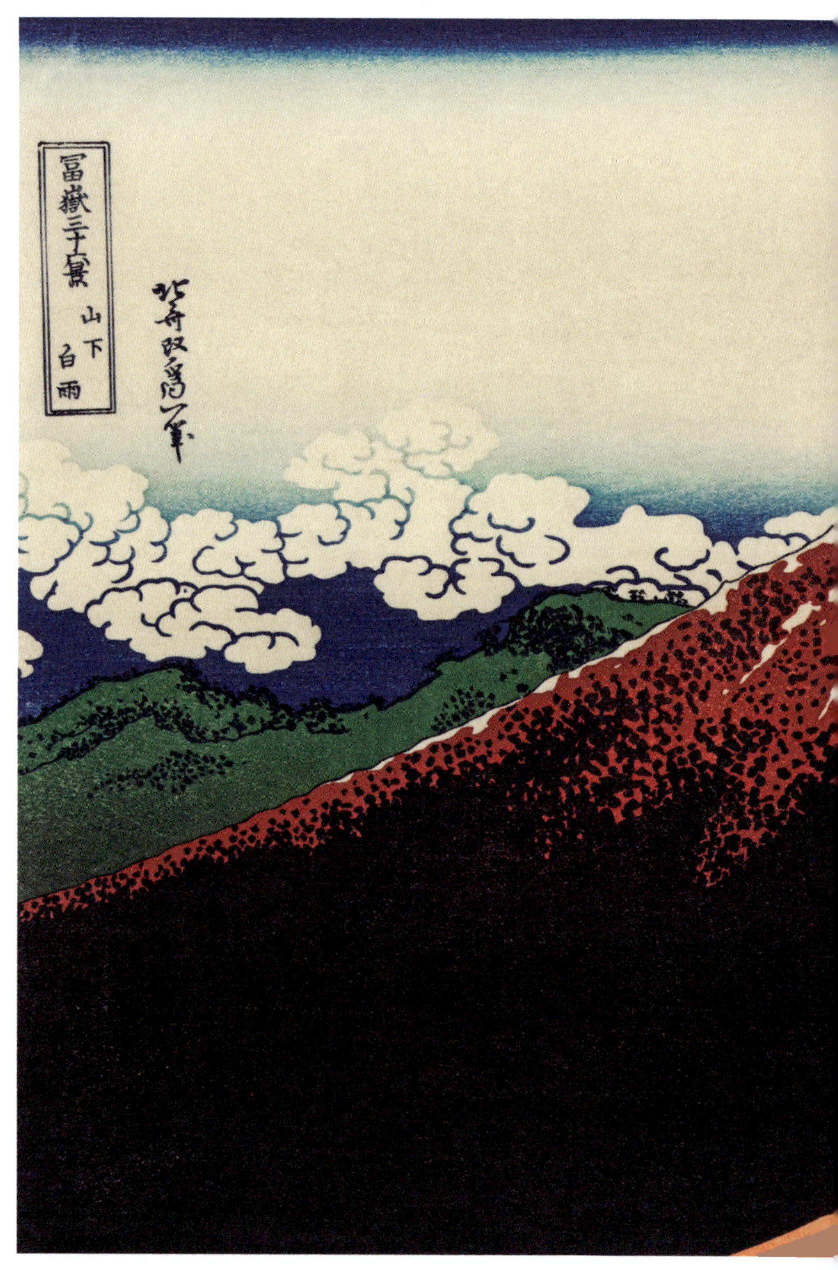

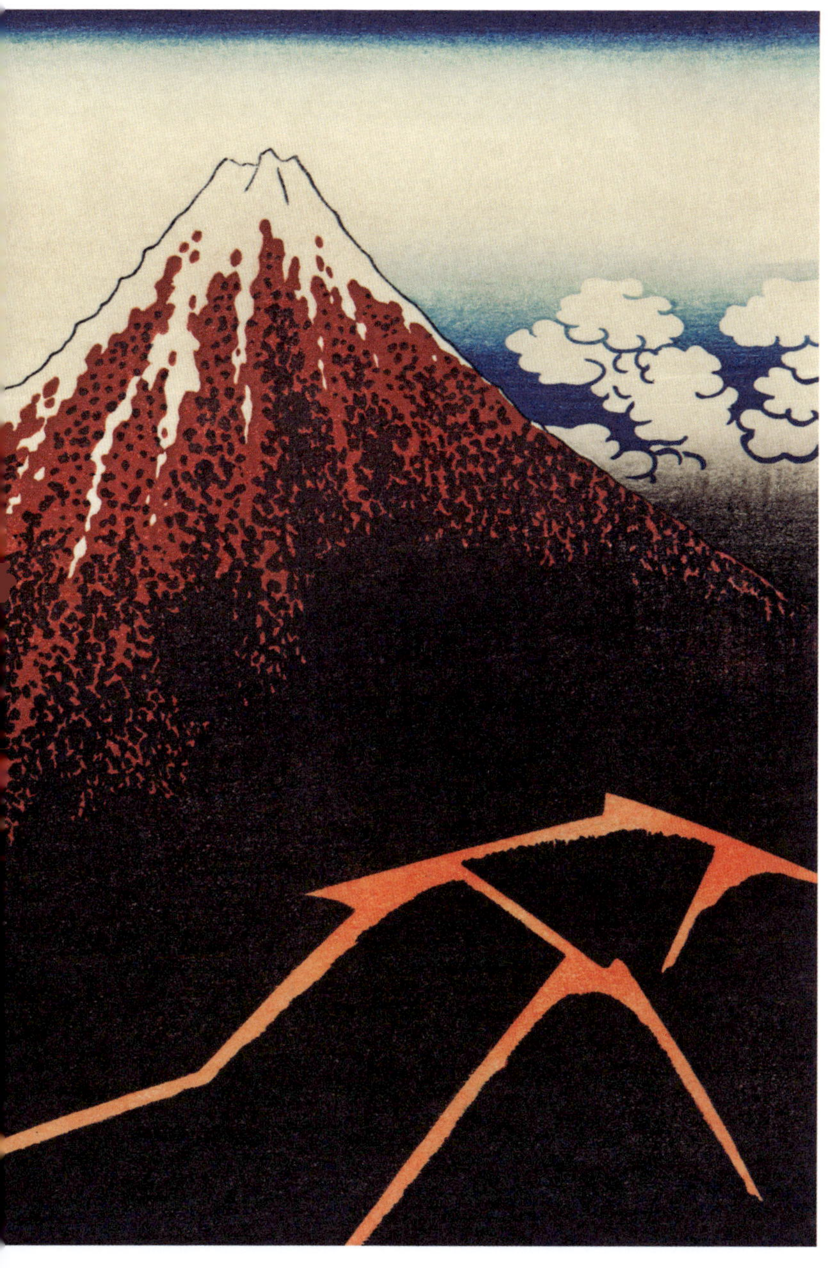

Under the Wave off Kanagawa from the series *Thirty-six views of Mount Fuji*

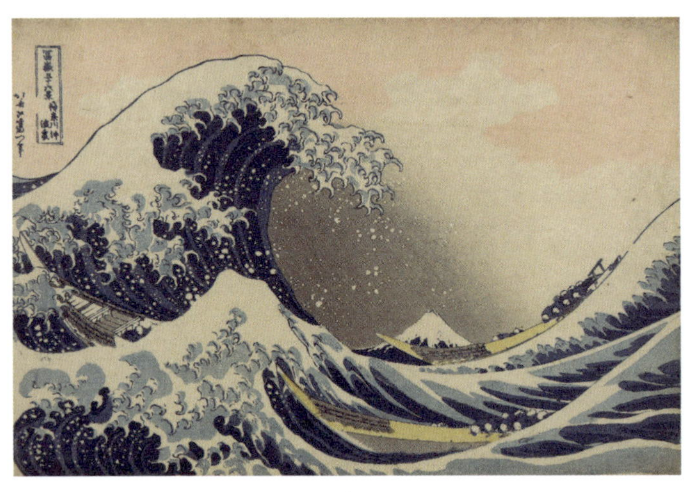

Woodblock print,   c. 1830-1832
ink and colour
on paper
25.7 cm × 37.9 cm
(10⅛ in × 14⅞ in)

Commonly known as *The Great Wave*, this artwork is so famous around the world that it can be hard to see with fresh eyes. But imagine for a moment being an Edo resident in the early 1830s, or a French Impressionist painter a few decades later, and viewing this masterwork for the first time!

The print depicts three *oshiokuri* (cargo boats), which transported goods to Edo, in the undulating sea off Kanagawa. Their crews hunker down as they approach a great wave that towers above them. The stylised design of the cresting wave's seafoam evokes talons, and the droplets of water resemble hailstones. In contrast to this moving force, the distant Mount Fuji stands serene.

East Asian landscape painting was traditionally focused on mountains and water, and Hokusai had made images of large waves in the early 1800s when he was experimenting with European-style perspective. Now, at the height of his artistic powers, he synthesised these elements to create an iconic image of humanity's tie to the natural world.

While the use of Prussian blue is integral to each print impression, this later impression is particularly notable for the pink sky and yellow boats (for further details on the series' colours and impressions, see *Kajikazawa in Kai Province* on page 104).

Under the Wave off Kanagawa from the
series Thirty-six views of Mount Fuji

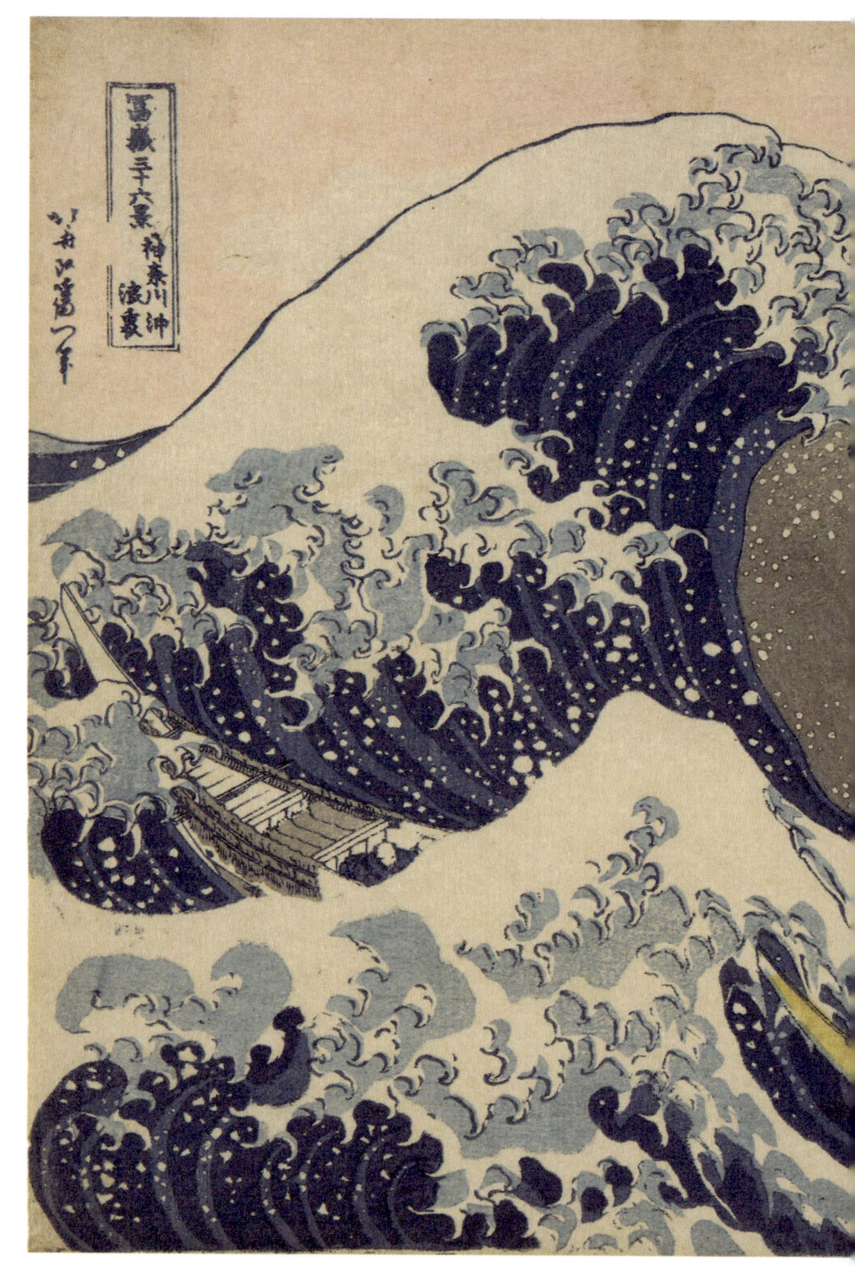

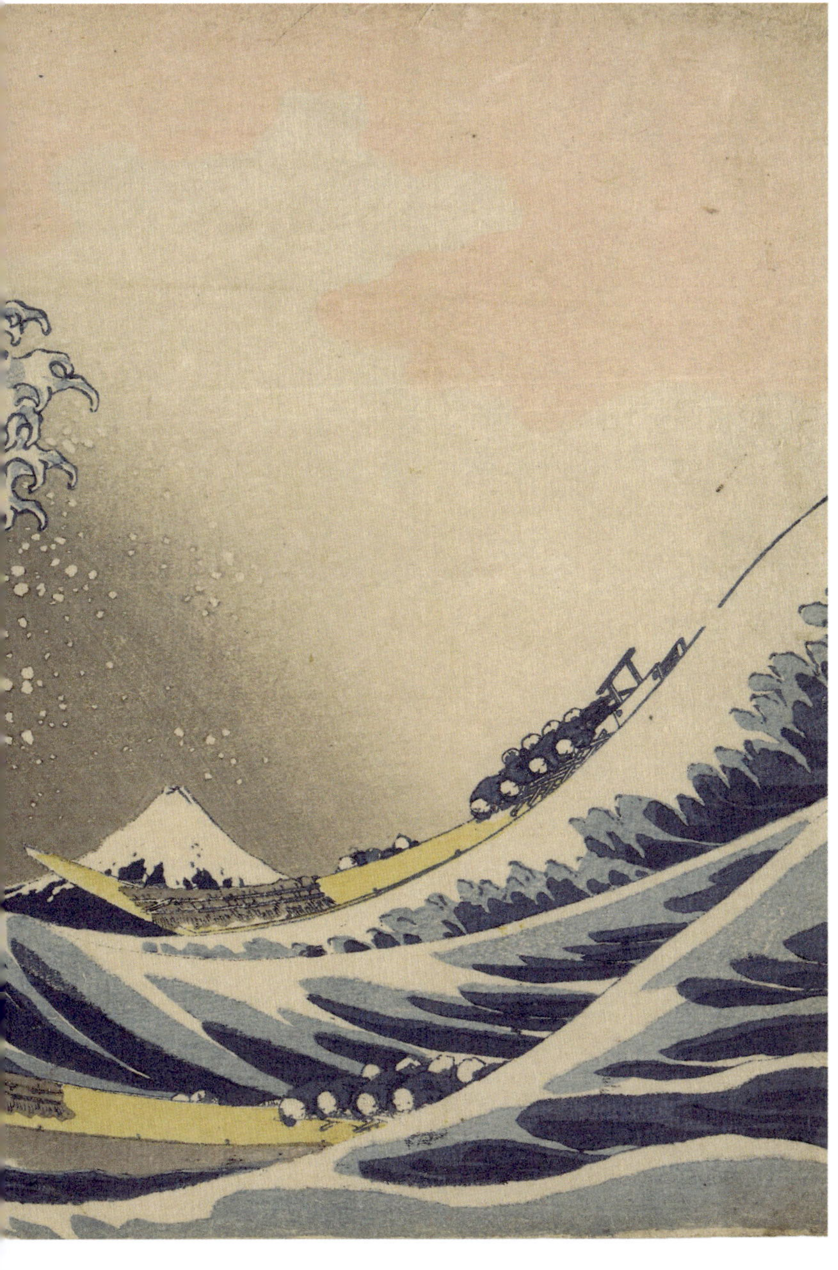

Kajikazawa in Kai Province from the series *Thirty-six views of Mount Fuji*

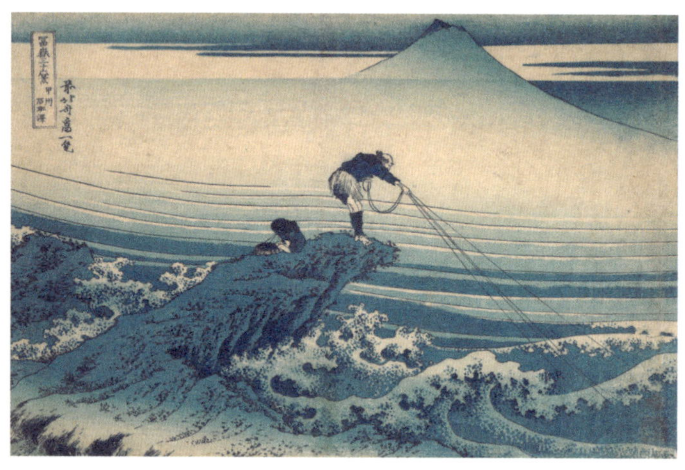

104

Woodblock print,   c. 1830-1832
ink and colour
on paper
25.4 cm × 38.4 cm
(10 in × 15⅜ in)

In an 1831 advertisement for *Thirty-six views of Mount Fuji*, the publisher describes the prints as being made in the *aizuri* (blue) technique.

The importation of Prussian, or Berlin, blue in the 1820s was largely responsible for this artistic development. A synthetic pigment made in Europe, Prussian blue was more vibrant, had a broader tonal range, and was longer lasting than natural dyes. Prints of the *Thirty-six views* made significant use of this pigment, though they also employed traditional indigo.

This early impression of *Kajikazawa in Kai Province* reveals the poetic effect of the *aizuri* technique. Later impressions (additional prints made from the same woodblock) frequently have more added colours, and other prints in the series used additional colours from the start. *Kajikazawa in Kai Province* is also magisterial in composition. By mirroring the form of Mount Fuji in the triangle created by the rocky outcrop, the figures of the fisherman and his son, and the fishing lines, Hokusai unites humankind with the landscape. Yet there is poignancy in the fisherman's precarious position and the power of the water below.

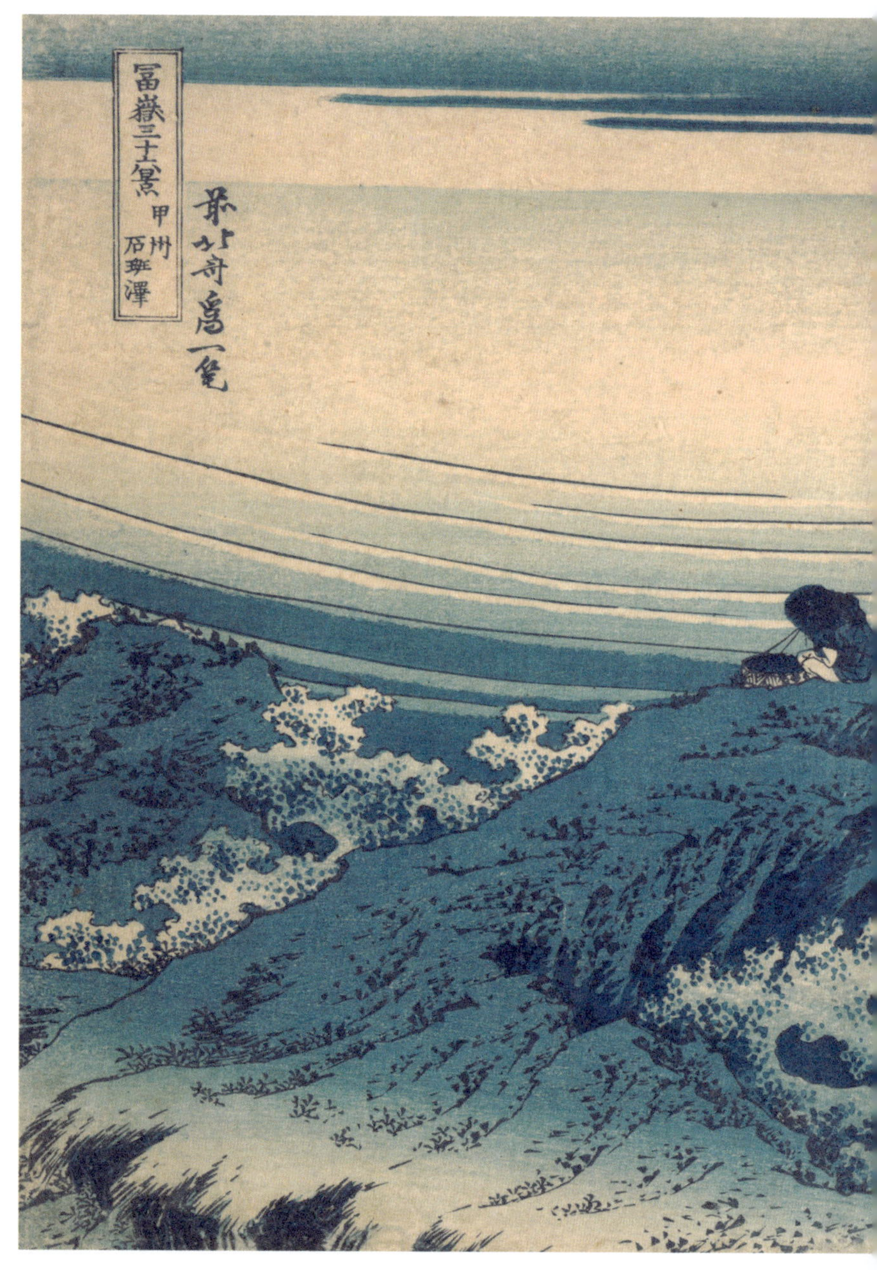

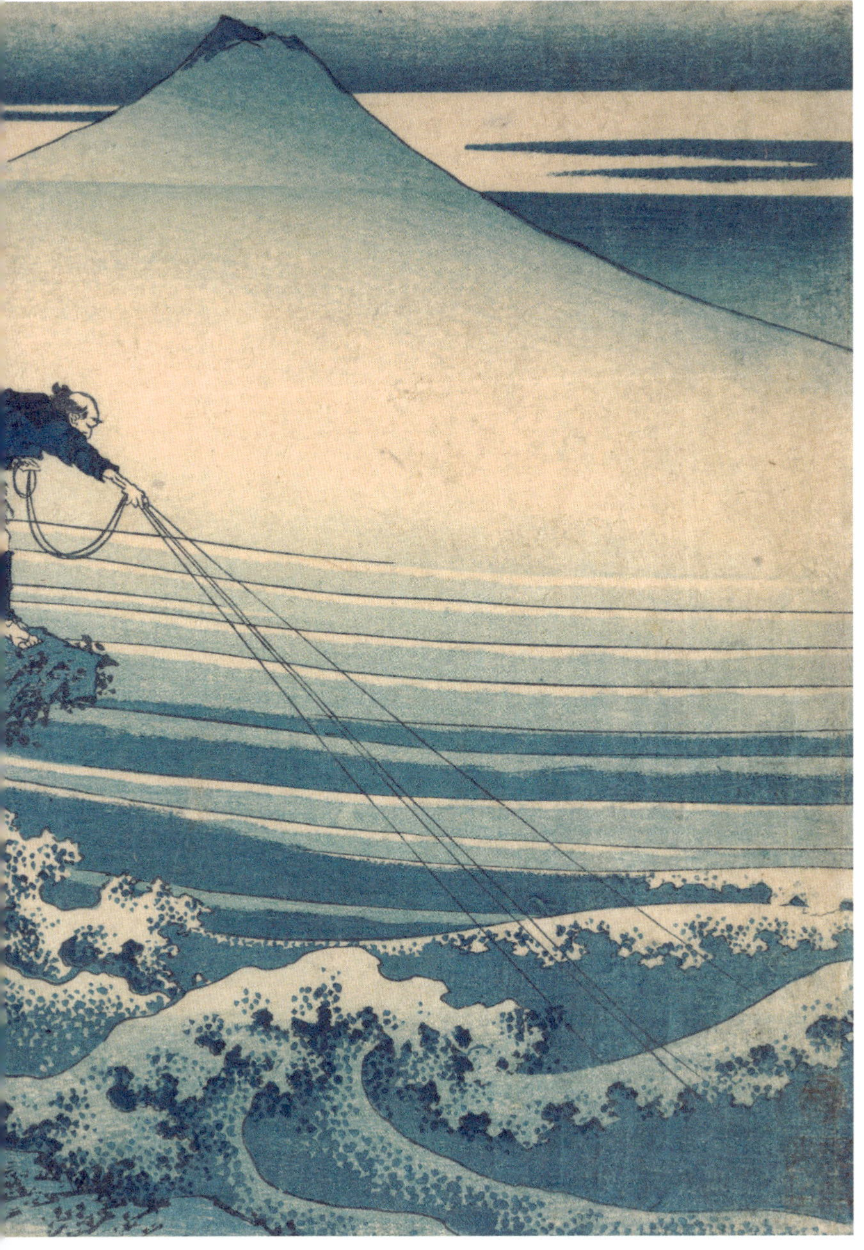

Ejiri in Suruga Province from the series *Thirty-six views of Mount Fuji*

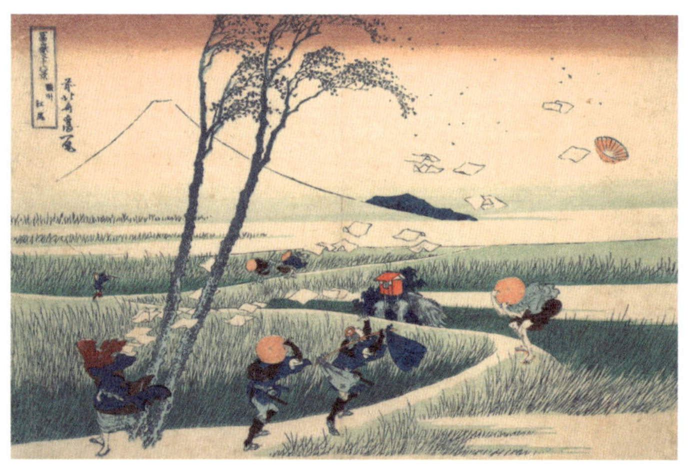

Woodblock print,   c. 1830-1832
ink and colour
on paper
25.1 cm × 37.5 cm
(9⅞ in × 14¾ in)

This delightful picture is a humorously empathetic account of humankind's vulnerability to the forces of nature. Caught out by the effects of a blustery day, figures on a marshland path struggle to keep their balance and their belongings. A man's hat has already blown off, while a woman with an unruly headscarf has lost a stack of tissue paper to the wind. In the sky, these papers accompany leaves blown from the bending trees.

If we compare this print with *Sazai Hall at the Five Hundred Arhat Temple* (page 112), we can see the striking formal variety of the *Thirty-six views*. The latter picture offers a distant view of Mount Fuji from the Sazai Hall veranda. The volcano is largely covered in snow but its base is depicted in deep blue, a colour mirrored by the band of sky at the composition's top edge.

By contrast, the uppermost band in this impression of *Ejiri in Suruga Province* is a rose hue, which is repeated in the colours of the figures' hats. We are now much closer to Fuji, here represented by a concise blue line. The mountain's still, immutable form is quite a foil to the chaotic human comedy taking place below.

Ejiri in Suruga Province from the series
Thirty-six views of Mount Fuji

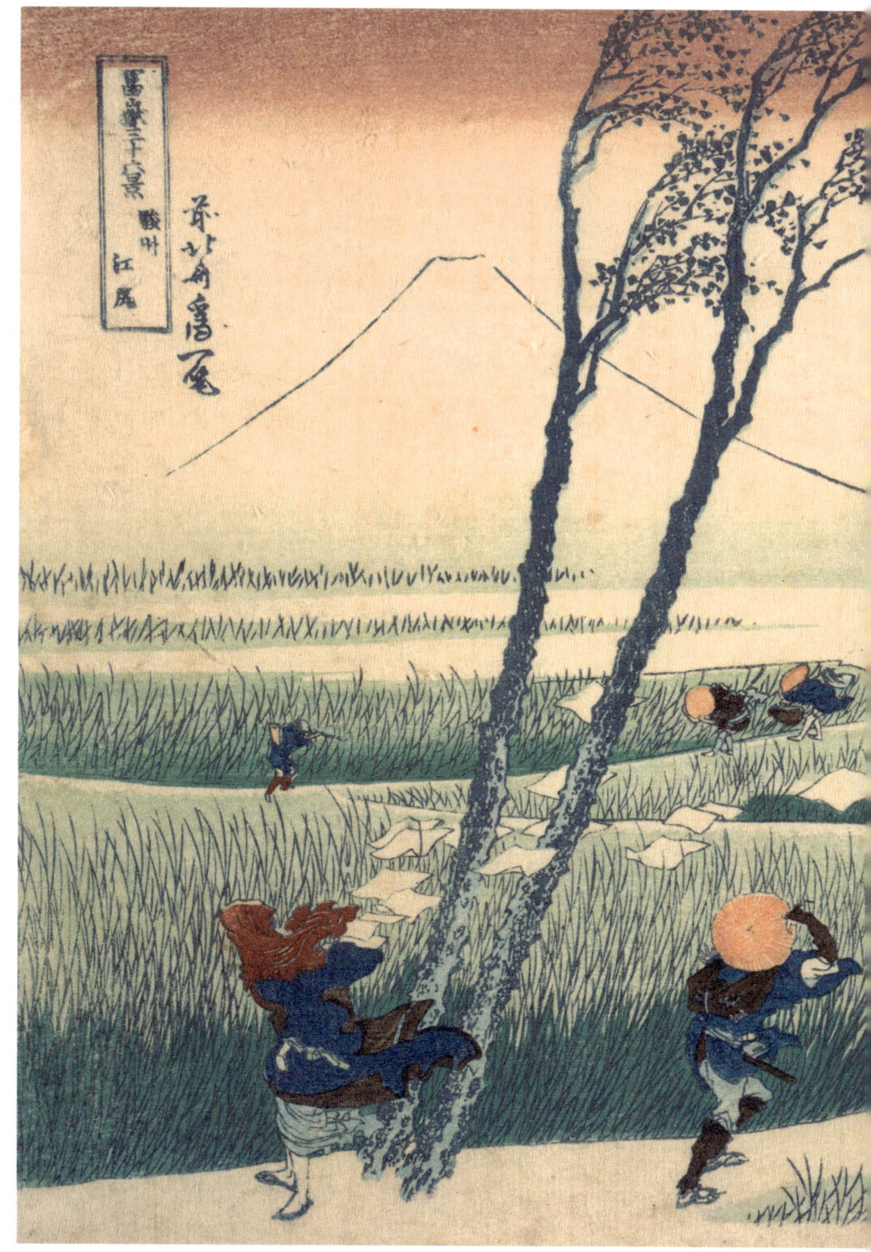

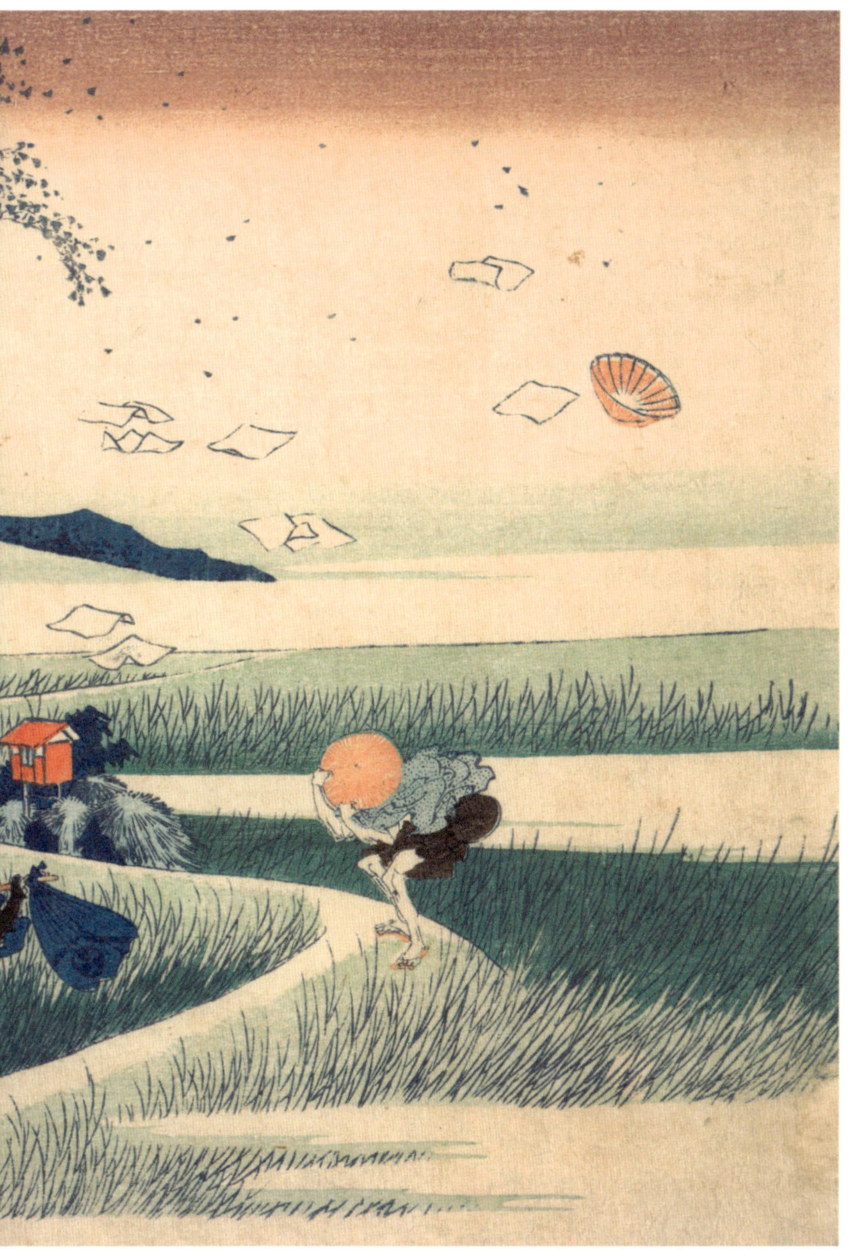

Sazai Hall at the Five Hundred Arhat Temple from the series *Thirty-six views of Mount Fuji*

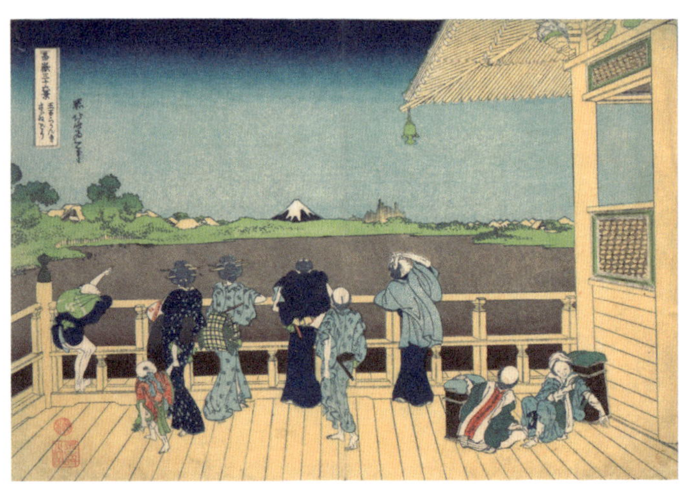

Woodblock print,
ink and colour
on paper
26 cm × 38.7 cm
(10¼ in × 15¼ in)

c. 1830-1832

With its depictions of pilgrims and sightseers, this image reveals a major impetus for the creation of Hokusai's *Thirty-six views*. Earlier works, such as *Hamamatsu* (page 56) from c. 1806, responded to a growing demand for travel images, but by the 1830s the desire to travel had reached a crescendo. Affordable prints were ideal mementos, or images of inspiration.

Journeys were often made as spiritual pilgrimages, but pleasurable stops en route and scenic sites were also drawcards. The Five Hundred Arhat Temple was an important Buddhist site in Edo, and this print depicts the viewing platform adjoining its spiralling Sazai (turban shell) Hall. Two pilgrims drop their belongings on the right, while daytrippers admire the distant view of Fuji. Echoing the natural form of the mountain are the spires of a lumberyard, one of which Hokusai depicts in close-up in *Tatekawa in Honjō* (page 116).

The combination of demand for travel images and Hokusai's exquisitely drawn, engaging scenes meant that his *Thirty-six views* was a sensation in Japan and, a few decades later, overseas. *Sazai Hall* inspired Claude Monet's early Impressionist masterpiece *The Garden at Sainte-Adresse* (1867).

Sazai Hall at the Five Hundred Arhat
Temple from the series Thirty-six views
of Mount Fuji

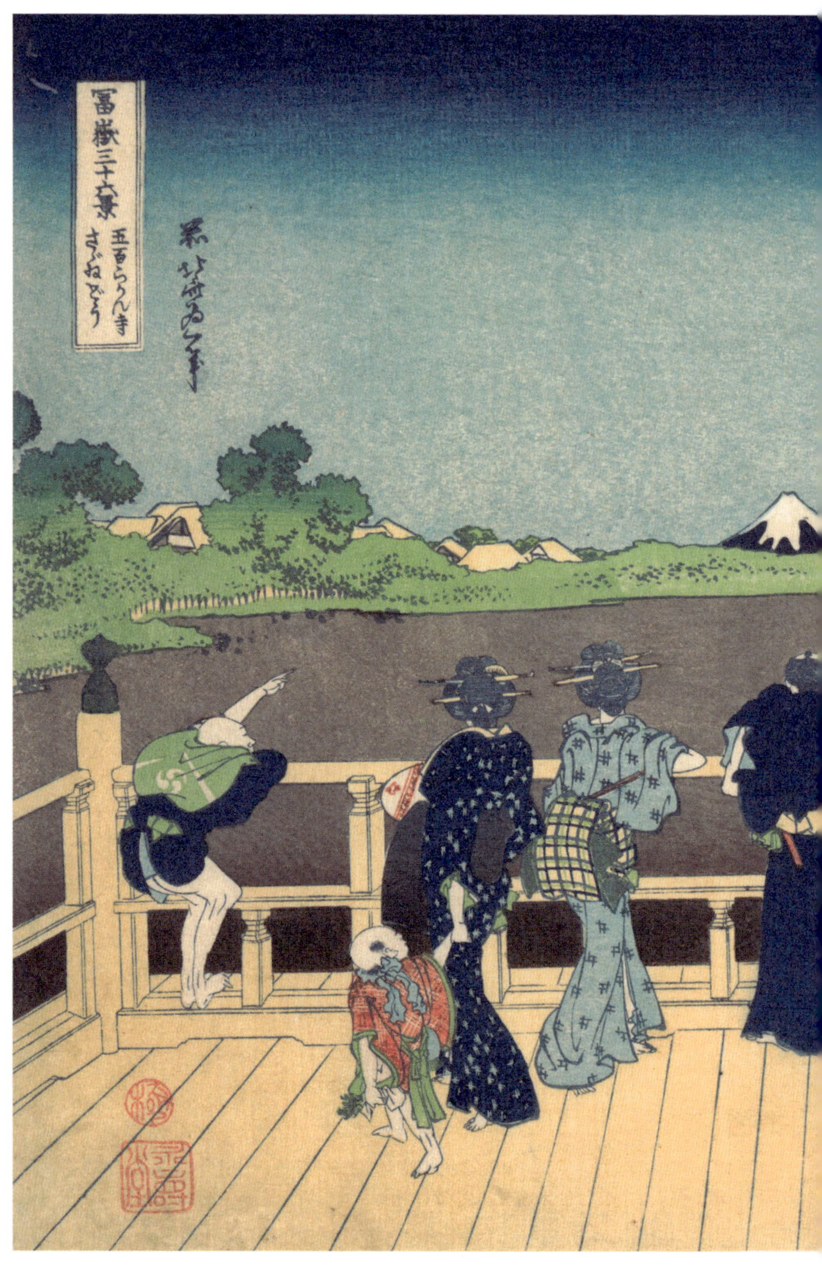

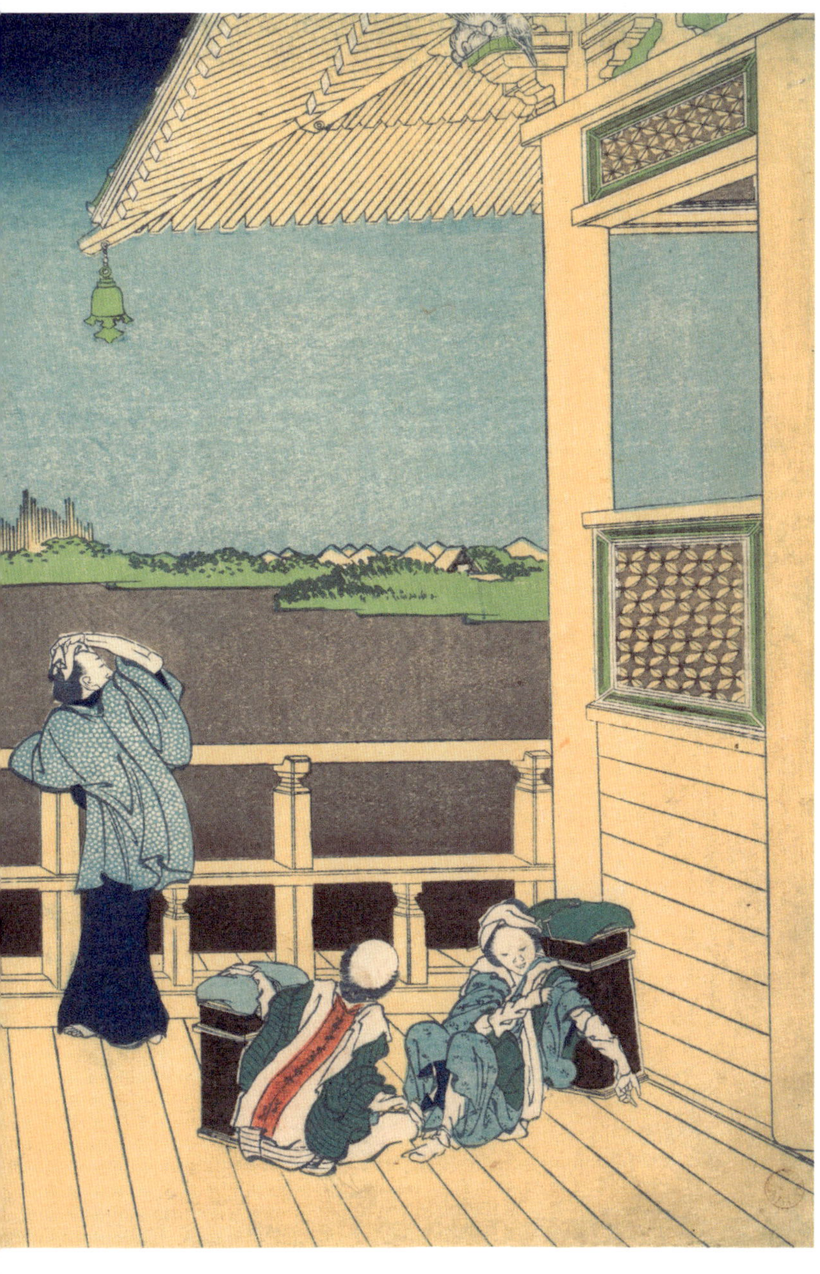

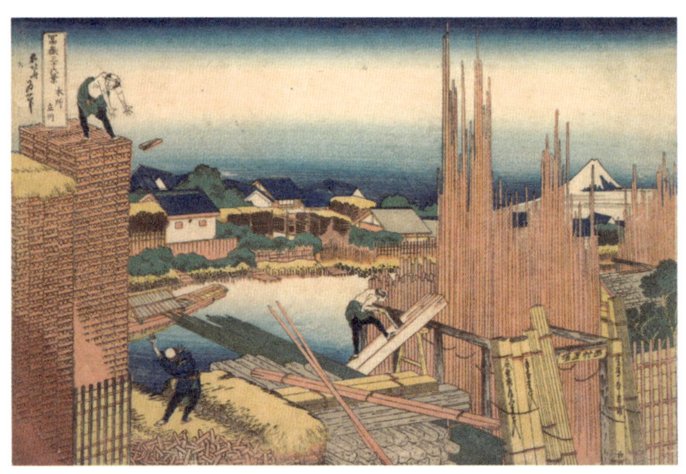

Woodblock print,   c. 1830-1832
ink and colour
on paper
25.6 cm × 38.1 cm
(10⅛ in × 15 in)

The charm of this depiction of a lumberyard on the
Tatekawa River in Edo's Honjō area relies on a novel
combination of subject matter and compositional layout.
As viewers, we're located in an elevated position, looking
across to the men working in the yard and beyond to the
surrounding landscape. The quiet stillness of Mount Fuji
contrasts with the animated gestures of the workmen as
one throws supplies to another. These consist of short
wood pieces that are being stacked in an alarmingly tall
pile. This playful verticality is mirrored by the long, thin
planks on the right, and by the distant Fuji, which is
tucked off to the side.

The inscriptions on the wooden boards in the piece's
foreground remind us of the commercial nature of
these affordable prints and alert us to their creator's
wry humour. These unabashed advertisements reference
the publisher and where the prints could be bought. One
particular inscription suggests that this was the first of
the ten additional views created after the original thirty-
six. It reads 'New edition of Thirty-Six Fuji in stock'.

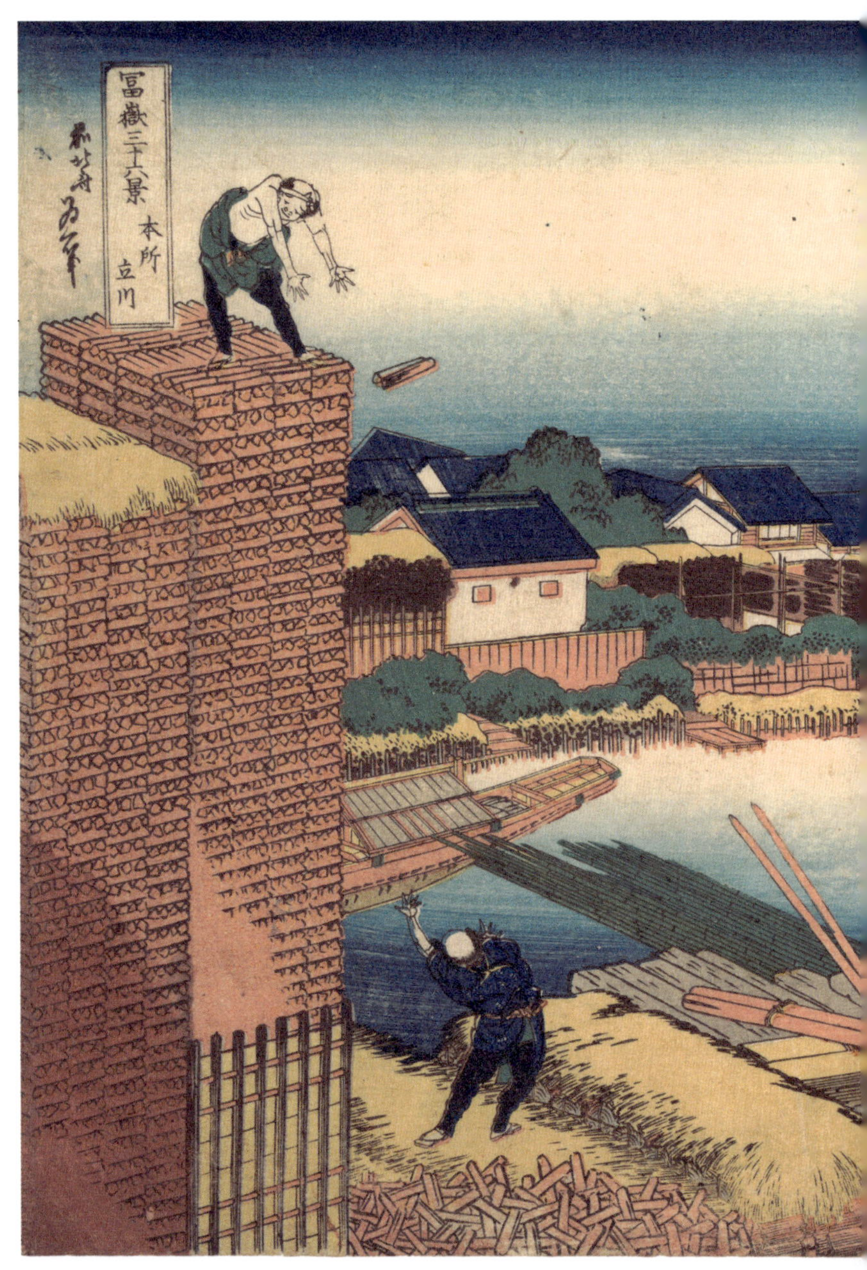

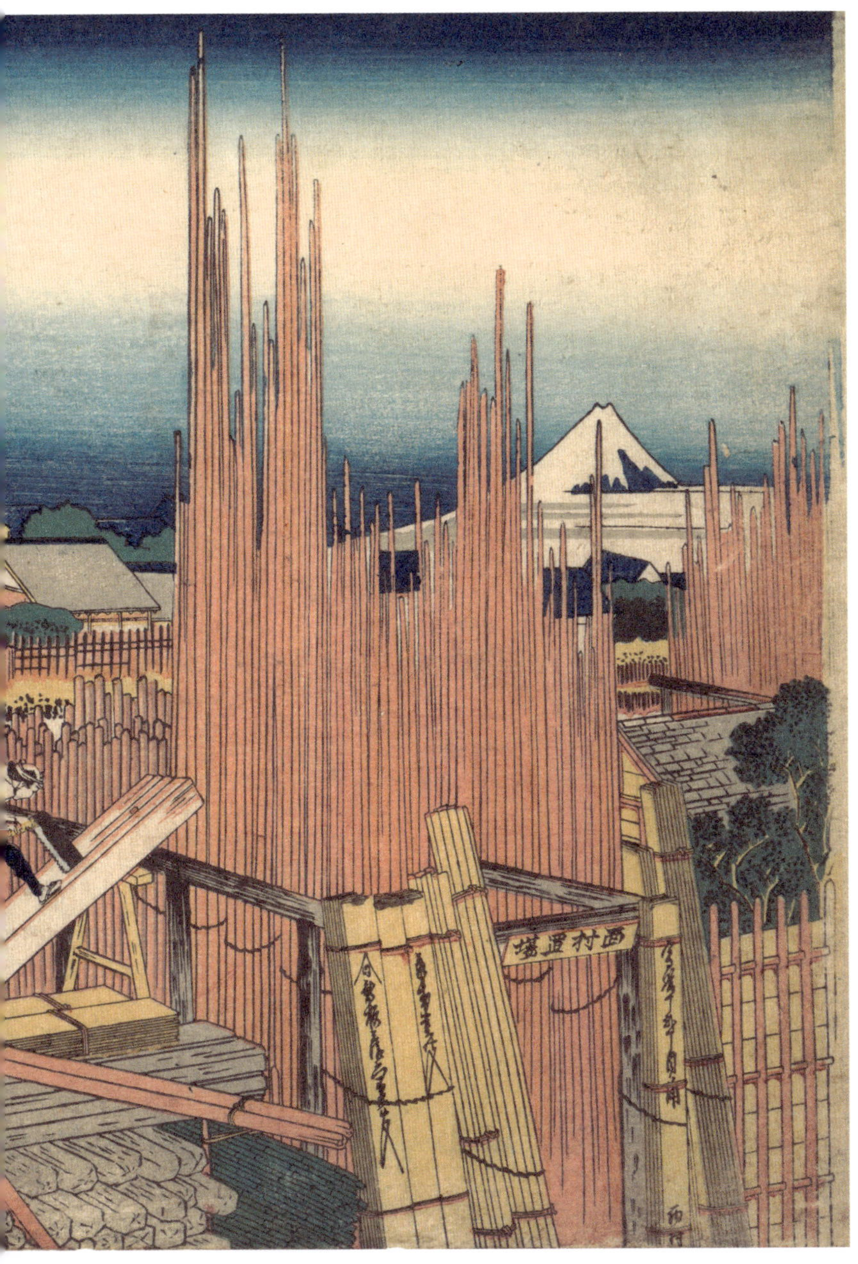

Carp Swimming by Water Weeds

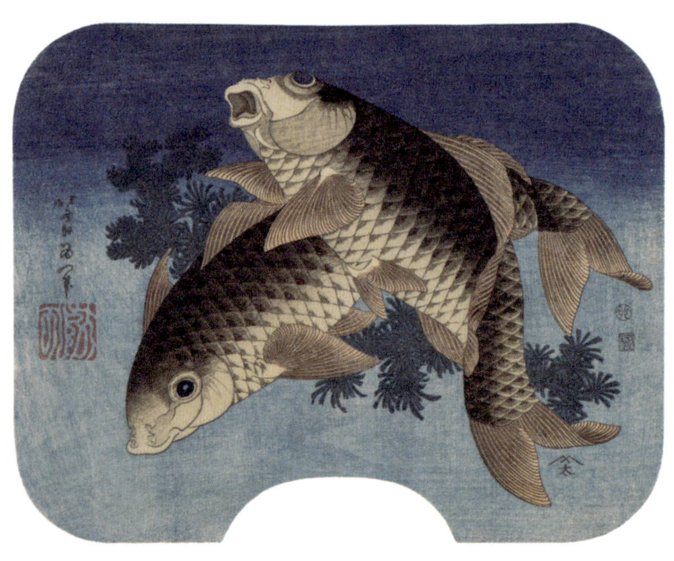

Woodblock print,   c. 1831
ink and colour
on fan
24.2 cm × 29.2 cm
(9½ in × 11½ in)

Hundreds of thousands of *ukiyo* prints still exist in museums and private collections, but this is a fraction of the many published. They were, after all, affordable, mass-produced images that weren't necessarily intended to be kept forever. Fan prints, or *uchiwa-e*, were also extremely popular, but even more ephemeral; as everyday items used during the summer, they didn't tend to last too long. For instance, among the tens of thousands of illustrations Hokusai created, only a few fan prints have survived.

It's surprising, then, that Hokusai took such care in the making of *uchiwa-e*, treating them as one-off images rather than as a collection. But fan prints, like this design of two carp swimming, were items that would be seen out and about in Edo. This may explain why Hokusai added his red Katsushika seal to this work – a seal he tended to reserve for paintings.

Shaped ready to be mounted on a rigid bamboo frame, *Carp Swimming* is suitably eye-catching. The Prussian blue background, with its skilful gradation from a deep to a light tone, is especially beautiful. It is characteristic of a group of fan designs that provided cooling hues for the hot summer days.

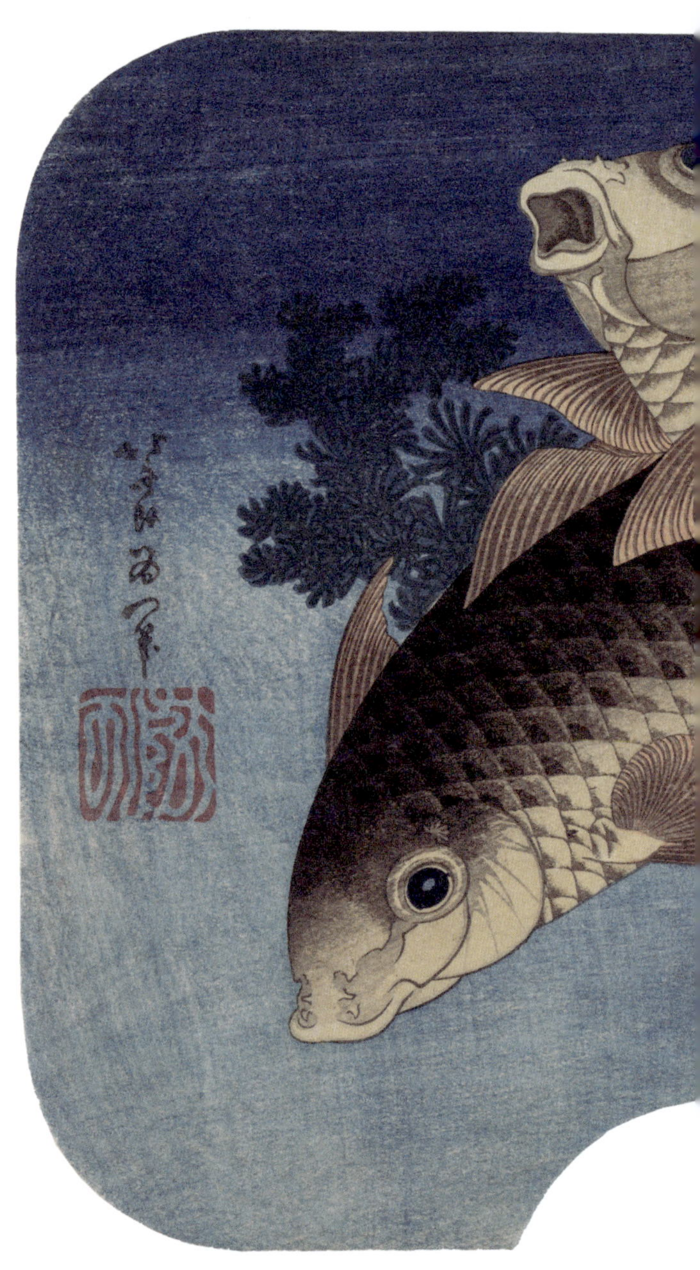

c. 1831

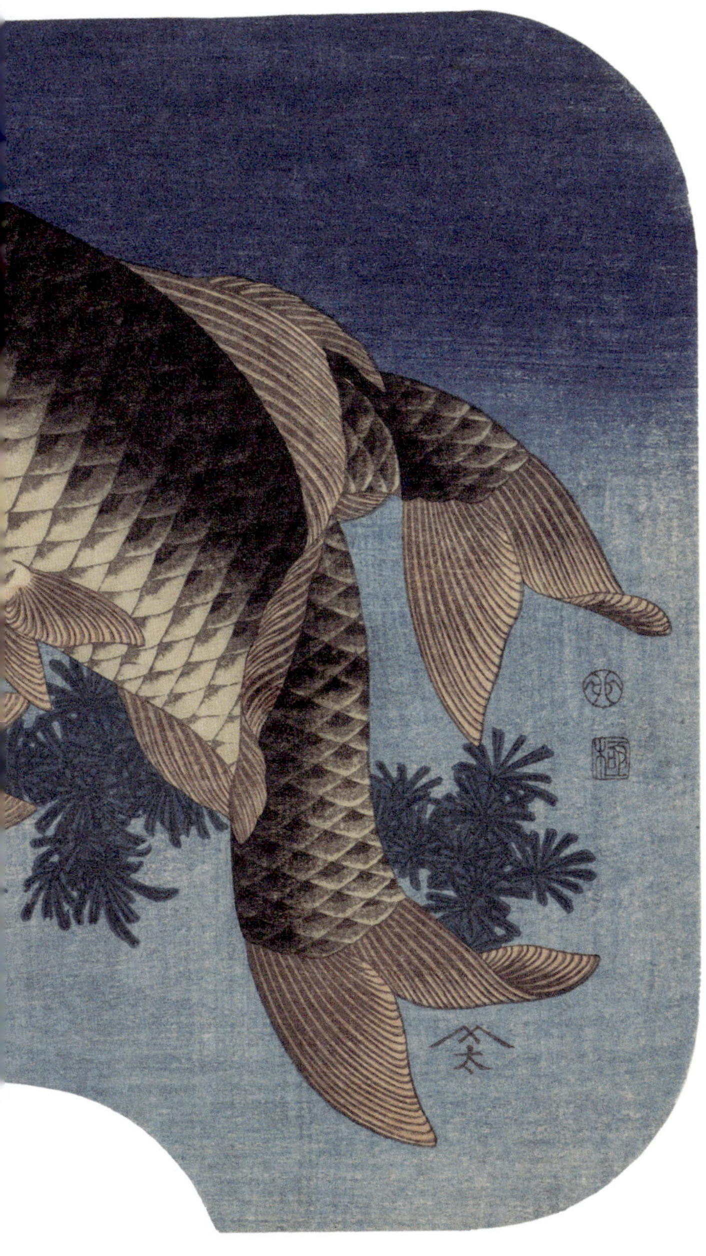

Oiwa from the series *One hundred [ghost] tales*

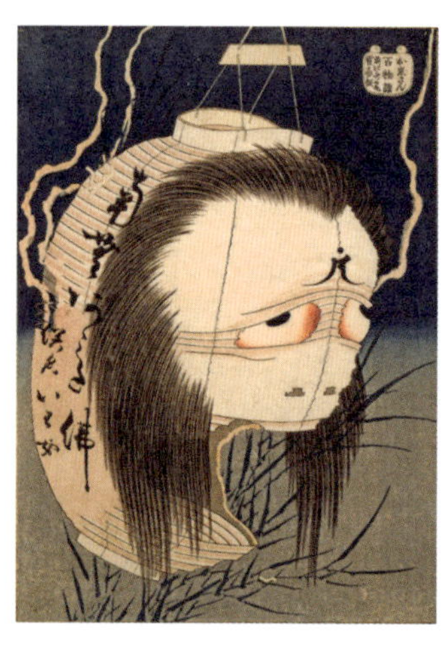

Woodblock print,   c. 1831-1832
ink and colour
on paper
25.6 cm × 16.1 cm
(10⅛ in × 6⅜ in)

The title of this series refers to a popular tradition of gathering together at night to tell ghost stories. After each tale, a light would be extinguished and, when all was dark, an apparition was said to appear. In this case, the ghost that has appeared is Oiwa, whose story derives from the kabuki play *Yotsuya Kaidan*. One of Japan's most famous ghost stories, it tells how a rival for her husband's love sent Oiwa a poisonous face cream that disfigures her. Her husband then abandons her and Oiwa, in a rage, accidentally kills herself. In the afterlife, she swears revenge.

What is particularly disturbing, though also rather ingenious, is that Oiwa's face emerges from a paper lantern. During Obon, an annual Buddhist festival, people in Japan light lanterns to guide their dead ancestors as they come to visit the living. Here, Oiwa doesn't simply visit; she takes over the lantern, her gaping mouth appropriating a burnt section of the paper.

Hokusai's astounding characterisation of the tragic Oiwa is augmented by the print's colouring. Oiwa's pale skin and bloodshot eyes are offset by the deep blue background, which suggests a haunted abyss. A prayer for Oiwa's soul appears on the lantern's side.

Oiwa from the series
One hundred [ghost] tales

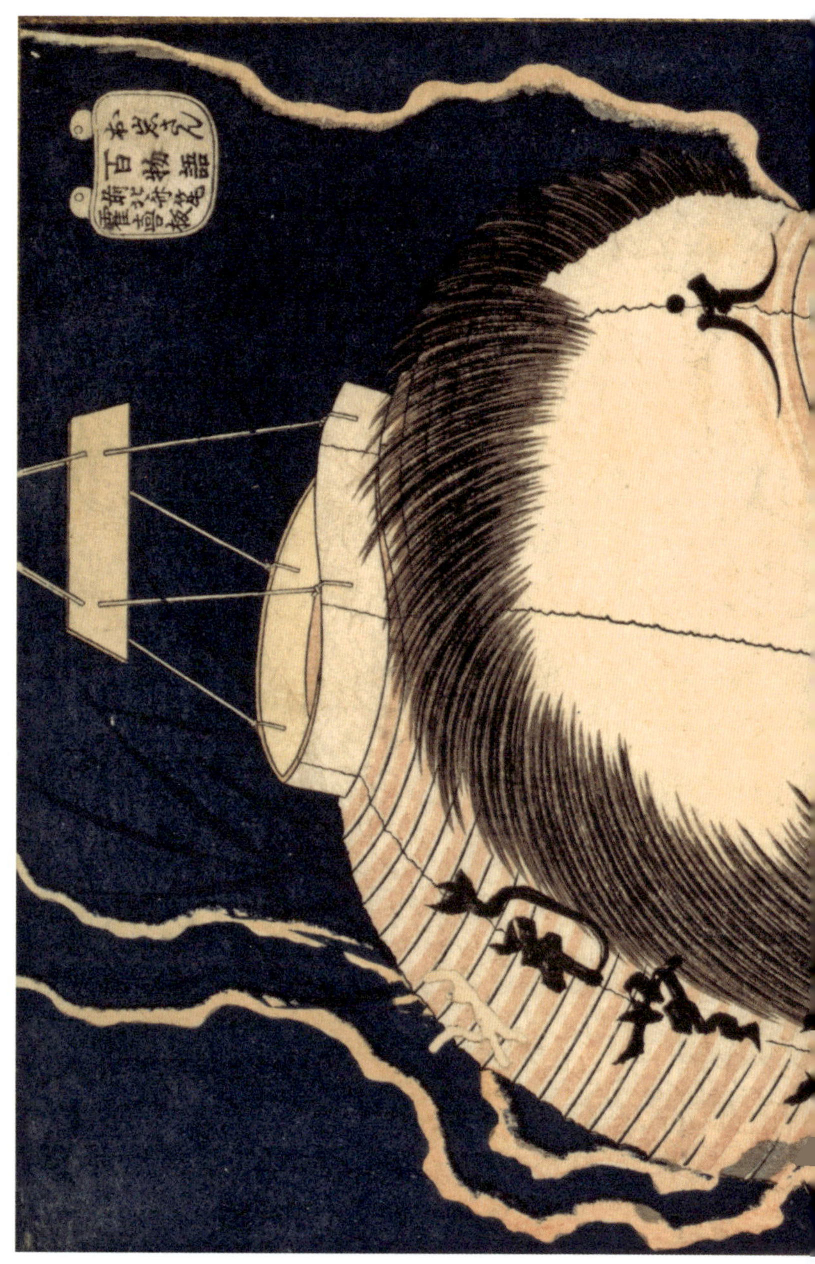

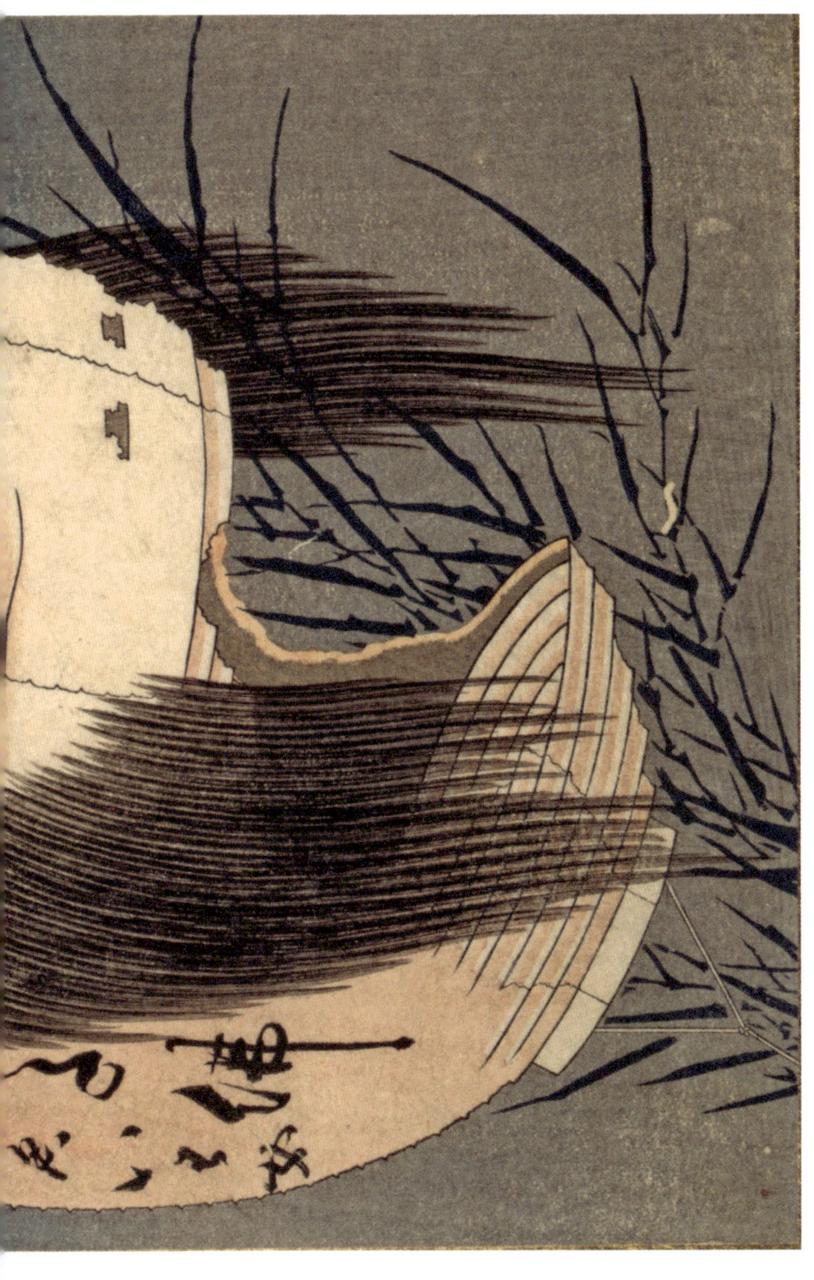

Kohada Koheiji
from the series
*One hundred
[ghost] tales*

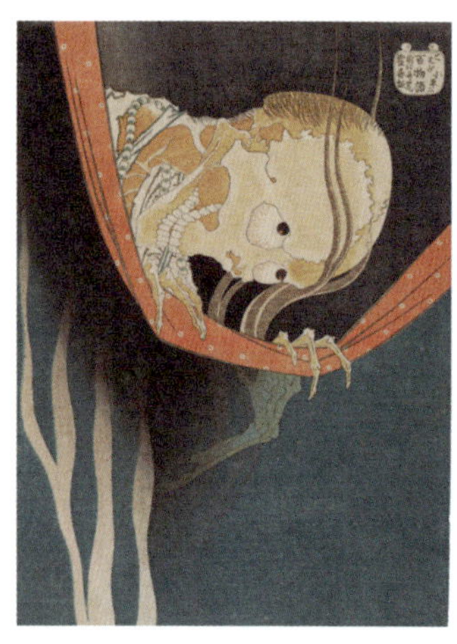

Woodblock print,   c. 1831–1832
ink and colour
on paper
26.5 cm × 18.9 cm
(10⅜ in × 7½ in)

Hokusai's depictions of ghosts are startlingly modern. Their demonic features respond to a fascination with the supernatural that is with us as much today as it was in Edo Japan. *Kohada Koheiji* is from the same series as *Oiwa* (page 124). While one hundred ghost tales may have been intended, these are two of only five prints that have come down to us. Each is similarly macabre in tone, though not without black humour.

Kohada Koheiji was a travelling actor who, in an ironic twist, was typecast as playing ghosts. His wife was embarrassed by this and took a lover, who eventually drowns Koheiji in a swamp. Naturally, Koheiji returns to haunt them. Here he is seen peering over the mosquito net that enshrouds their bed. His skeletal form – with bony fingers and maniacal grin – is made even more gruesome by the continued presence of hair, muscles and skin.

The forms below Koheiji have frequently been interpreted as flames or smoke, though perhaps even more significant is their resemblance to grasses found in a swamp, the site of Koheiji's death. The blue-green colour of the net similarly recalls his tragic end, and are his eye sockets shaped like shells?

Kohada Koheiji from the series
One hundred [ghost] tales

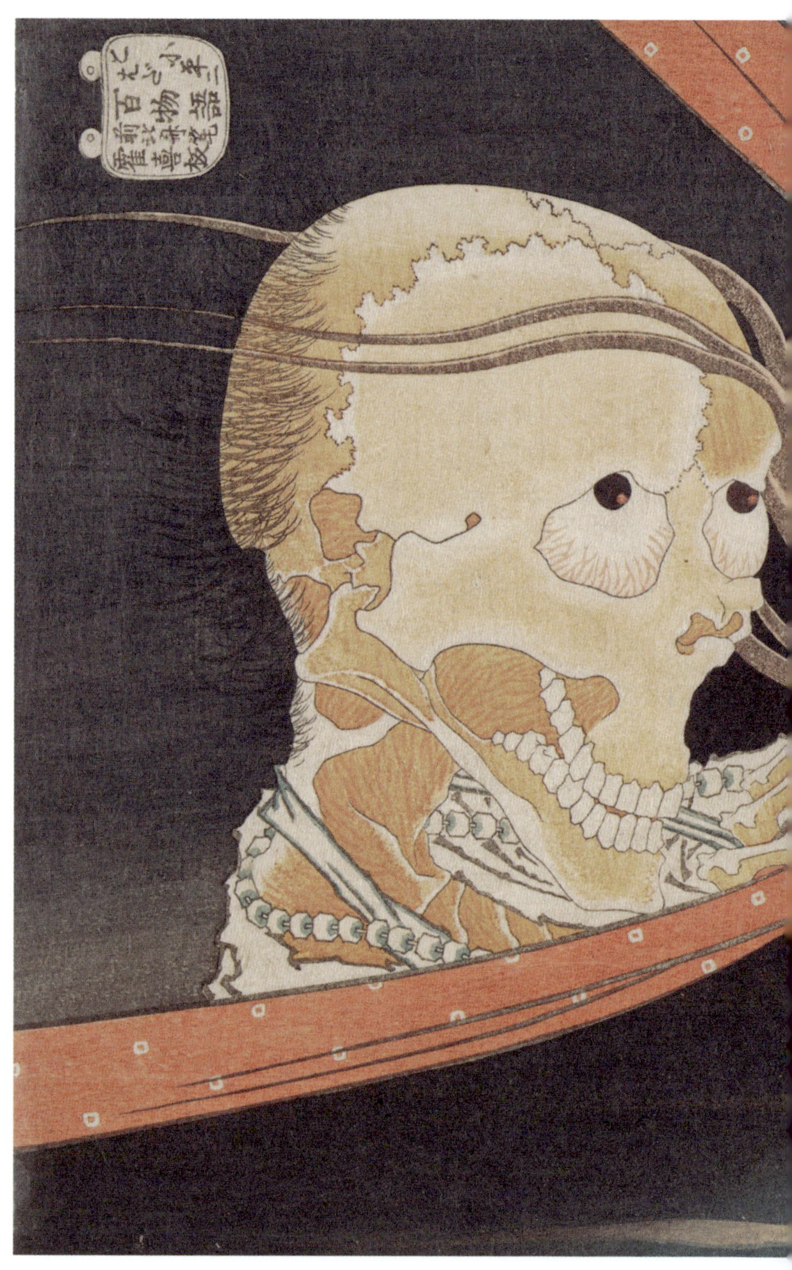

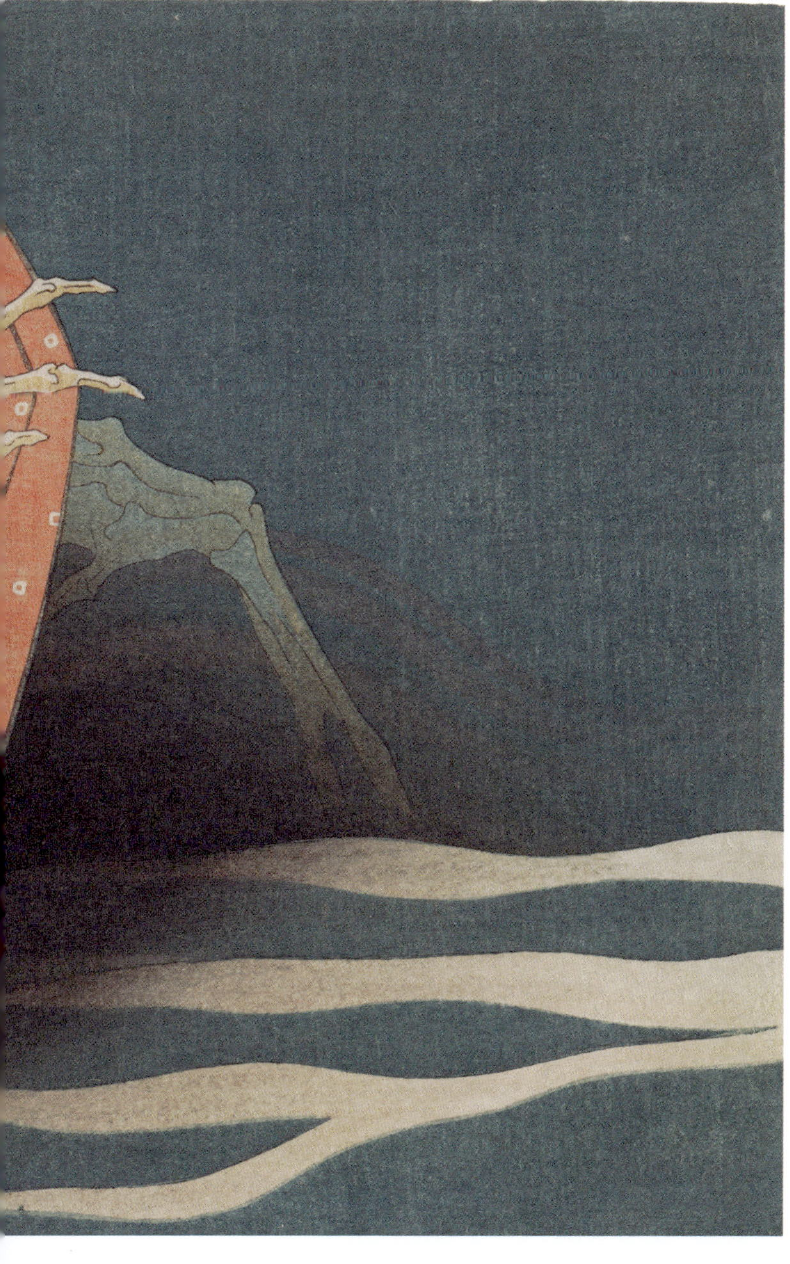

Poppies from the
series *Large flowers*

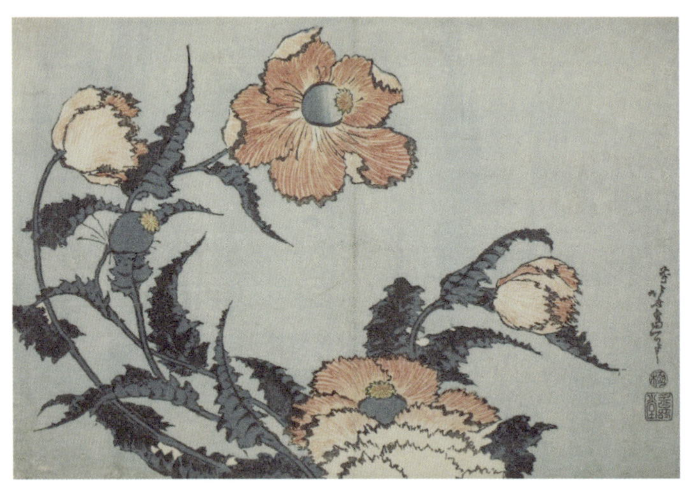

132

Woodblock print,   c. 1831-1832
ink and colour
on paper
25.4 cm × 36.5 cm
(10 in × 14⅜ in)

In his study of Hokusai, Richard Lane notes that it was unavoidable that this composition be compared with *The Great Wave* (page 100). It's an astute observation. In each print, the wind or other environmental forces cause the subject – the poppies; the wave – to curve into an arc from the left. But not only that: both works, in their respective genres, are masterpieces.

The series from which *Poppies* derives is known as *Large flowers* in the West. Ten prints have been recorded, all of a horizontal *ōban* (large) format, the same as *The Great Wave*. During the highly productive 1830s, Hokusai worked on both landscapes and these more intimate views of the natural world. Indeed, while there are precedents for *kacho-ga* (bird and flower pictures) in Chinese Ming (1368–1644) paintings, and in Edo Japan, Hokusai's approach was novel.

If we again compare *Poppies* with *The Great Wave*, we can see how both subjects seem infused with life. In the *Large flowers* series, this is in part achieved by the close-up view of the flowers, as though the artist depicts their portraits. In *Poppies*, the animistic quality is furthered still by the rendering of the plant's wind-blown forms, and the energetic movement of Hokusai's brush.

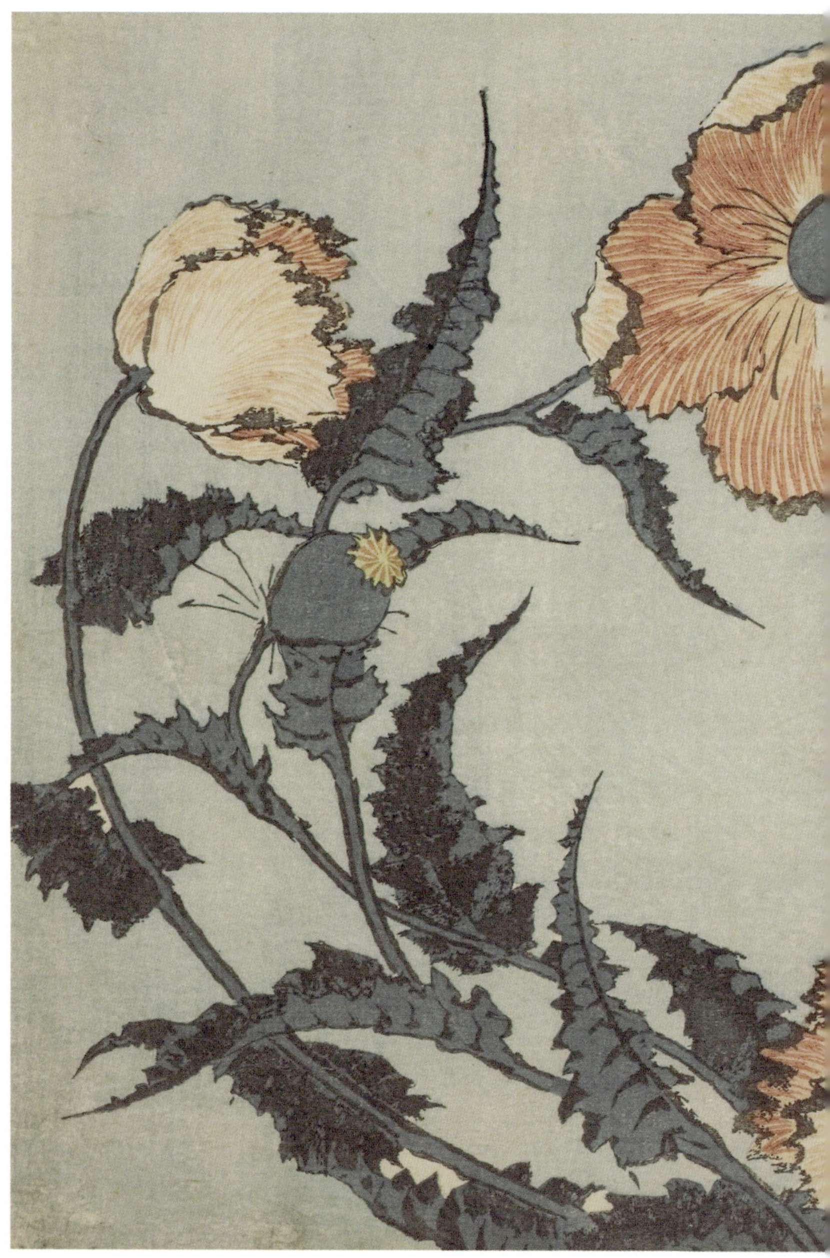

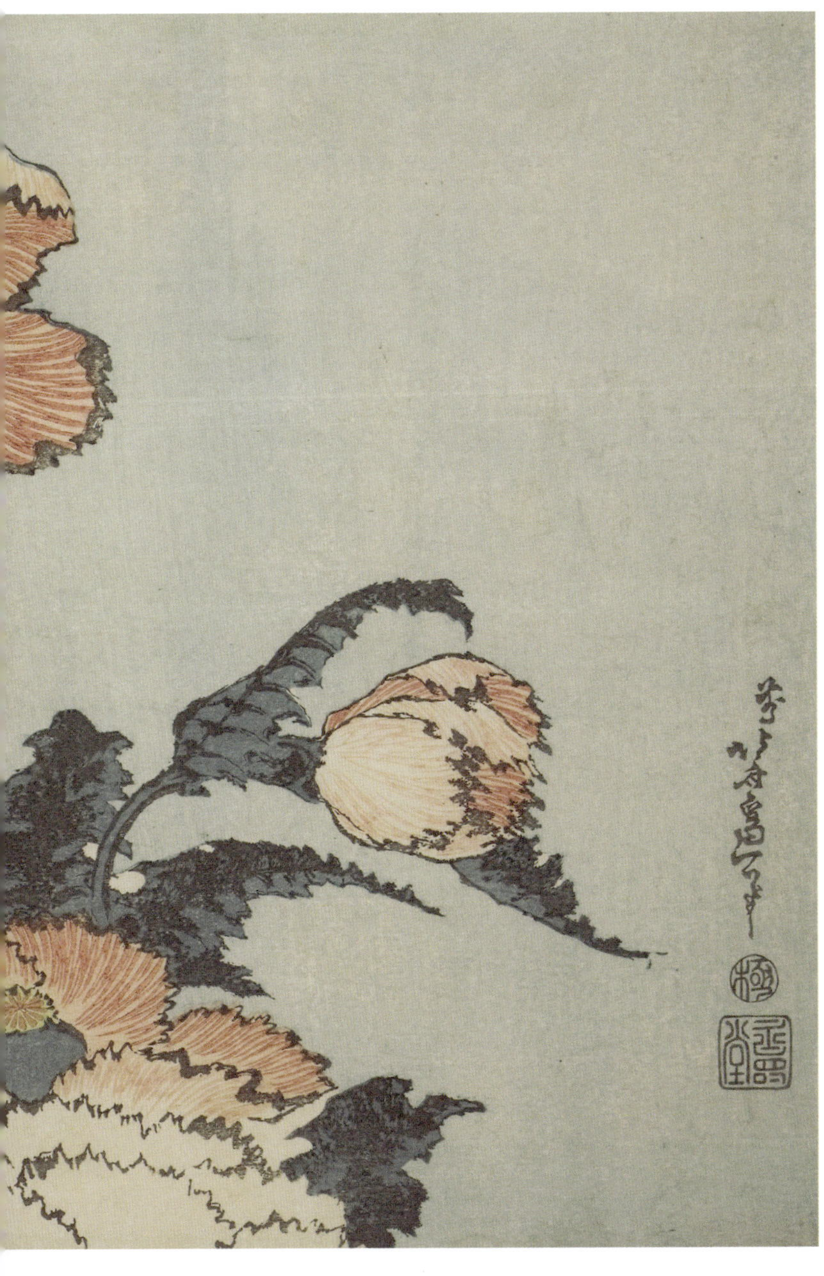

Snow on the Sumida River from the series *Snow, moon, blossoms*

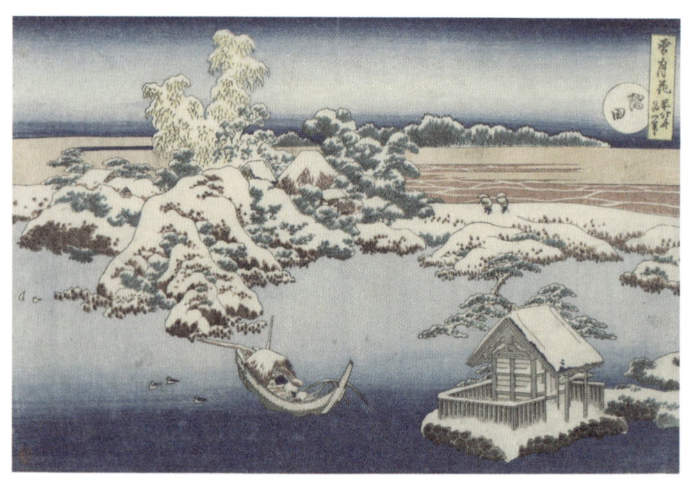

Woodblock print,   c. 1832-1833
ink and colour
on paper
24.8 cm × 36.8 cm
(9¾ in × 14½ in)

Snow, moon and blossoms, or *setsugekka*, are the 'three whites' of the natural world traditionally celebrated in Japan. The tripartite representation of winter snow, the autumn harvest moon, and spring cherry blossoms was a common theme in art of the Edo period. Around 1832, Hokusai contributed to the genre with a three-part series. This illustrates each motif at a notable landmark: the Sumida River in Edo; the Yodo River, an important waterway connecting Kyoto and Osaka; and Mount Yoshino, a famous spot to view cherry blossoms near Nara.

Snow on the Sumida River captures the ethereal beauty and quiet of a landscape blanketed with snow. The precise location is not given, but it has been suggested that this is Mukōjima in Edo. If we view this print alongside *Shower at the New Yanagi Bridge* (page 52) from 1806, the area's rural tranquillity makes quite a contrast to the bustle of the central city. Also distinctive is how the current landscape, washed in blues and crisp white, is now the picture's main subject. Yet the fisherman in the foreground, and the two figures walking towards the nearly hidden houses, are essential for establishing the scene's poetic lyricism.

Snow on the Sumida River from
the series Snow, moon, blossoms

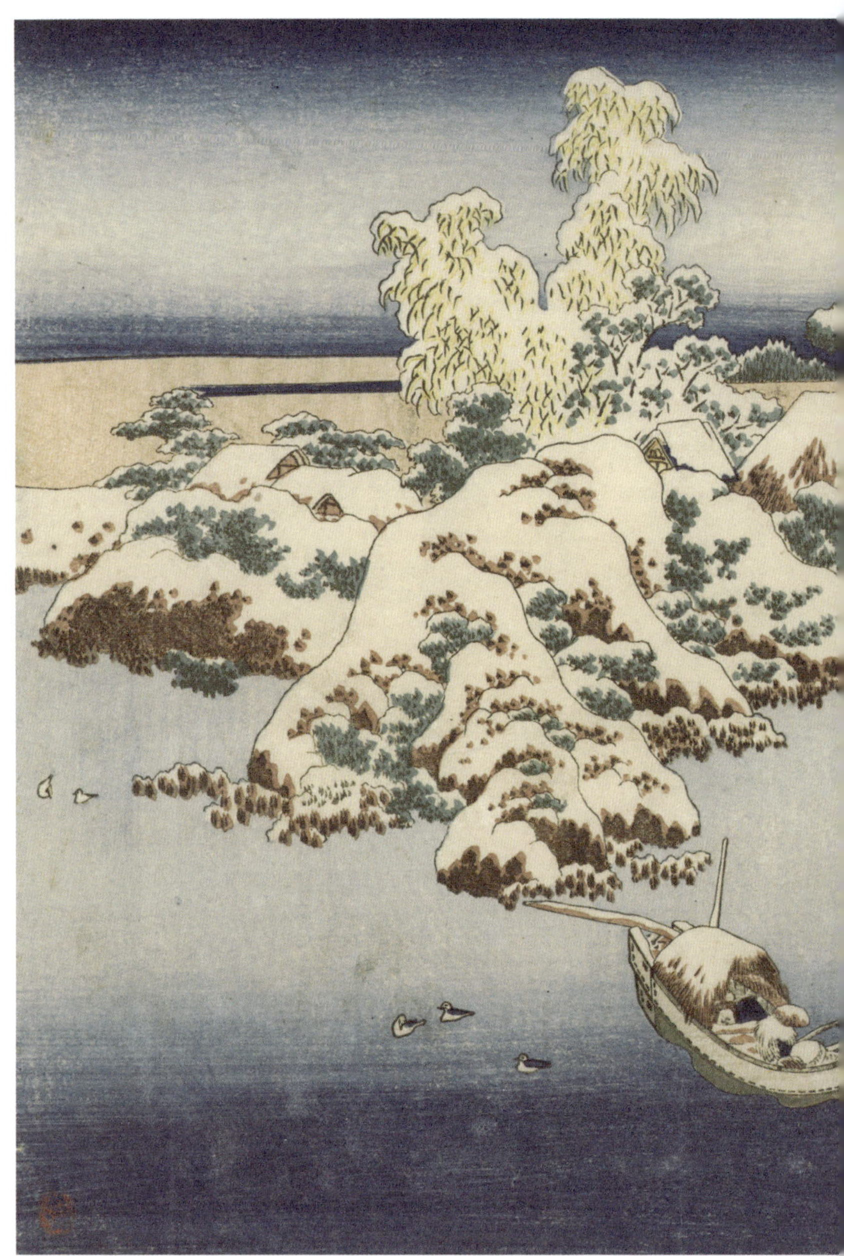

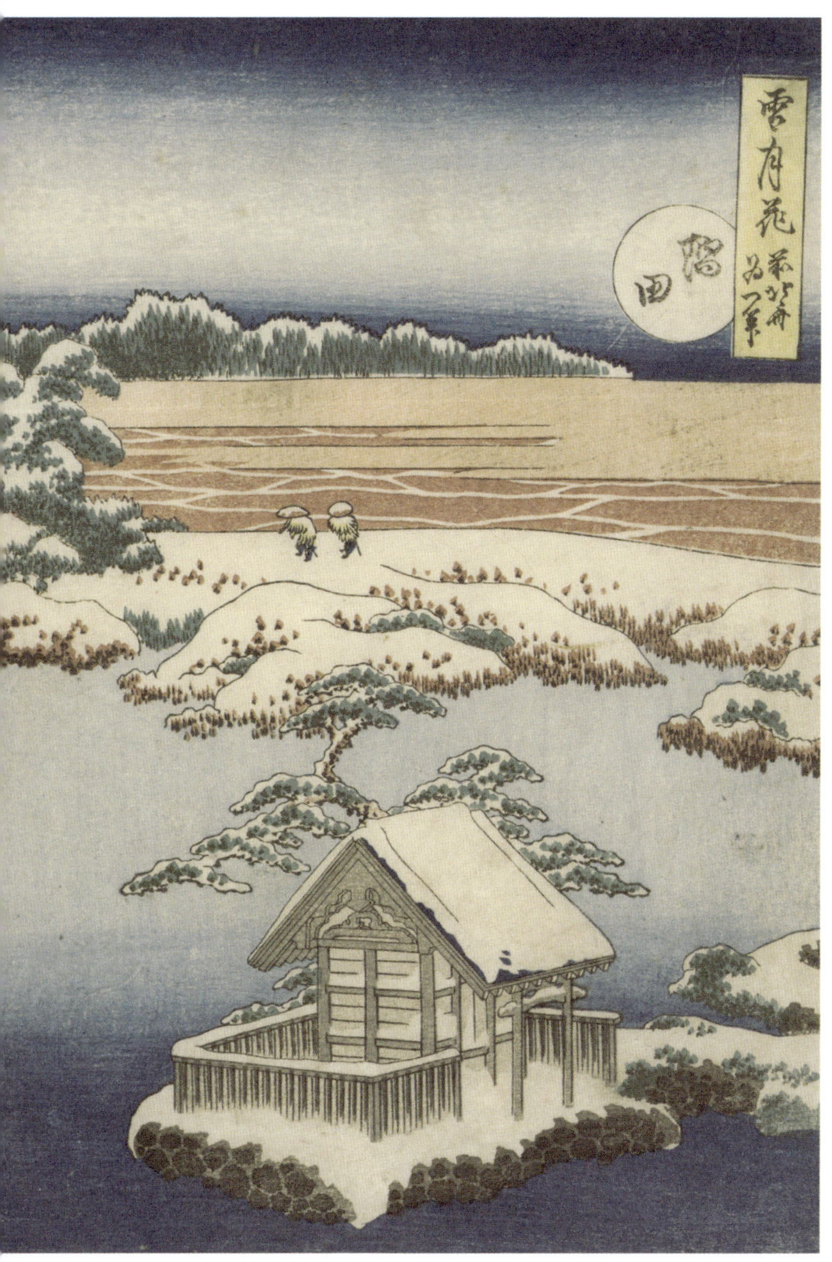

Voice of the Lake at Rinkai from the series *Eight views of Ryūkyū*

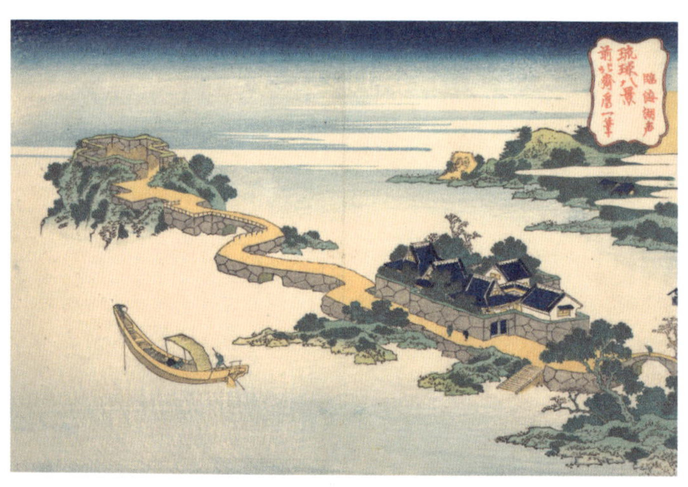

Woodblock print,
ink and colour
on paper
24.8 cm × 36.8 cm
(9¾ in × 14½ in)

c. 1833

In 1832 a court embassy from the Ryūkyū Islands in the far south-west of Japan came to Edo to pay its respects to the ruling shogun. Okinawa Prefecture now encompasses roughly two-thirds of these islands, but in this period the Ryūkyū archipelago was still a semi-independent kingdom that paid tribute to both China and Japan. At a time when Japan was cut off from the rest of the world, the 200-strong embassy of distant islanders, dressed in traditional Chinese-style clothing, was a subject of intense fascination for the people of Edo, Hokusai included.

In his *Eight views of Ryūkyū*, Hokusai emphasises the exotic, fairytale nature of these faraway islands. The artist had never been to the Ryūkyūs; he worked from a 1757 Chinese account that was reprinted in Japan in 1831. The views are quite different from those of the Mount Fuji series, where we are *inside* the landscape. As this print shows, those of Ryūkyū instead offer a bird's-eye view of the scene below, furthering the allure of the isolated. That the picturesque, winding causeway seems to float as much in the sky as in a lake only serves to heighten the sense of the storybook.

Voice of the Lake at Rinkai from
the series *Eight views of Ryūkyū*

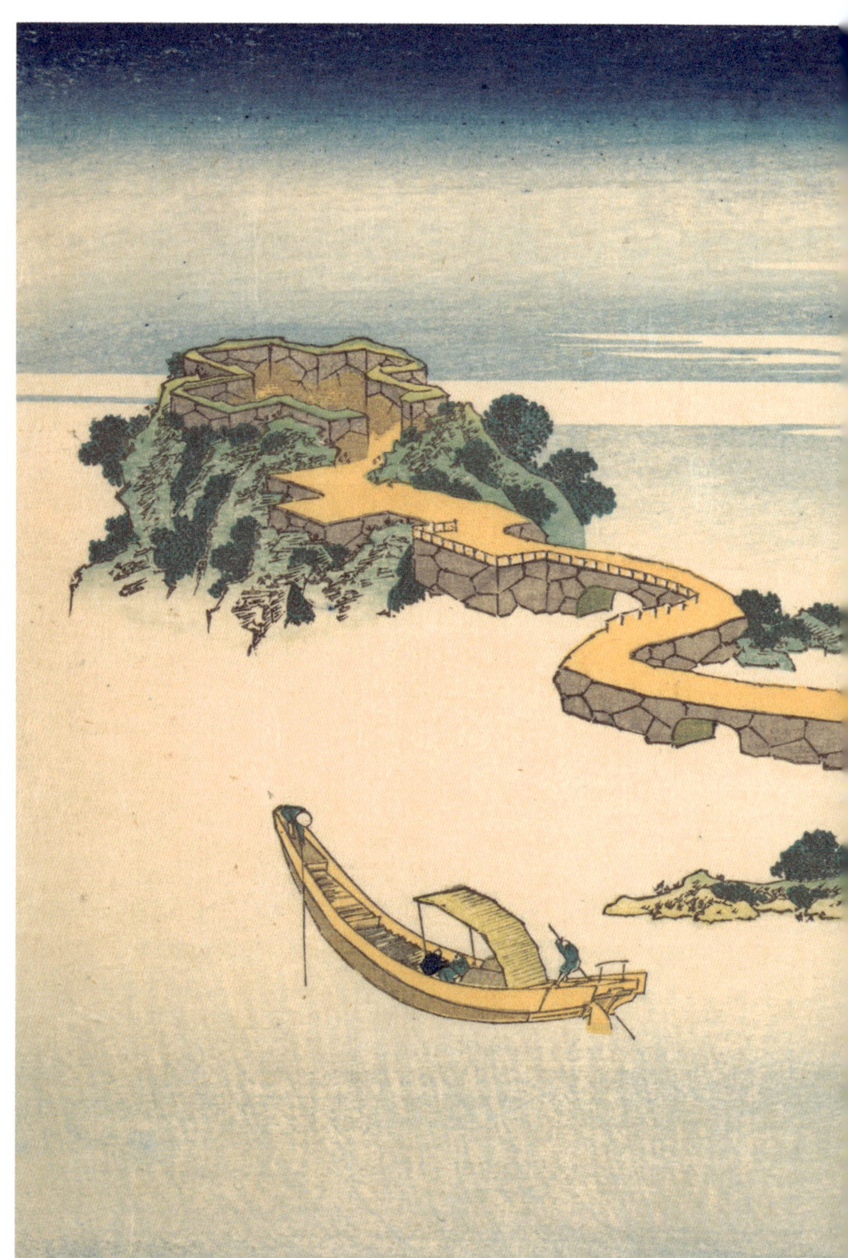

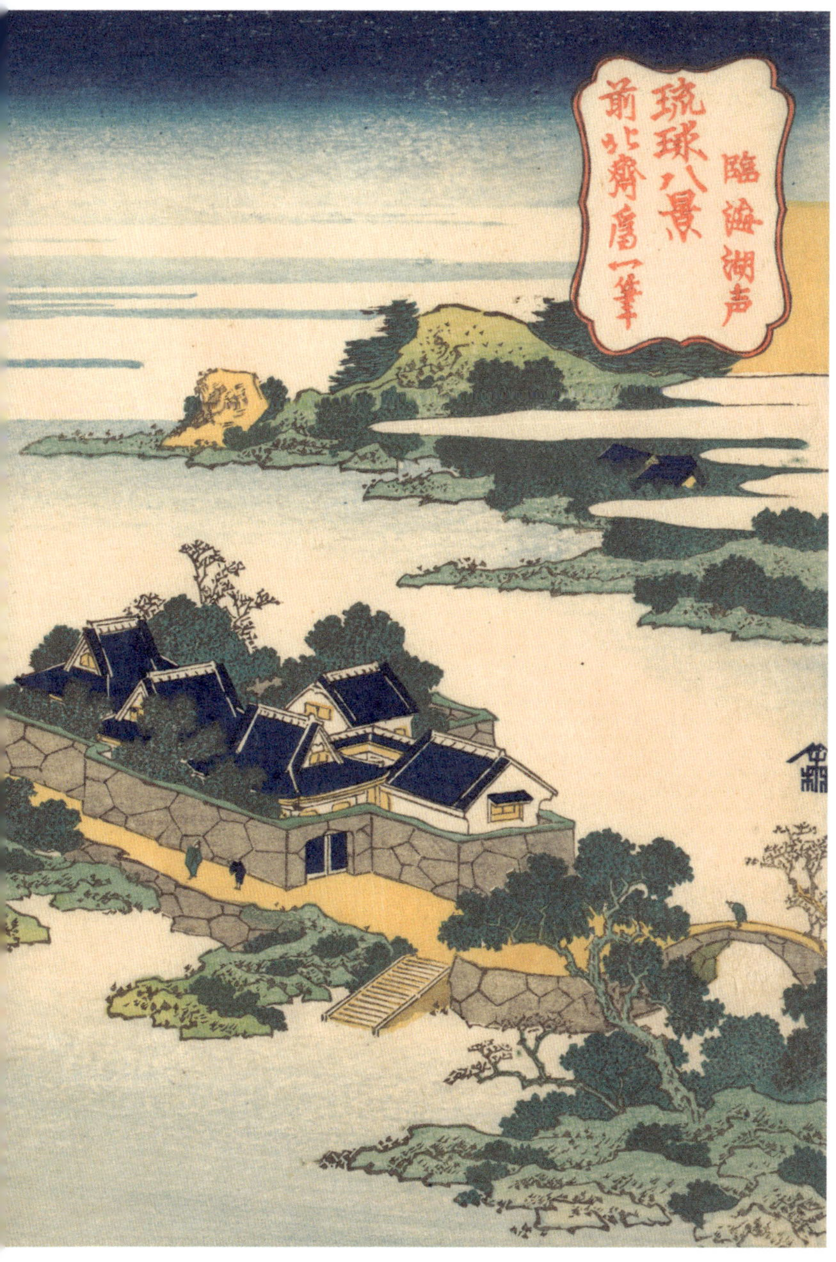
臨海湖声
琉球八景
前北斎為一筆

Amida Falls in the Far Reaches of the Kiso Road from the series *A tour of waterfalls*

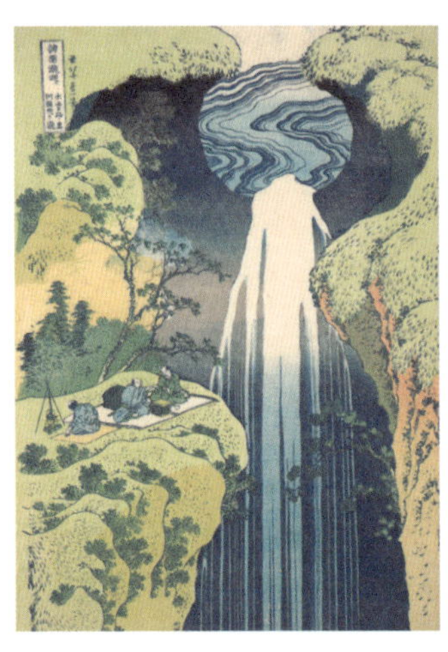

Woodblock print,
ink and colour
on paper
37.5 cm × 26 cm
(14¾ in × 10¼ in)

1833-1834

Hokusai's representations of nature are often described as animistic. The idea that natural phenomena possess a spirit or soul is a belief in Shintō, the indigenous religion of Japan, which has long coexisted with Buddhism. Waterfalls are one feature of the landscape that have traditionally been revered, and in the early 1830s Hokusai created a distinctive series on this subject.

A tour of waterfalls illustrates eight waterfalls in different Japanese provinces. Complementary with the subject matter, they are all in the vertical *ōban* format. Some of the falls Hokusai likely visited, while others were studied in gazetteers or derived, at least in part, from Hokusai's imagination.

Amida Falls is perhaps the series' most striking image. The waterfall is believed to be the incarnation of the Buddha Amida, and with the round, head-like top and flowing 'limbs', there is certainly a sense that the falls contain a living presence. Particularly novel is how Hokusai has depicted the pool at the top of the waterfall as though we're looking at it from above, while we view the falling water straight on. The inclusion of the small figures on the left emphasise the waterfall's monumental presence.

Amida Falls in the Far Reaches
of the Kiso Road from the series
A tour of waterfalls

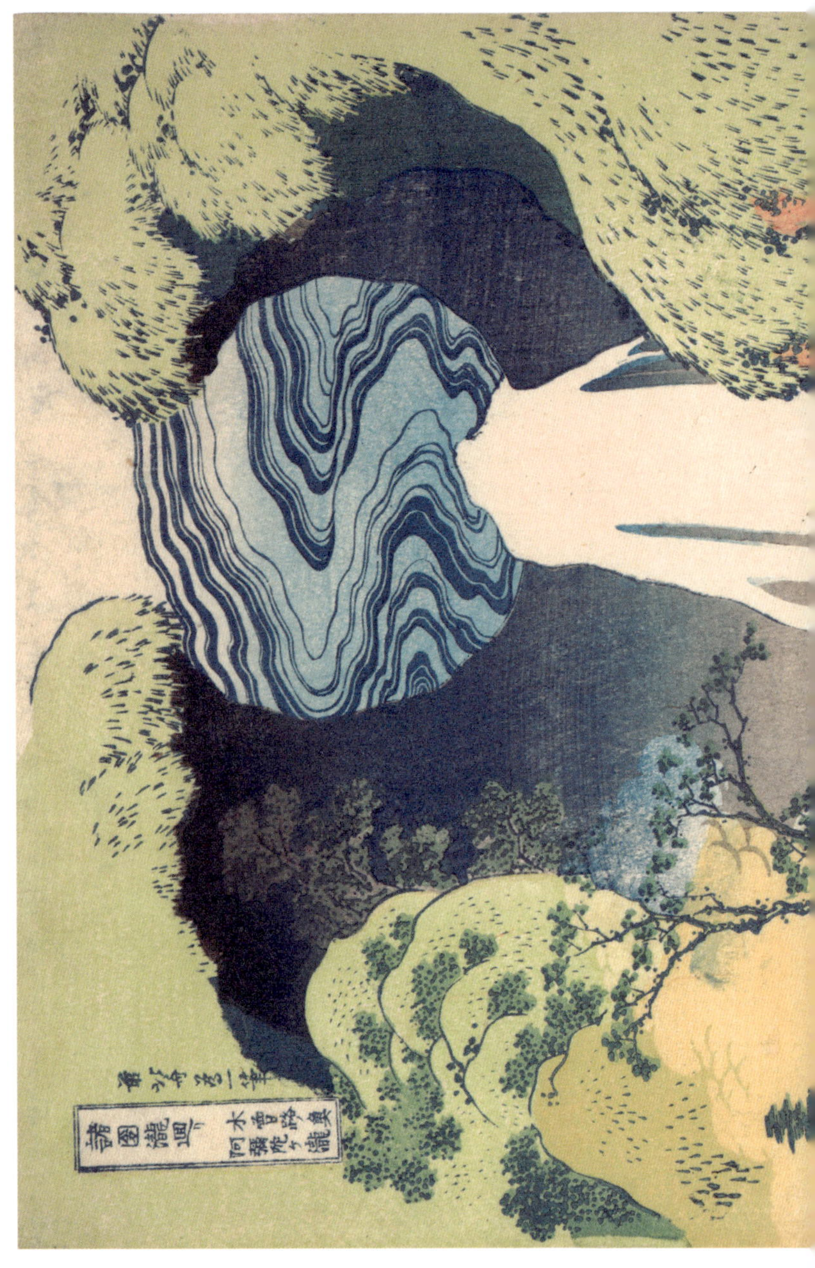

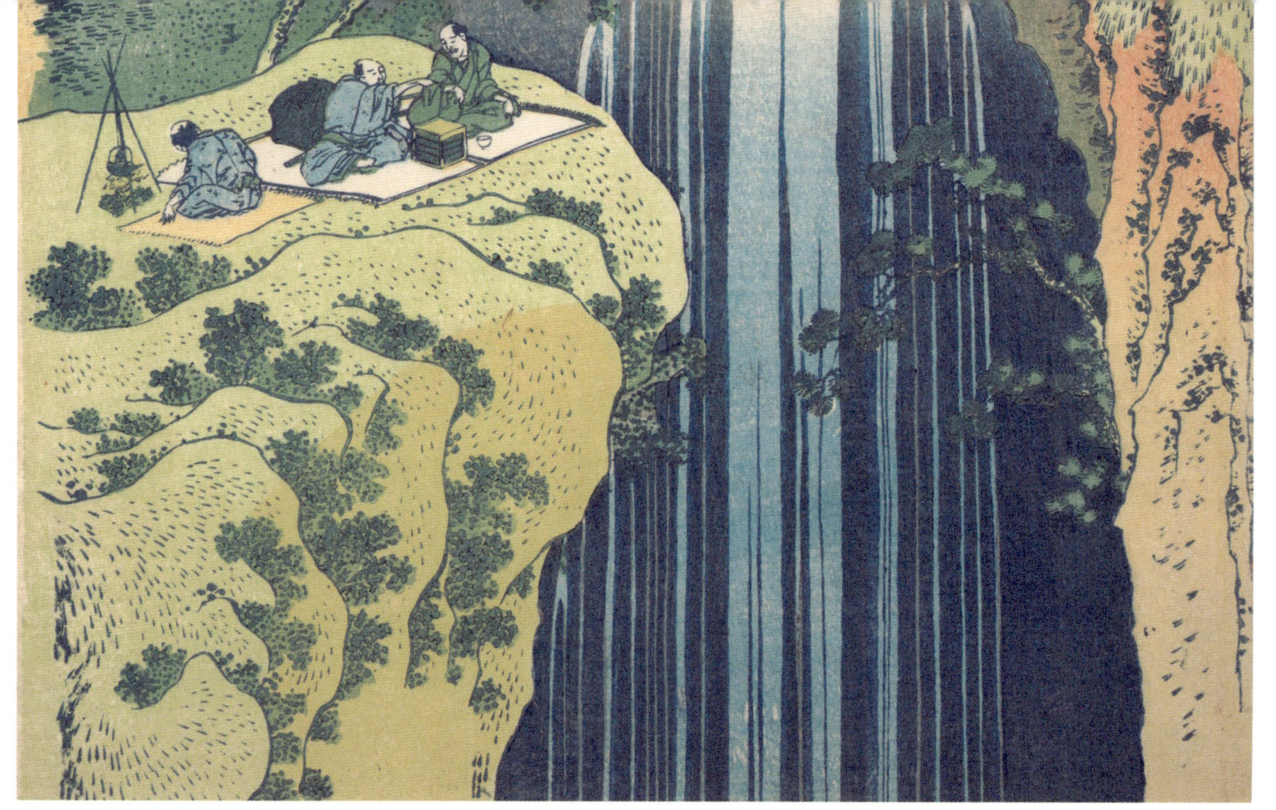

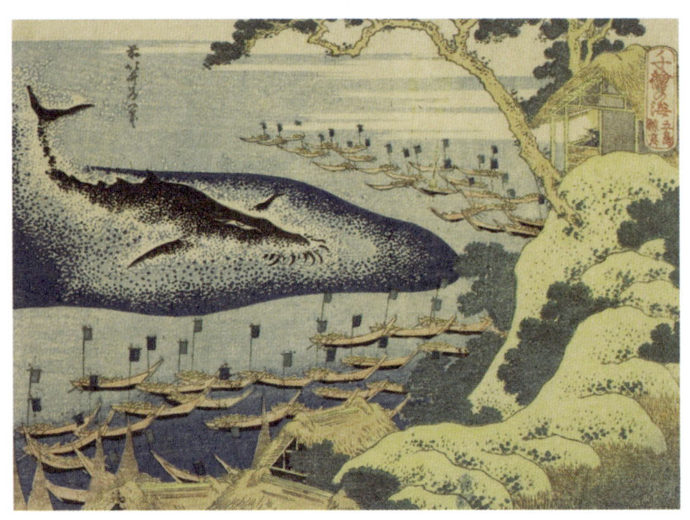

Woodblock print,
ink and colour
on paper
19 cm × 25.7 cm
(7½ in × 10⅛ in)

1833-1834

In *Kajikazawa in Kai Province* (page 104), from the series *Thirty-six views of Mount Fuji*, a man fishing represents humankind's inextricable connection to the natural world. The print, like so many others by Hokusai, also reveals the artist's fascination and empathy for humankind and its labours within this world. The slightly later series *One thousand images of the sea* is likewise devoted to these themes.

Consisting of ten mid-sized *chūban* prints – smaller than Hokusai's contemporaneous landscape sets – the series features various scenes of fishing in both oceans and rivers. *Whaling off Gotō* depicts dozens of boats surrounding a whale by the Gotō Islands west of Nagasaki. Hokusai had never visited the area and the image was likely inspired by book illustrations as well as his own inventiveness.

Printed in black ink, the whale is the focal point of this striking composition. The leviathan slaps its tail in warning. The animal's immense power is conveyed by the deep blue area of surrounding sea that mirrors its form like a force field. This sense of strength is furthered by the contrast between the whale's size and that of the many small boats with their blue and green flags.

Whaling off Gotō from the series
One thousand images of the sea

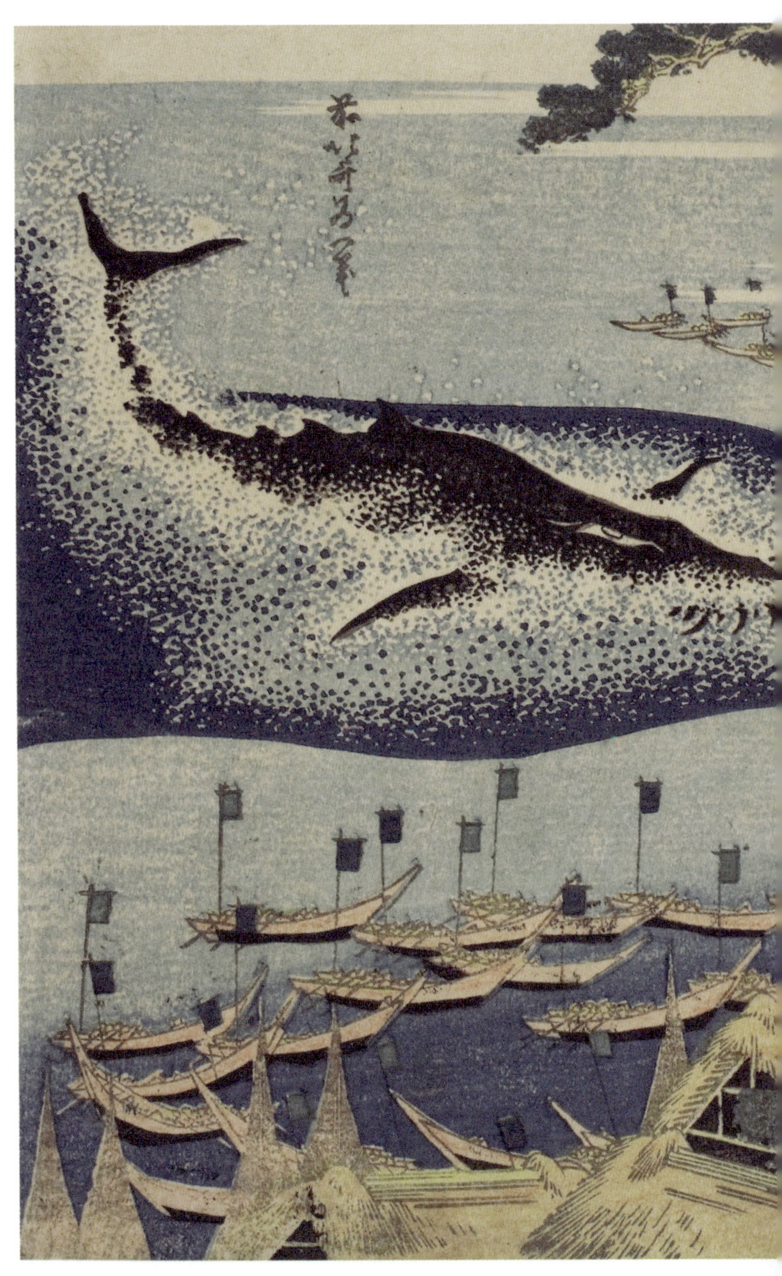

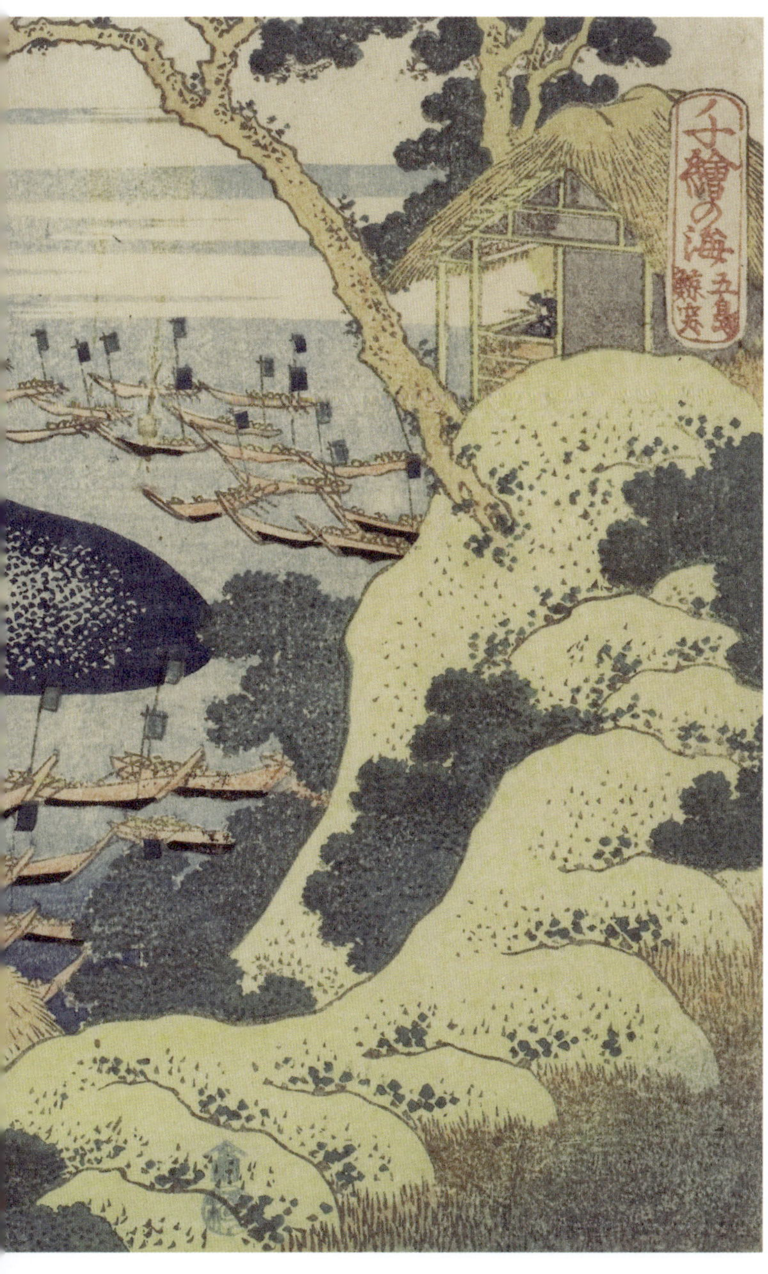
千繪の海
五島
鯨突

The Reed Gatherer (Tokusa-gari) from the series *A true mirror of Chinese and Japanese poetry*

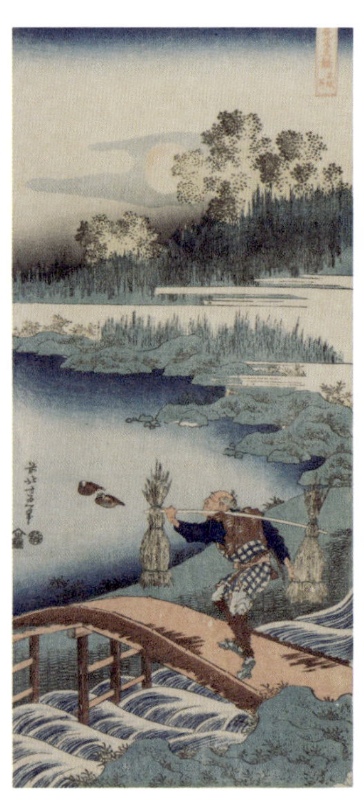

Woodblock print,   c. 1833-1834
ink and colour
on paper
52.1 cm × 23 cm
(20½ in × 9 in)

One in a series of ten, this *nagaōhan* (long-format) print recalls traditional Japanese hanging scrolls used to display paintings. Alongside this distinct formatting, the collection's subject matter and refined printing – with significant use of Prussian blue – suggests that the publisher, Moriya Jihei, had a particularly cultured audience in mind.

The theme of the series is classical Chinese and Japanese literature. Certain prints represent a poet or poem from one or the other country, but there is frequent intermingling of Chinese and Japanese subject matter. *The Reed Gatherer* is based on a play from Noh theatre, the ancient Japanese dance-drama that preceded kabuki.

In the play *Tokusa* (*Reeds*), an elderly reed gatherer is reunited with his son who disappeared long ago. A poem by Minamoto no Nakamasa, which is quoted within the play, is likely Hokusai's source for this scene of the gentleman alone on a quiet, moonlit autumn evening. It is typically Hokusai in its tender portrayal of a figure toiling in the landscape. With back and knees slightly bent, the old reed gatherer reaches back his right hand to steady his rear bundle as the stream undulates below.

The Reed Gatherer (Tokusa-gari)
from the series A true mirror
of Chinese and Japanese poetry

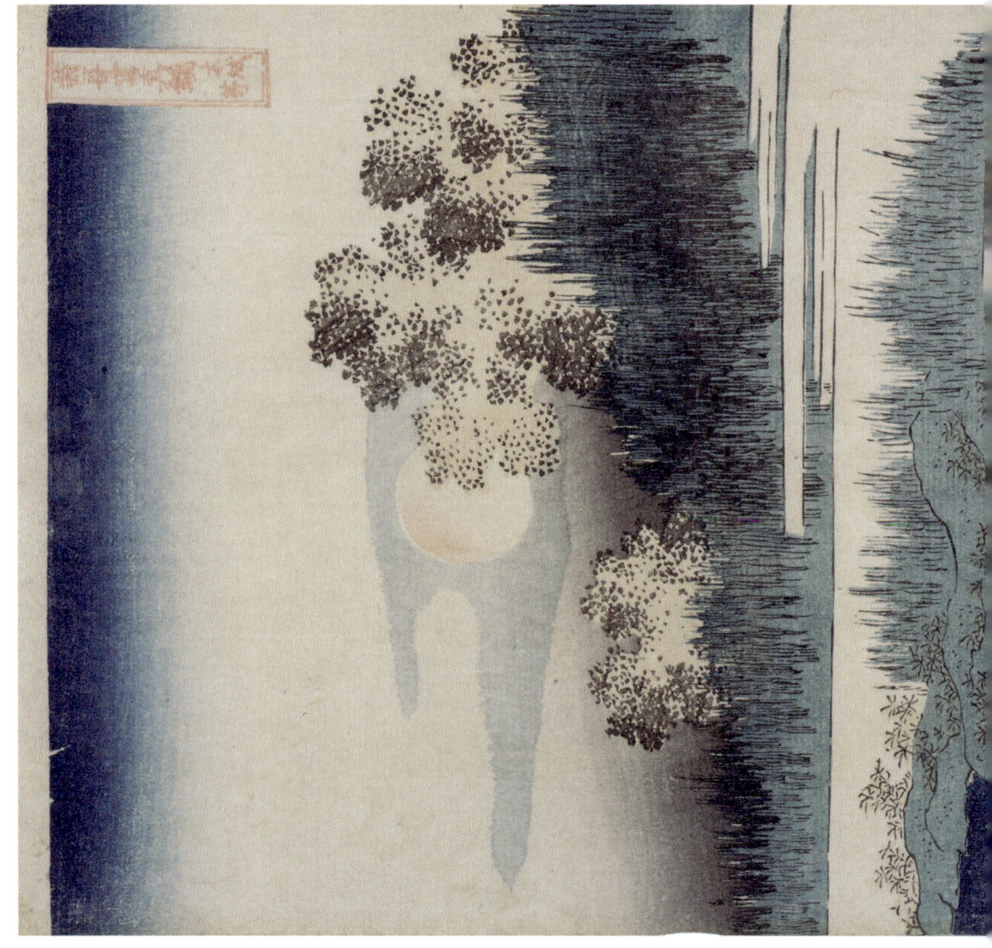

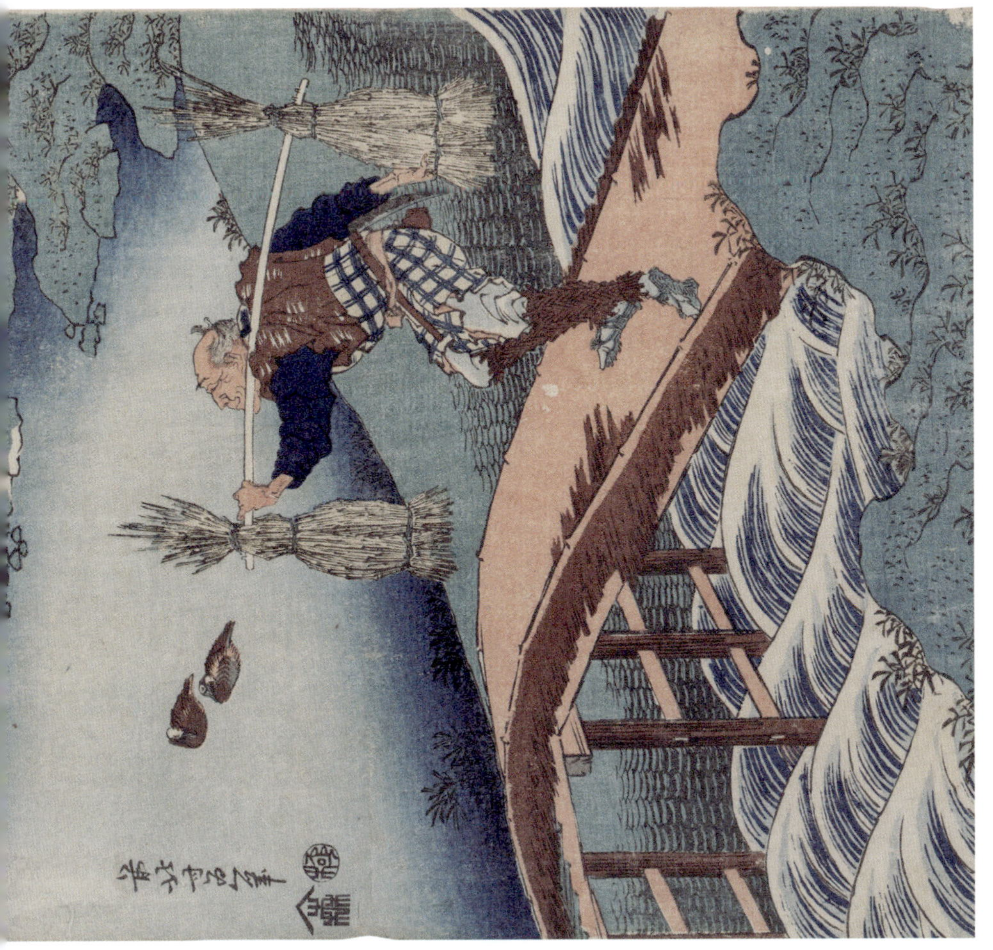

Cranes on
a Pine Tree

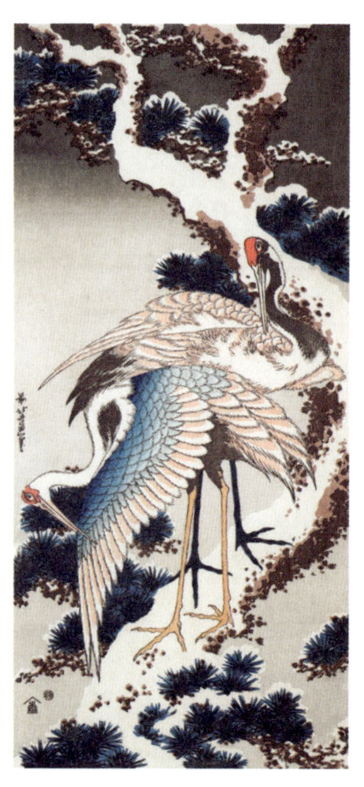

Woodblock print,   1833-1834
ink and colour
on paper
51.9 cm × 23.3 cm
(20⅜ in × 9⅛ in)

Cranes on a Pine Tree is one of five in a set of nature prints that depict animals traditionally regarded as auspicious. Like *The Reed Gatherer* (page 152) and the other works in that series, these are all *nagaōban* (long-format) prints. Both collections were published around the same time by Moriya Jihei, and their large size and impressive print designs indicate that they were intended as more affordable substitutions for scroll paintings.

Here, two red-crowned cranes, symbols of luck and longevity, have landed on a gnarled, snow-covered pine tree. The work combines Hokusai's keen eye for observation with a striking decorative quality. Set within a closely cropped scene, the curve of the pine branch provides an ideal stage for the two large birds. Their wings and long necks echo the curvature of the tree, just as their usual snow-white feathers in fact reflect the blue and russet of the surrounding vegetation.

In contrast with his partner's deep blue legs, the foremost crane's yellow legs create a visually arresting note (try covering these up to see the difference it makes). And, in a customarily Hokusai gesture, the cranes seem to observe us as much as we observe them.

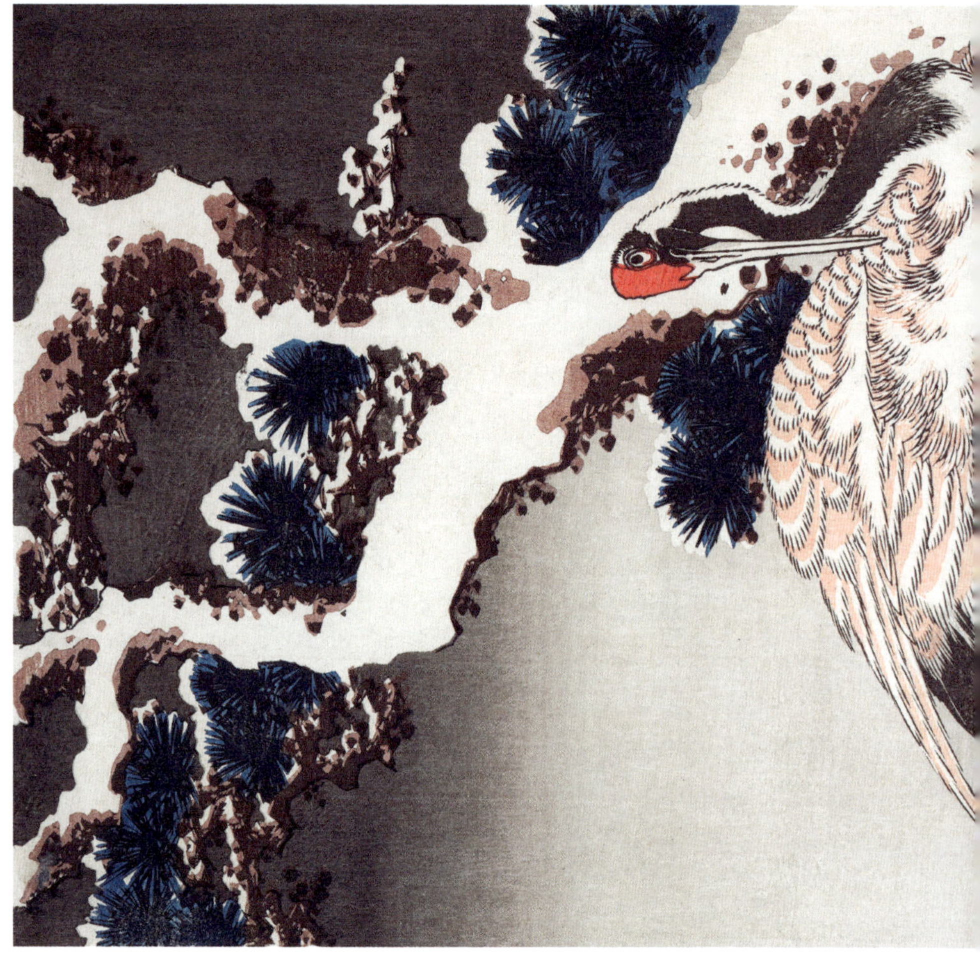

Cranes on a Pine Tree

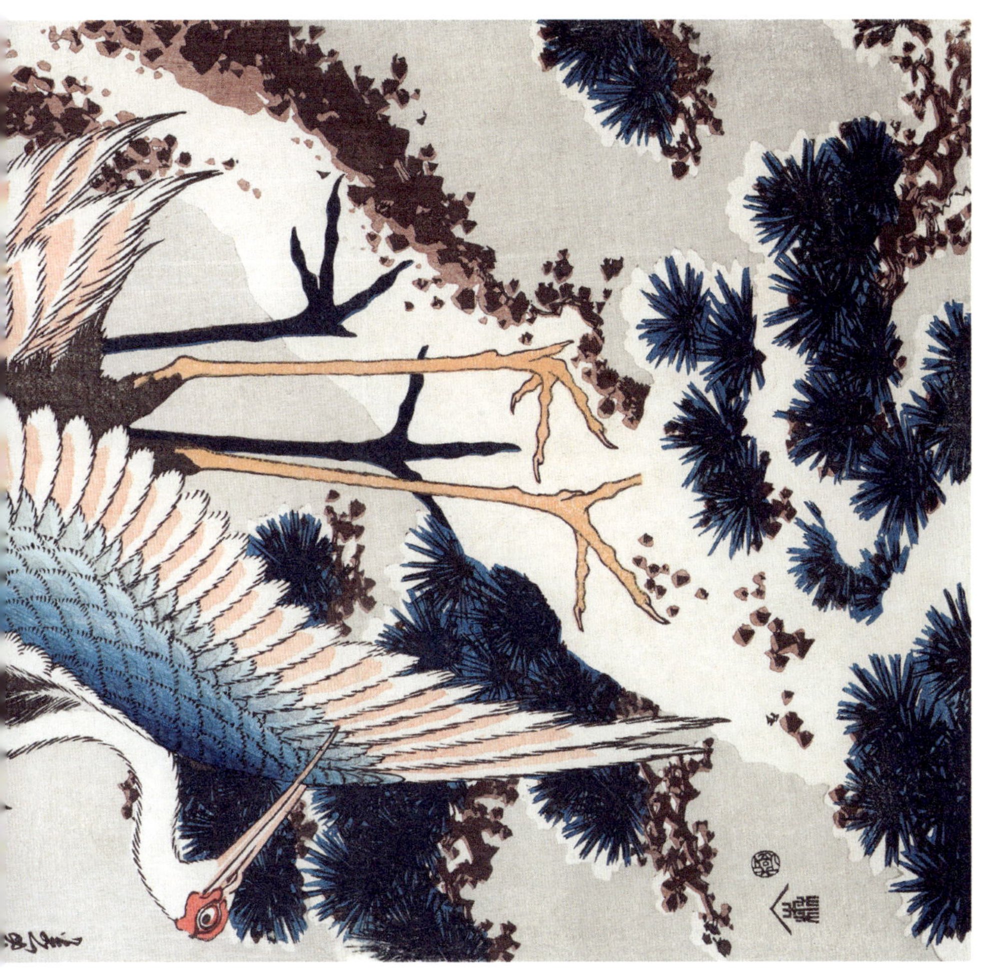

Kamakura no Gongoro Kagemasa and Torinoumi Yasaburo Yasunori

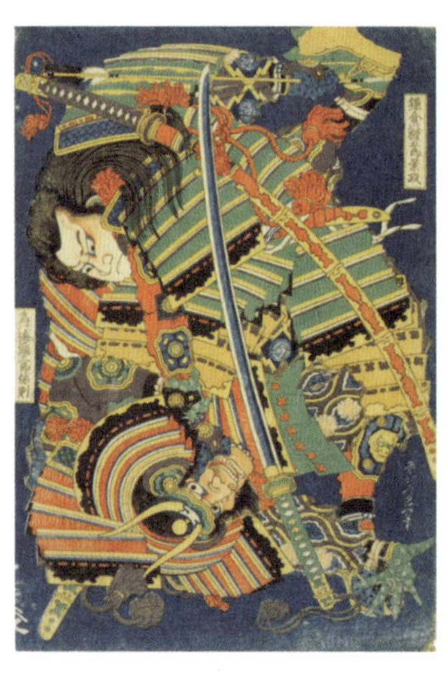

160

Woodblock print,   c. 1833-1834
ink and colour
on paper
37.2 cm × 25.3 cm
(14⅝ in × 10 in)

Alongside Hokusai's prolific production of landscapes, nature motifs and ghost images in the early to mid-1830s, he also made an untitled series on the theme of warrior combat, of which five prints are known. As in the aforementioned works, the use of Prussian blue infuses the compositions with bold vitality.

This print depicts the samurai hero Kagemasa and his enemy Yasunori, though the design is so colourful and convoluted that it is hard to figure out exactly what is going on. Heads pop out among the kaleidoscopic pattern of armour (including the small face of a demon on an arm guard); swords cross; and a booted foot appears at the upper edge of the composition while a gloved hand appears at the bottom.

Kagemasa, who is shown here overpowering his foe, is famous for continuing to fight in battle after being shot in the eye with an arrow. While it takes a moment to see, this act is referenced by the hand holding an arrow at the top of the print. Kagemasa is also the central figure in one of the most well-known kabuki plays, *Shibaraku*, and his determined facial expression recalls those of Hokusai's early actor portraits, such as *Ichikawa Ebizō* (page 16).

Kamakura no Gongoro Kagemasa
and Torinoumi Yasaburo Yasunori

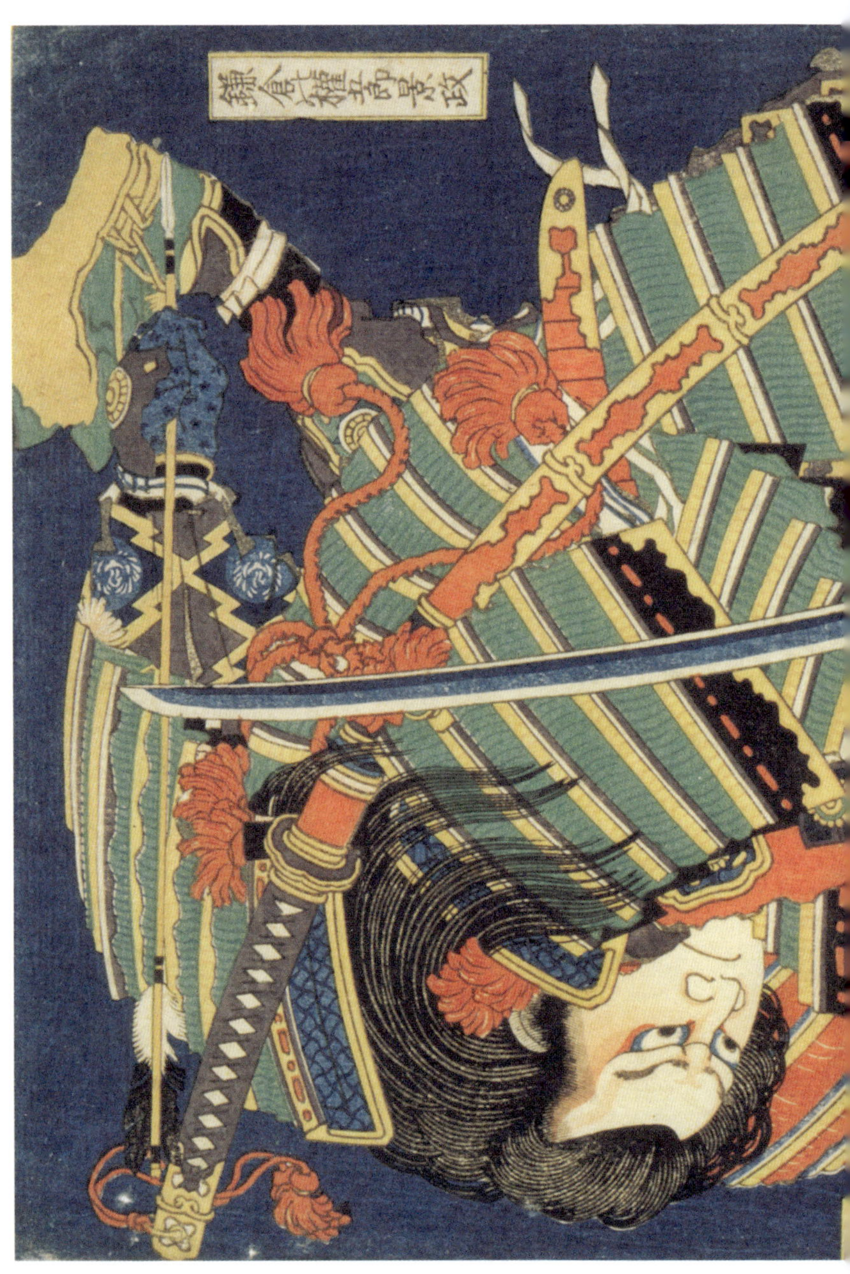

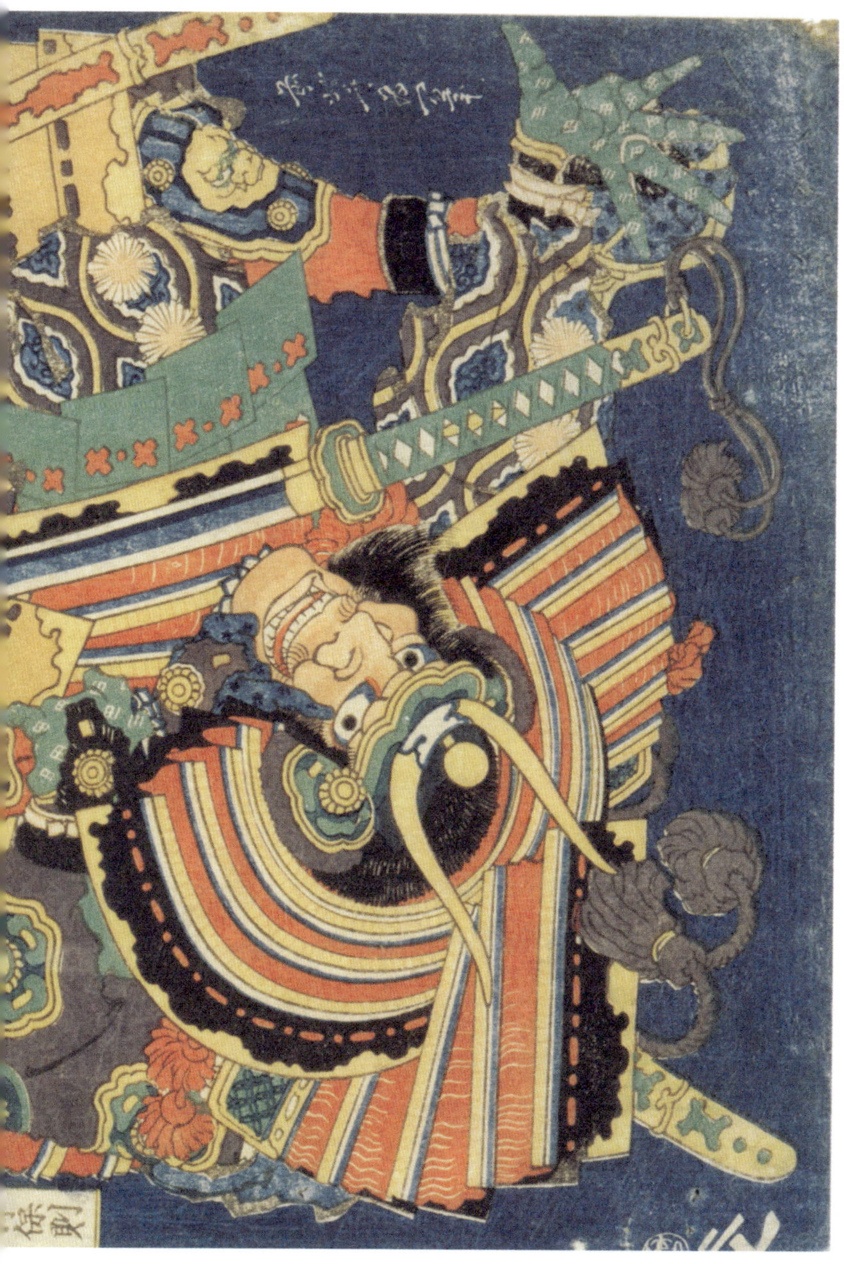

Suspension Bridge on the Border of Hida and Etchū Provinces from the series *Rare views of famous bridges in various provinces*

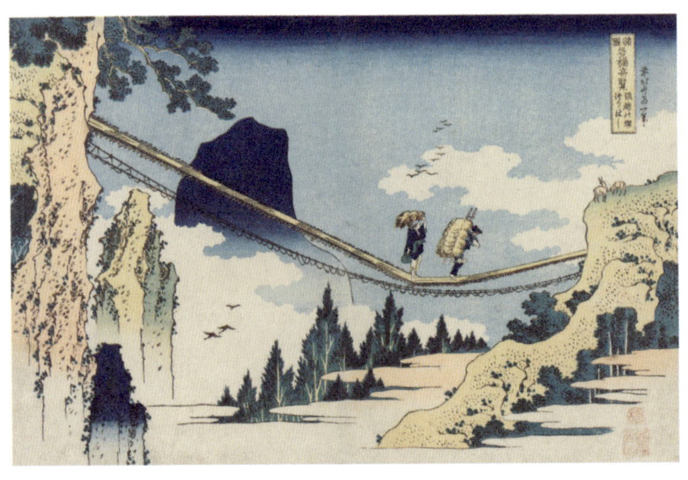

Woodblock print,   c. 1834
ink and colour
on paper
25.3 cm × 37.6 cm
(10 in × 14¾ in)

Although *Thirty-six views of Mount Fuji* is the most famous, Hokusai actually created a plethora of magnificent landscape series in the early 1830s. After working together on *Thirty-six views* and *A tour of waterfalls*, the same publisher, Eijudō, issued the eleven-print series from which this work derives.

Bridges seem to have held a particular enchantment for Hokusai. He sketched them in the *Manga* and, around 1823, he depicted a landscape filled with fifty-plus bridges in a large woodblock print. The scenes in *Rare views*, like in *A tour of waterfalls*, were in part based on existing descriptions, and partly depended on Hokusai's imagination. This blending of fact and fantasy is evident in this astonishing view.

The figures crossing the suspension bridge are characteristic of the hard-working people Hokusai empathised with, but the rest of the work recalls a dreamscape. The incredibly perilous-looking bridge stretches across a great chasm between rocky outcrops. These rise above conifer trees that are largely covered by low-lying clouds. A dark-blue mountain in the distance furthers the grandeur of the natural scene, which the woman on the bridge contemplates as she takes a momentary pause.

Suspension Bridge on the Border of Hida and Etchū Provinces from the series Rare views of famous bridges in various provinces

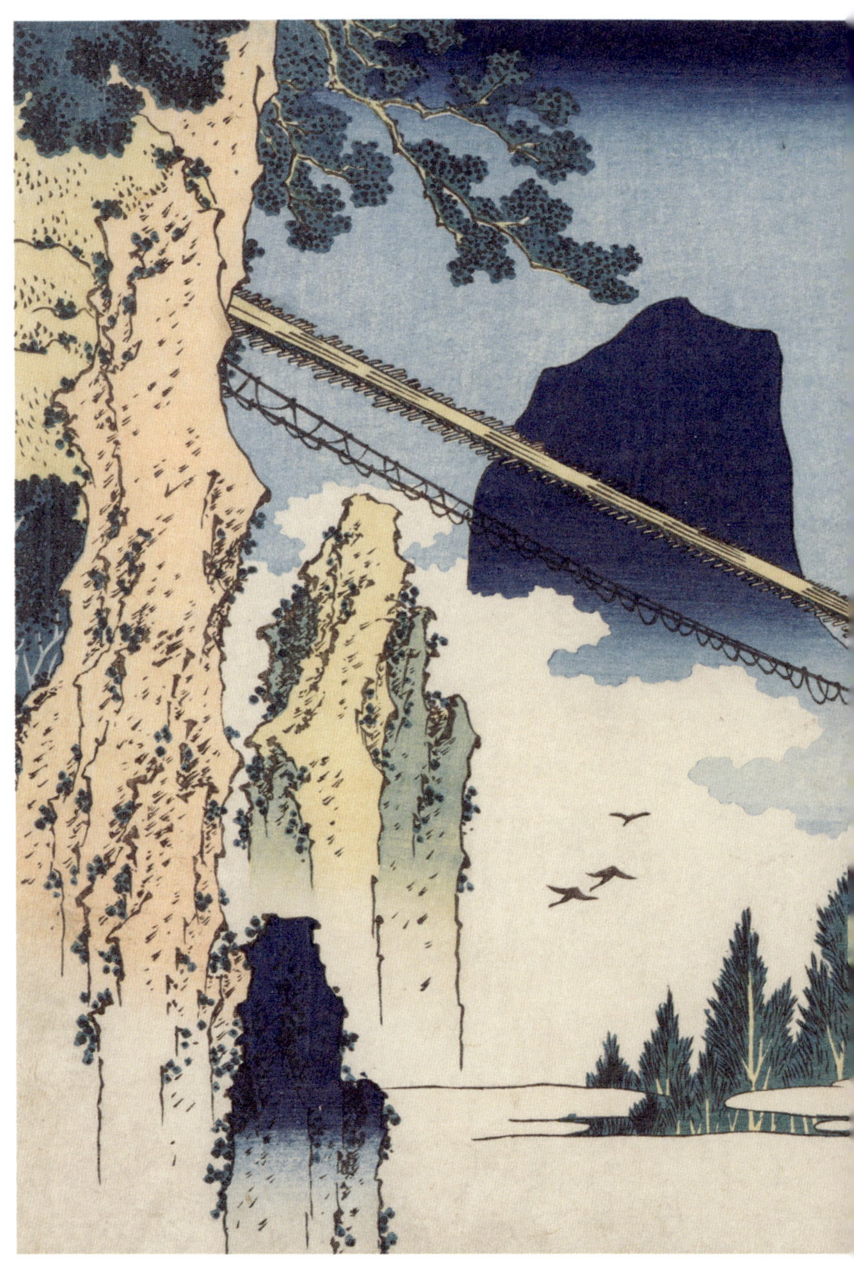

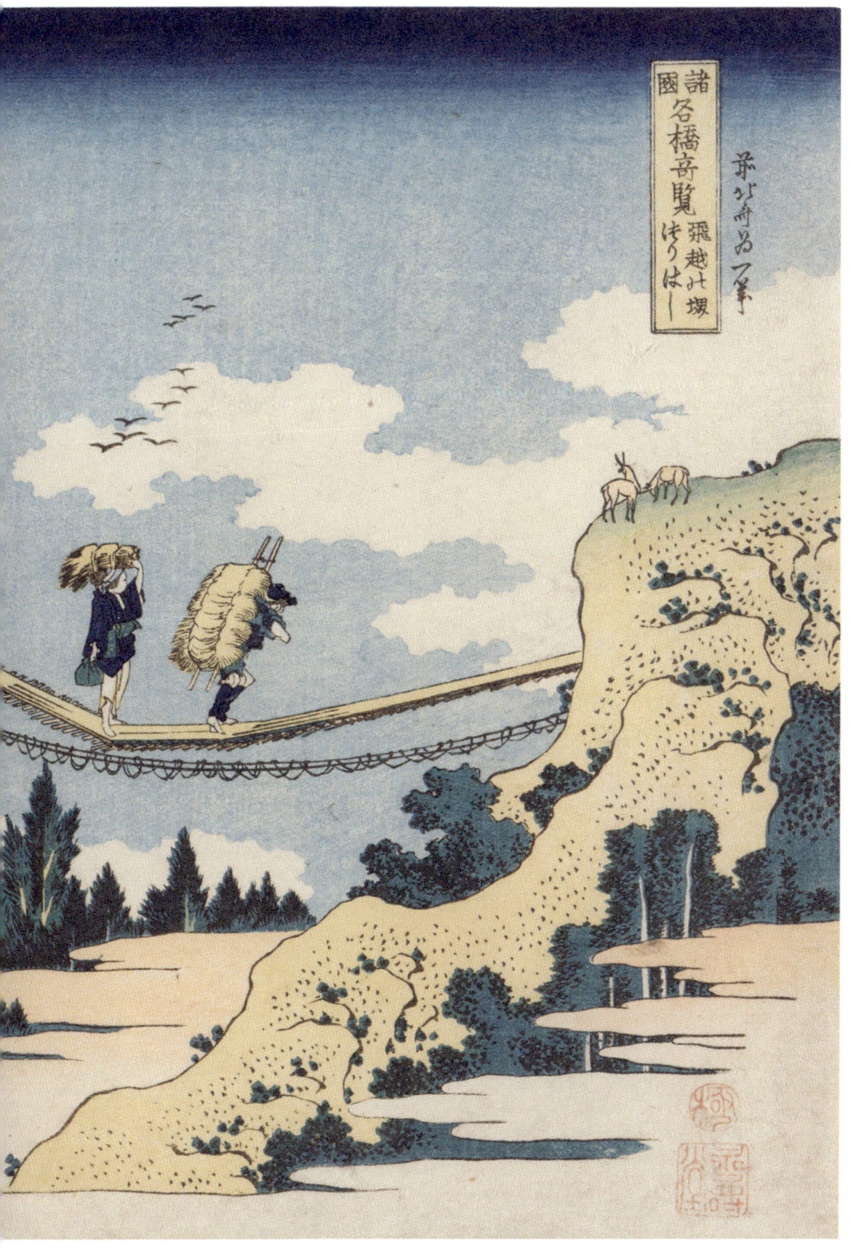

諸國名橋奇覧　飛越の堺つりはし
前北斎為一筆

Bullfinch and Weeping Cherry from the series *Small flowers*

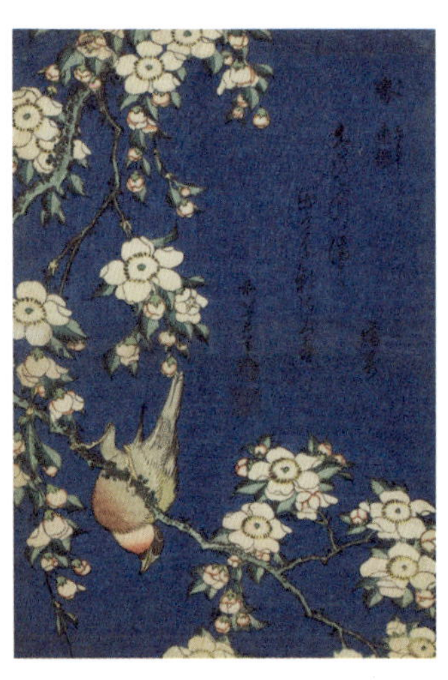

Woodblock print,   c. 1834
ink and colour
on paper
25.4 cm × 19.1 cm
(10 in × 7½ in)

After the so-called *Large flowers* series, the same
publisher, Nishimuraya Yohachi, issued another ten
'pictures of birds and flowers'. These are in a vertical
chūban (medium) format and are therefore known as
the *Small flowers*. Viewing *Poppies* (page 132), from the
Large series, alongside the present work reveals their
distinct styles.

The inscribed verse in *Bullfinch and Weeping Cherry*
tells us that the bird has landed on the branch when the
cherry tree is damp with morning dew. Our view here
is up towards the tree. Here the pale pink blossoms,
buds tinged a deep rose, and the male bullfinch, with its
pinkish-red breast and cheeks, all stand out against the
Prussian blue background.

Compared to *Poppies*, there is an opulence about this
print, almost as though it's enamelled. Aside from
the rich colouring, this effect is also achieved by the
generally thin and precise lines with which Hokusai
delineates forms. Look, for instance, at the outlines of
the blossoms and buds in this print alongside the raggedy
ones that render the poppies. This is not to say that one
is better than the other! In both prints, Hokusai's brush
celebrates nature's wonders.

Bullfinch and Weeping Cherry
from the series Small flowers

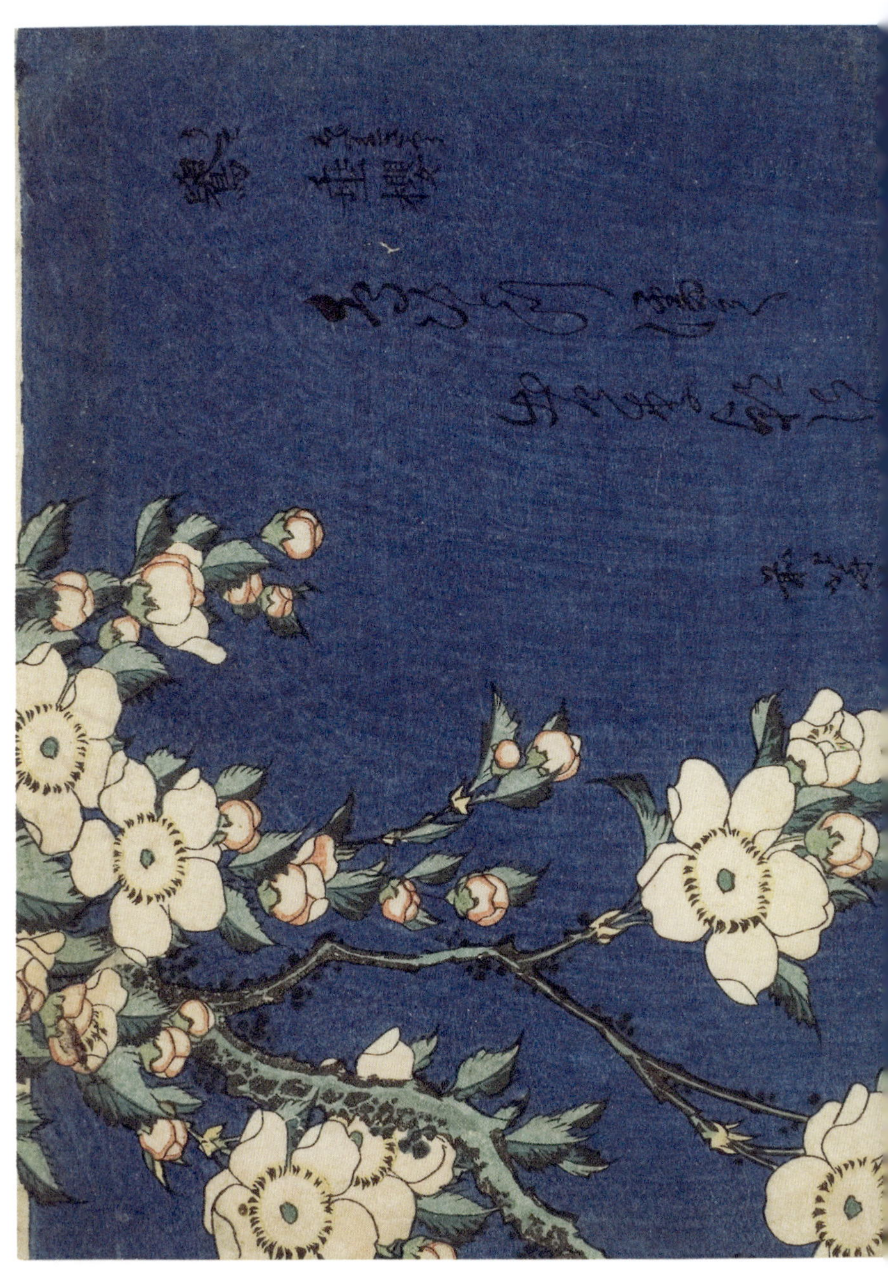

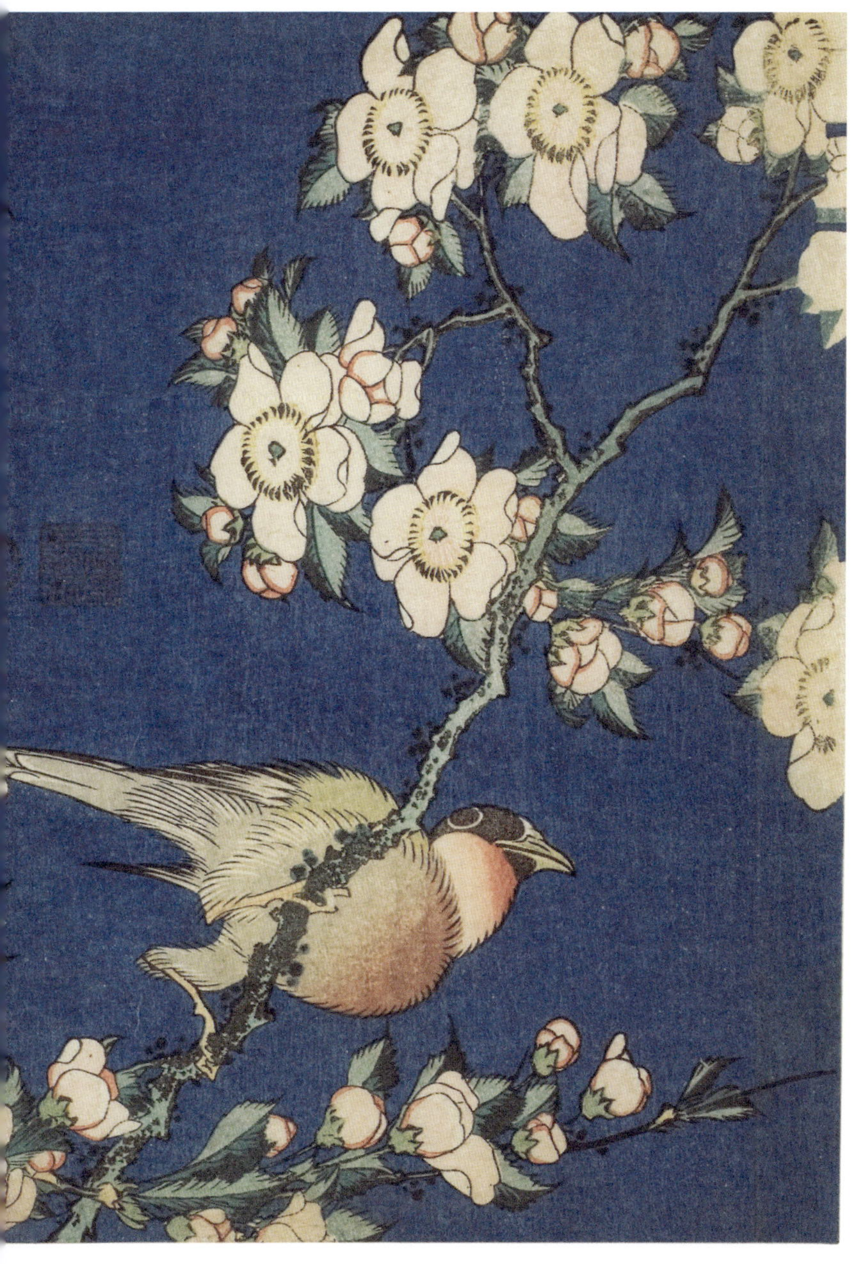

c. 1834

Fuji at Sea from the book *One hundred views of Mount Fuji*

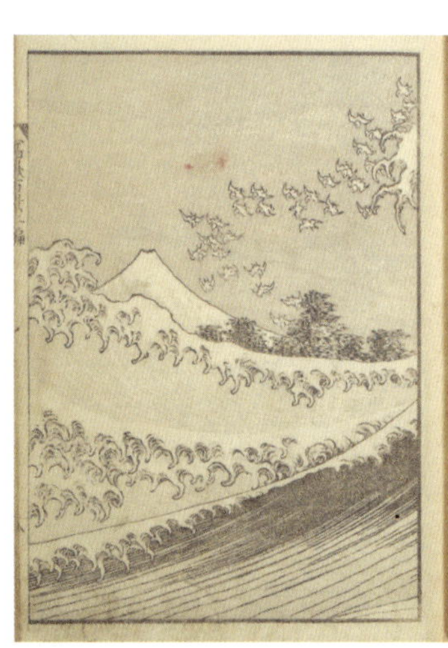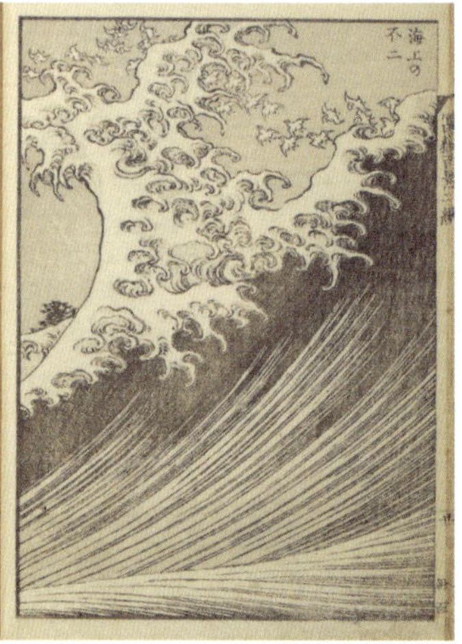

Woodblock print,
ink on paper
22 cm × 26 cm
(8⅝ in× 10¼ in)

1834-1835 &
c. 1849

While the *Thirty-six views of Mount Fuji* series is more well known, Hokusai's subsequent three-volume work depicting 102 views of the mountain is one of the greatest of all illustrated books. It's often considered to be Hokusai's masterpiece.

Hokusai was in his seventies when the first two volumes were published in 1834 and 1835. The Tenpō famine and economic crisis of the mid-1830s meant that the third volume was not issued until around 1849. Volume I's publication appears to have marked a new stage for Hokusai, for he then began to regularly use the new names Gaykō Rōjin, meaning 'Old man crazy to paint', and Manji, or 'Ten thousand', signifying longevity. Indeed, the belief that Mount Fuji is a source of immortality was undoubtably a key to Hokusai's fascination with the mountain.

In this double-page image, Hokusai reverses the position of the wave in his iconic *Under the Wave off Kanagawa* (page 100). Also in contrast to the earlier work, there is no evidence of human interaction in the natural world. Instead, in a startlingly delightful act of artistic bravura – and it takes a moment to notice this – the waves seem to have conjured a flock of darting plovers.

Fuji at Sea from the book
One hundred views of Mount Fuji

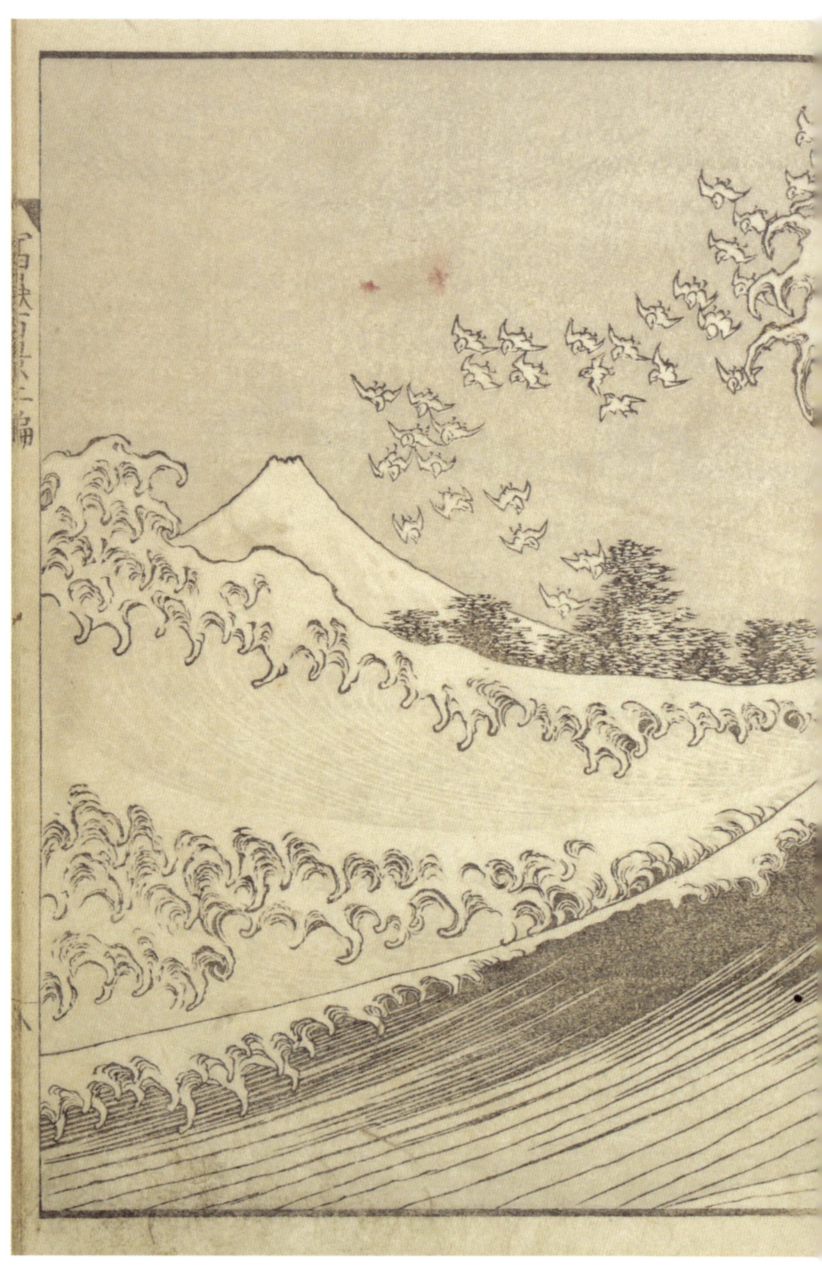

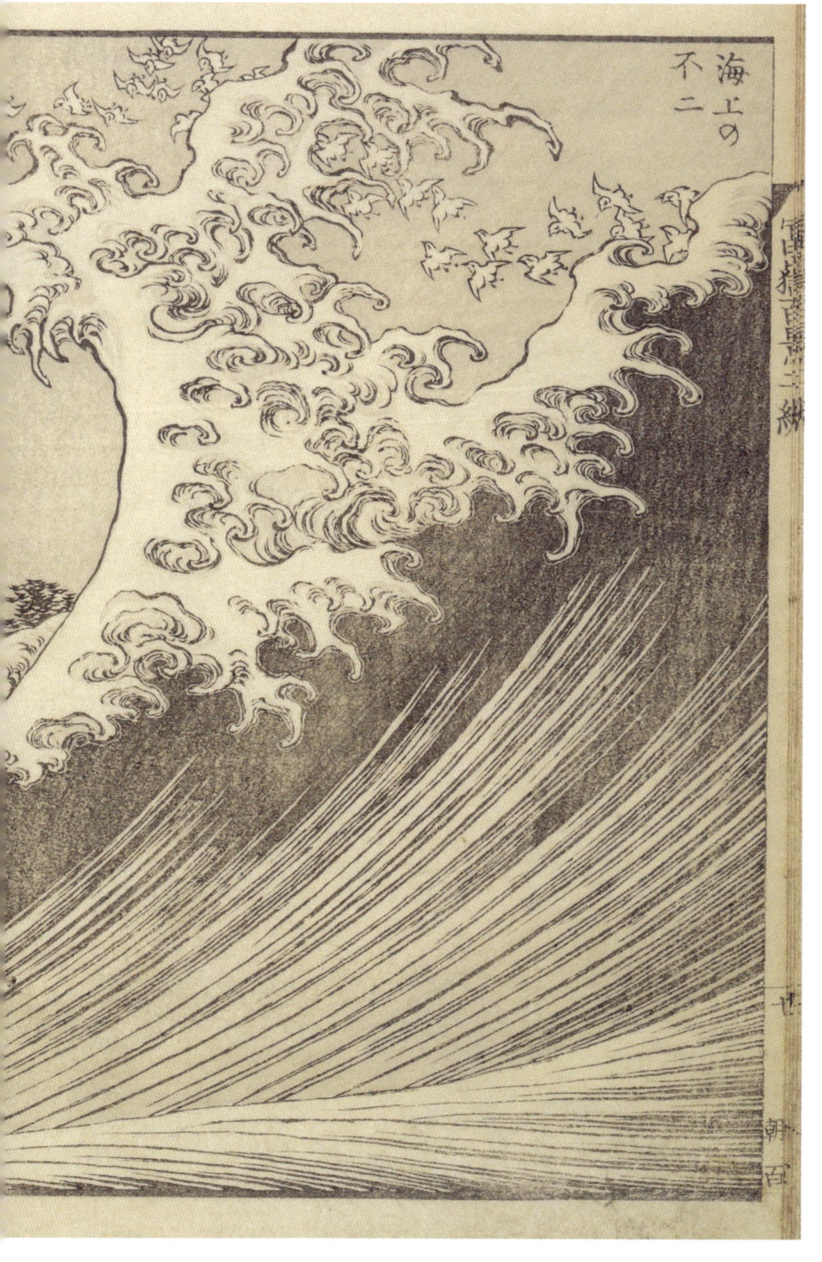
海上の
不二

*The Appearance
of Mount Fuji in the
Fifth Year of Kōrei*
from the book
*One hundred views
of Mount Fuji*

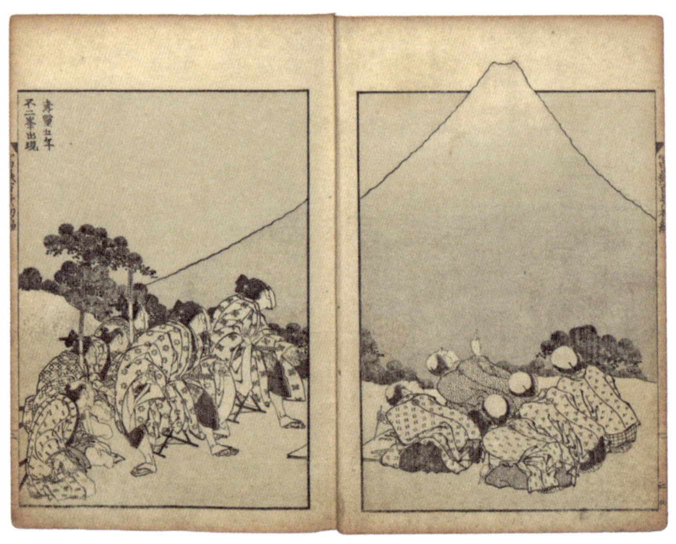

Woodblock print,   1834-1835 &
ink on paper   c. 1849
18.4 cm × 26 cm
(7¼ in × 10¼ in)

After a picture of the goddess of the mountain, this is
the second illustration to appear in *One hundred views of
Mount Fuji*. It represents the mythical moment when the
volcano was said to have appeared; such is Fuji's power,
it ruptures the page's top frame.

It was in the colophon of this book that Hokusai wrote his
now famous artistic statement. He begins by describing
how he had a 'mania' for drawing from the age of six.
Yet, while Hokusai says his works were published from
around the age of fifty, his perfectionism leads him to
dismiss those he made before he was seventy. It was only
at seventy-three that he felt he was able to 'partly fathom
the true quality of birds, animals, insects, and fish, and
the vital nature of grasses and trees'.

Looking forward, Hokusai hopes that by age eighty he
will have made further progress; by ninety he will see
things even more clearly; at one hundred his art will have
become 'truly wonderful'; and at age one hundred and
ten, 'each dot and each stroke will have a life of its own'.

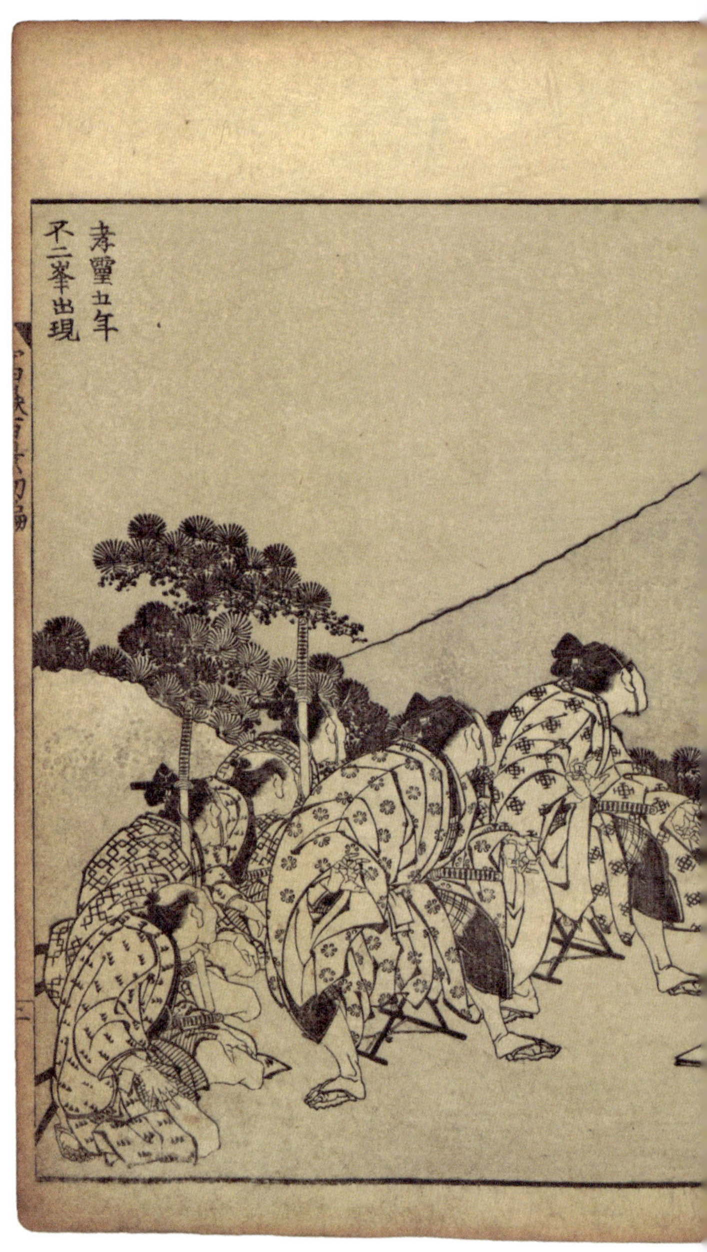

孝靈五年
不二峯出現

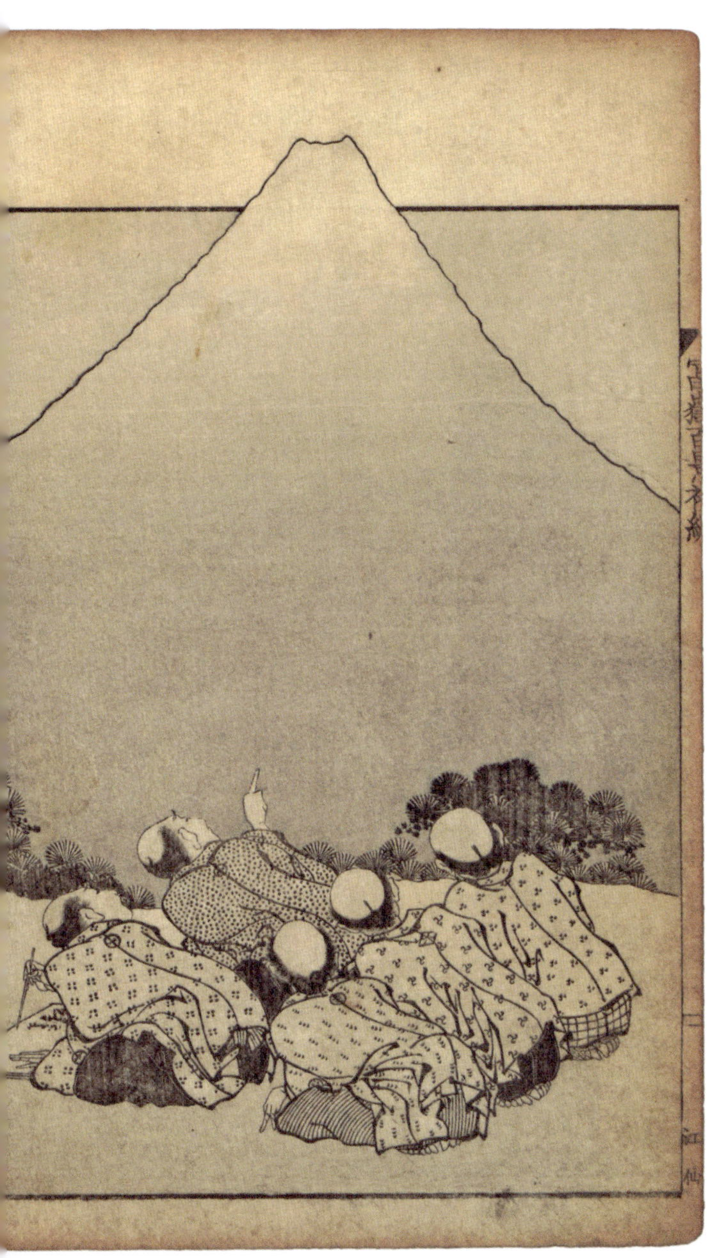

Self-Portrait as a Fisherman

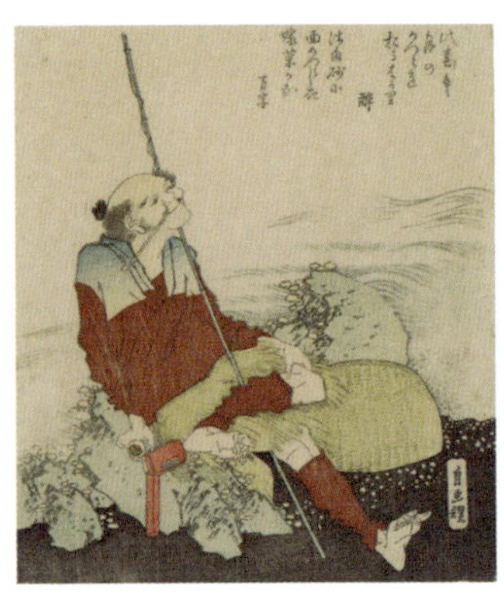

Woodblock print,
ink and colour on
paper with metallic
pigments
21.3 cm × 18.5 cm
(8⅜ in × 7¼ in)

So much of Hokusai's biography is shrouded in mystery, and yet throughout this book we gain glimmers of his life and insights into his personality. It therefore seems appropriate that this characterful study of a fisherman may, or may not, be a self-portrait.

Hokusai seems to have enjoyed being considered eccentric; he is famed for having lived in ninety-three residences, apparently because he would rather move than clean the house. With his down-to-earth sense of humour, we can imagine him being amused by this puzzle he's created. Certainly, this picture of a man content in nature seems to reflect Hokusai's personality well.

Further credence for the self-portrait hypothesis is given by the verses at the top of the *surimono* print. These are signed Manji, Hokusai's new art name (see *Fuji at Sea* on page 172), and Ei, shortened from Eijo, one of Hokusai's daughters. Known professionally as Katsushika Ōi (c. 1800–after 1857), Eijo was also an accomplished artist. After her mother (Hokusai's second wife) died, and her marriage ended in divorce, Eijo lived with and took care of her father for the last two decades of his life.

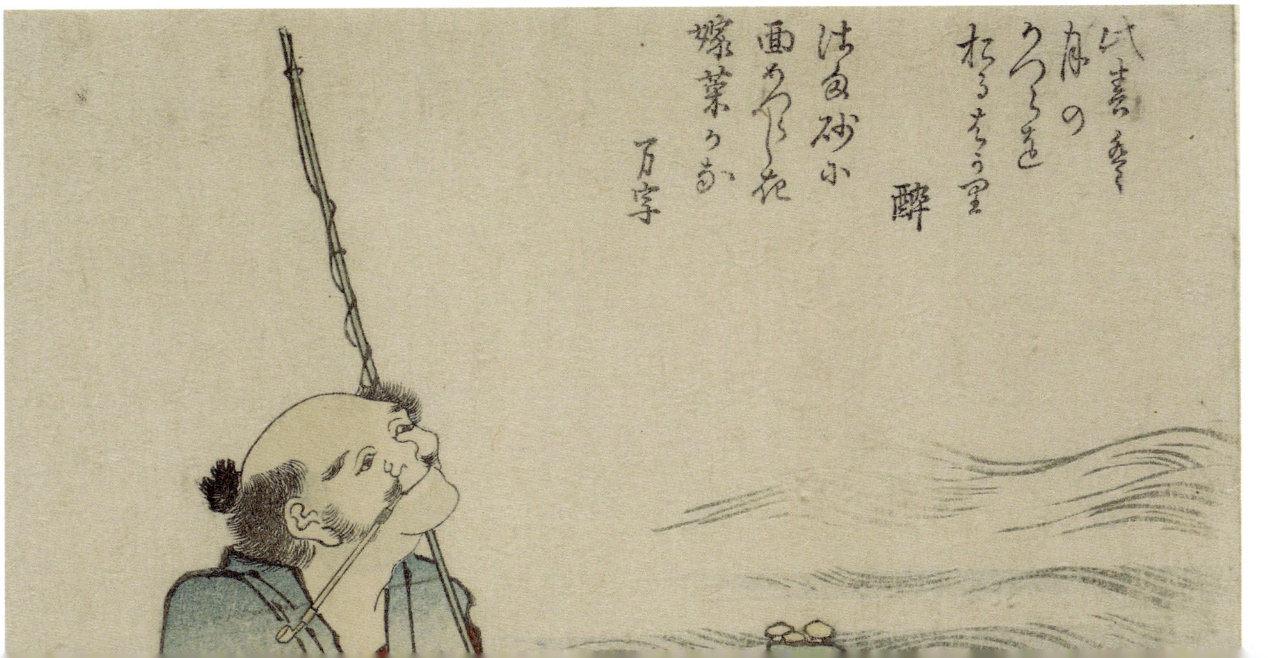
醉
万字

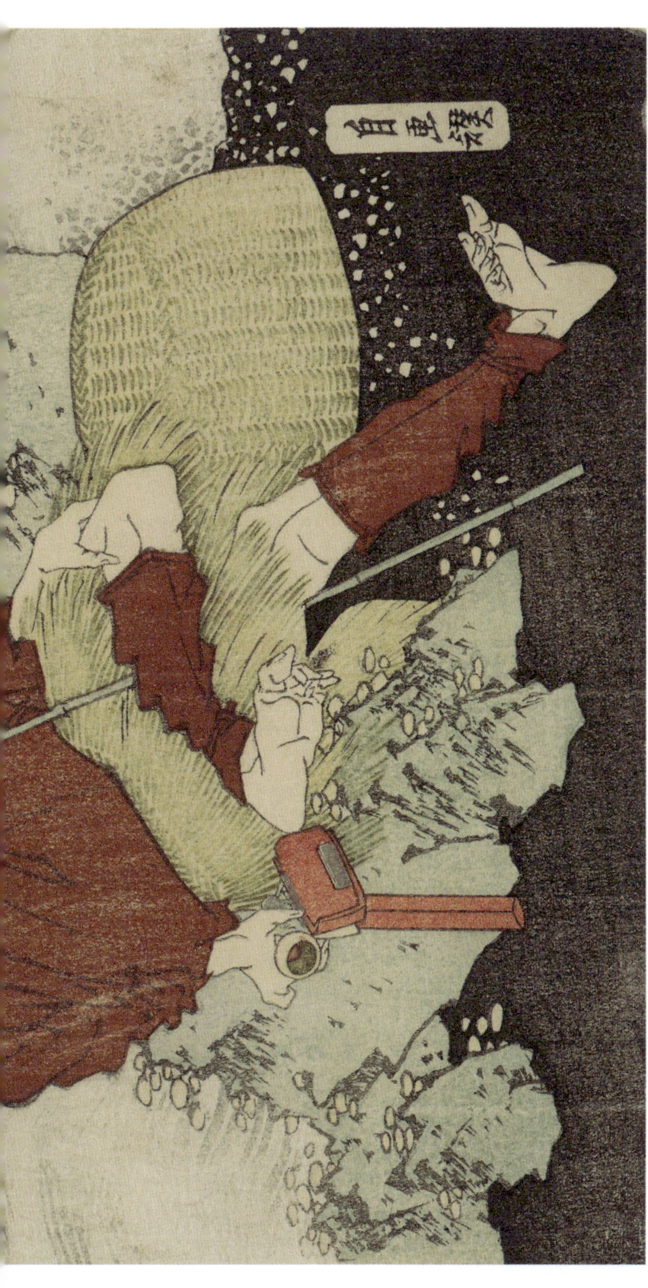

Poem by Minamoto no Muneyuki Ason
from the series *One hundred poems by one hundred poets, explained by the nurse*

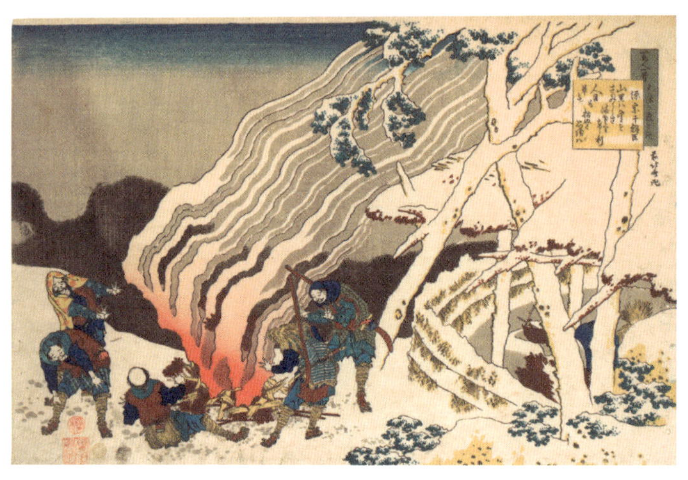

184

Woodblock print,   c. 1835-1836
ink and colour
on paper
25.1 cm × 36.8 cm
(9⅞ in × 14½ in)

This work is from the last colour print series Hokusai made. It's based on a popular anthology of classical poetry compiled around 1235 by the poet Fujiwara no Teika (1162–1241). Only twenty-seven of the designs were published, but more than sixty of Hokusai's woodblock-ready drawings have survived. The poem to which each image refers is included in the square cartouche in the top right. But the 'explanations' by 'the nurse' – that is, Hokusai – don't necessarily illustrate the poems directly; they are, instead, imaginative, and often allusive, responses by the artist.

This print's corresponding verse by Minamoto no Muneyuki Ason (d. 939) describes the loneliness of winter and its withering effect on people and plants. And yet the animated gestures of the hunters render this scene ebullient. Indeed, the contrast between the red fire, with its stylistic smoke patterns, and the snow-covered landscape makes this view one of the series' most striking. But perhaps it's in that contrast that the poem's melancholy is visualised, for the viewer is reminded that the hunters' cheerful presence is only fleeting.

Poem by Minamoto no Muneyuki Ason
from the series One hundred poems by
one hundred poets, explained by the nurse

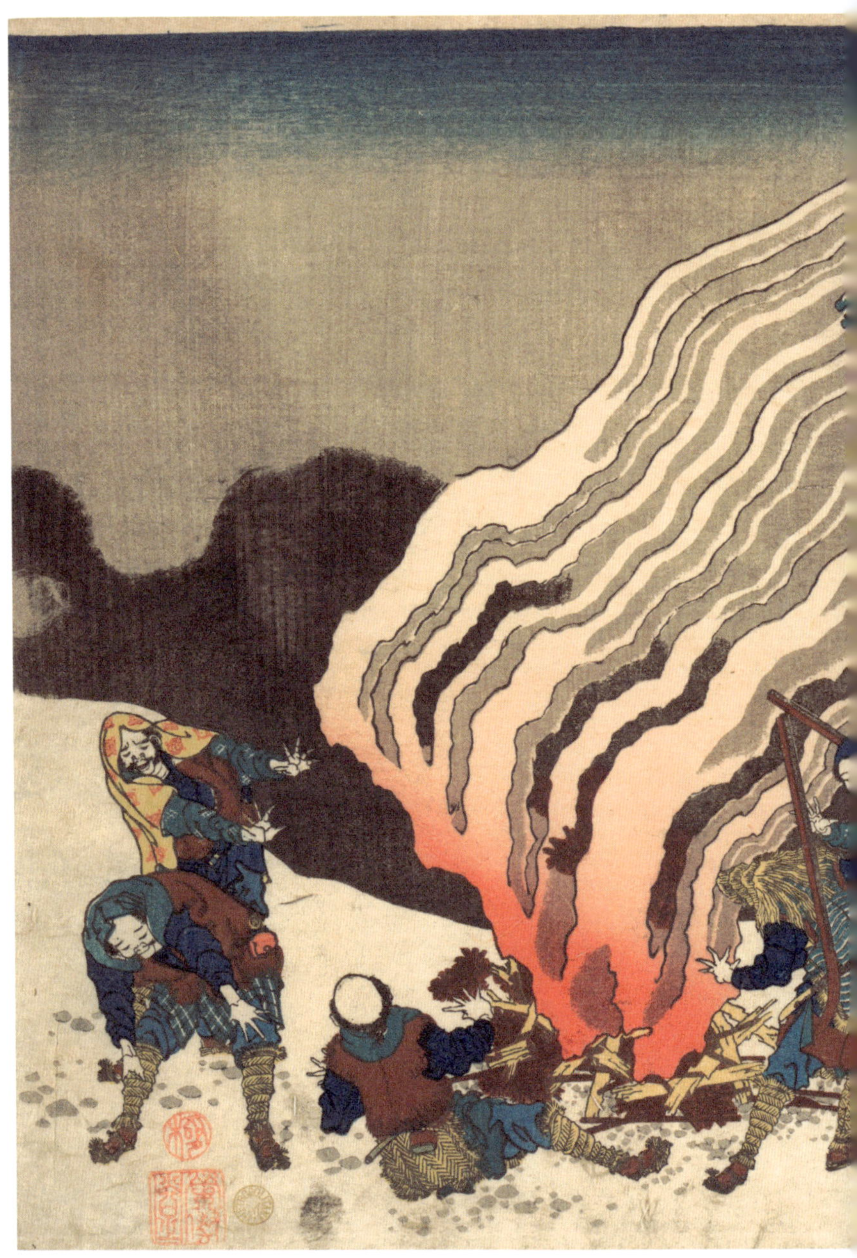

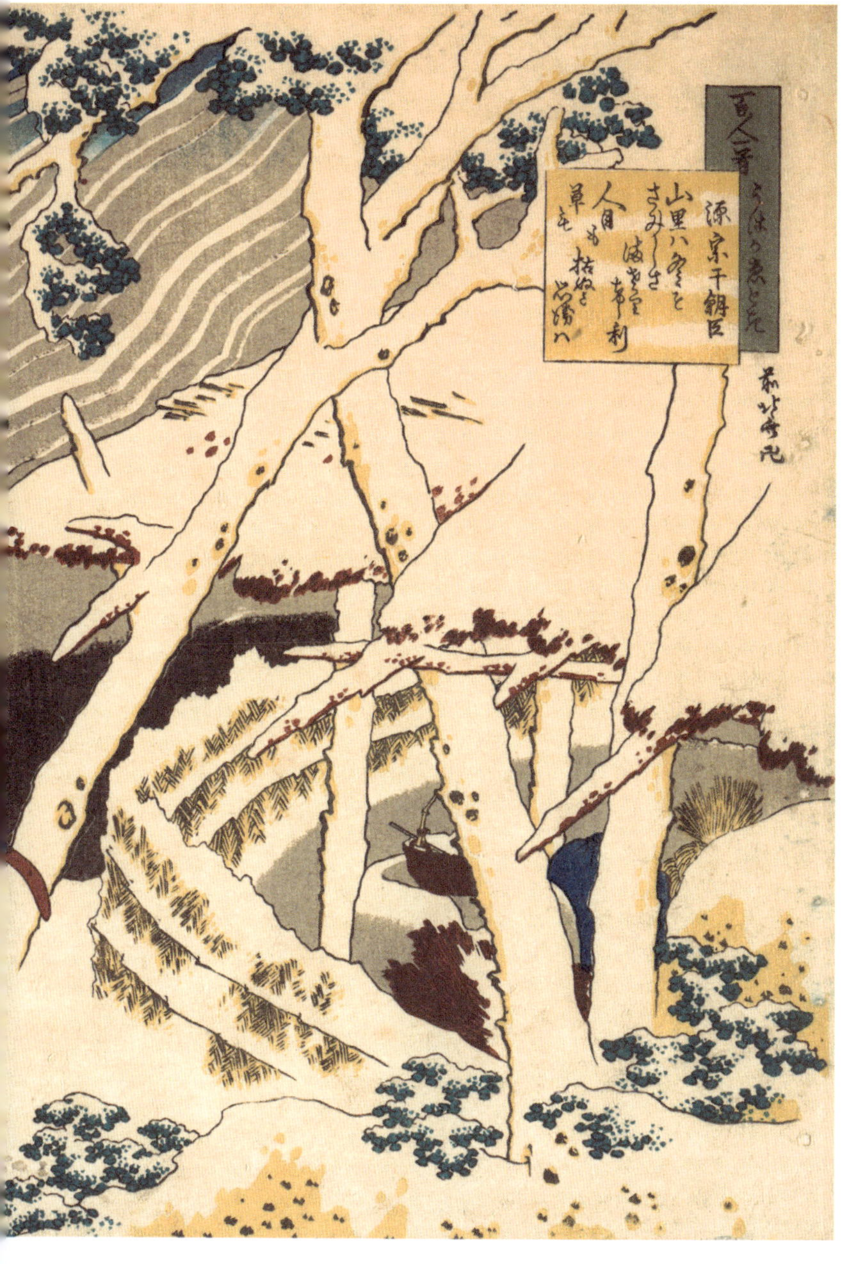
百人一首
うはのゑとき
源宗于朝臣
山里八冬そ
さみしさ
まさりける
人目も
草も
かれぬと思へハ
為北齊畫

Illustration from the book
The stirrups of Musashi

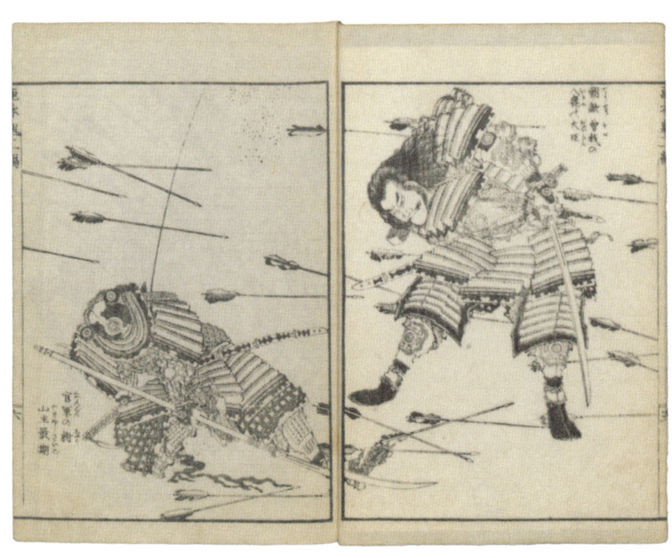

188

Woodblock print,
ink and colour
on paper
22.5 cm × 15.6 cm
(8⅞ in × 6⅛ in)

1836

In late 1834 Hokusai went into self-imposed exile. His retreat to Uraga, a coastal village around fifty kilometres (thirty miles) south of Edo, may have been to avoid his troublesome grandson or creditors – and the two were not unconnected – but the reason is not entirely clear. He of course continued to work, and it was in Uraga that he began his celebrated trilogy of 'warrior books'. Ever exacting, Hokusai wrote a joint letter to three Edo publishers in 1835 requesting the master woodblock-cutter Egawa Tomekichi be hired; Hokusai had been dissatisfied with other carvers.

The stirrups of Musashi, which derives its title from a place renowned for making horse stirrups, was the second volume published. With its sense of drama, formal complexity and intricate detailing, this double-page illustration is representative of the book's designs as a whole. Not only were the tales of the samurai thrilling to the general public, but, as Hokusai makes clear in the preface to the first volume, the designs were to be of use to artists. Here Hokusai has 'illustrated the correct movements of the human body, even under armour'. And to show that clearly, he needed a master carver.

Illustration from the book
The stirrups of Musashi

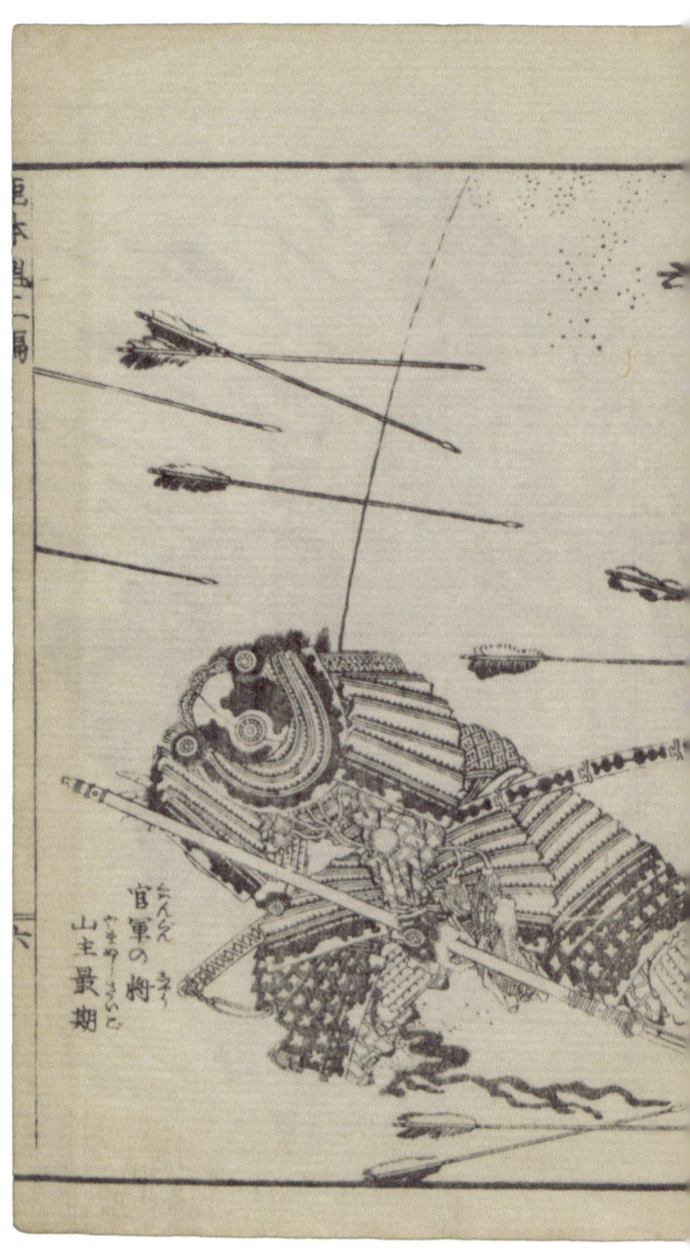

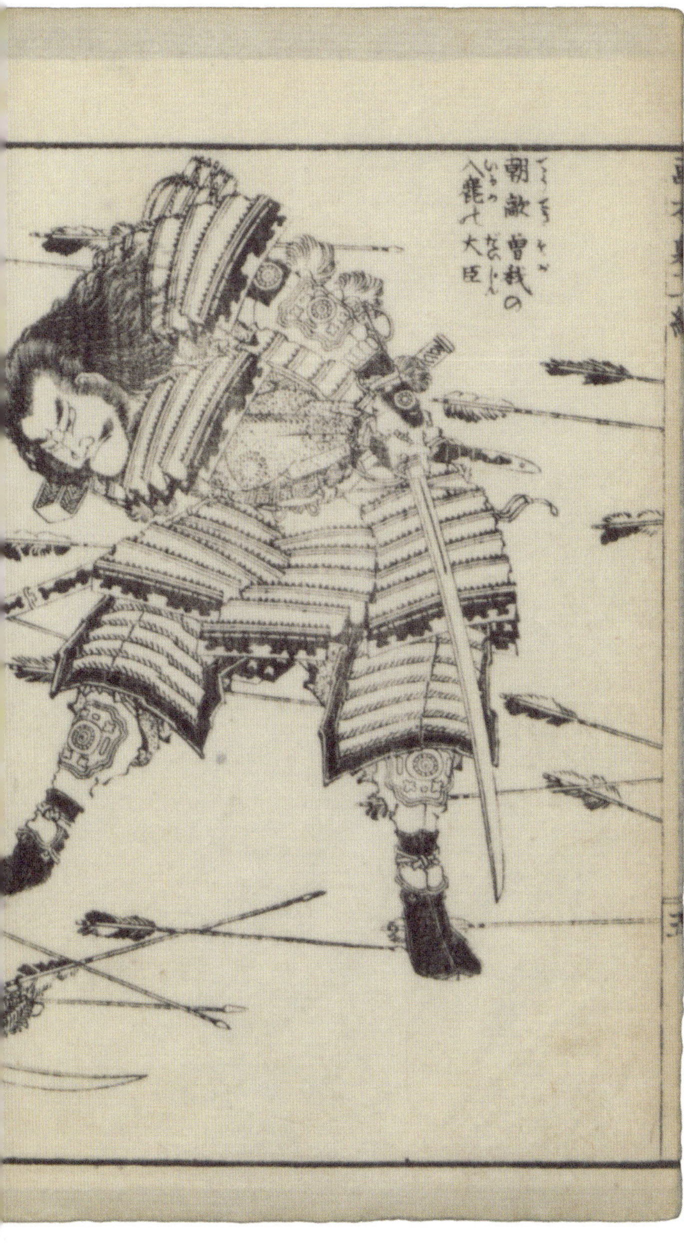

朝敵　曾我の
入道　大臣

Red Shōki,
Demon Queller

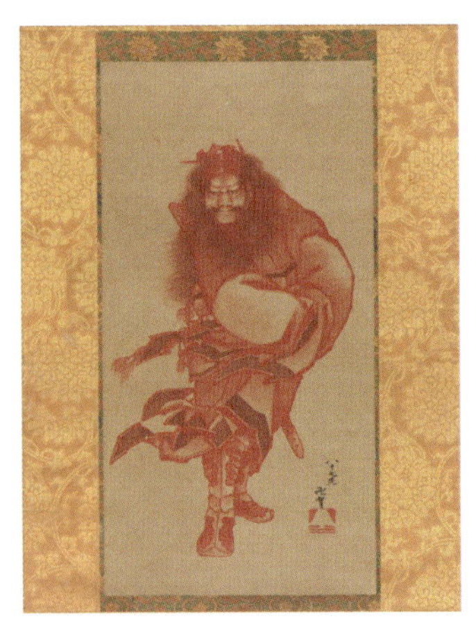

192

Hanging scroll, ink
and colour on silk
59.1 cm × 30.2 cm
(23¼ in × 11⅞ in)

After his voluntary exile from Edo (see Illustration from the book *The stirrups of Musashi* on page 188), Hokusai returned to the city in 1836. The Tenpō famine (1833–1837) was ongoing, and Hokusai and his daughter Ōi suffered a personal disaster in 1839 when their home was destroyed in a fire. Economic conditions meant that publishers frequently struggled at this time, and Hokusai was naturally impacted by this downturn. Over the next decade, as things improved, Hokusai continued to work on illustrated books, but he also began to devote more time to painting.

Hokusai's belief in Nichiren Buddhism was often reflected in his art, but he also drew upon less benevolent spirits (see *Kohada Koheiji* on page 128), as well as other protective talismans. He painted Shōki, the demon-quelling spirit of a seventh-century Chinese scholar, several times in his career. When painted in red, Shōki was said to guard against smallpox, of which there was an outbreak in Edo in 1846.

This powerfully expressive portrayal corresponds with Shōki's protective capabilities. His hair and beard, which surround his kindly but focused face, recall a lion's mane, while his bulky robes seem windswept, as though he has just arrived upon being summoned for help.

Red Shōki, Demon Queller

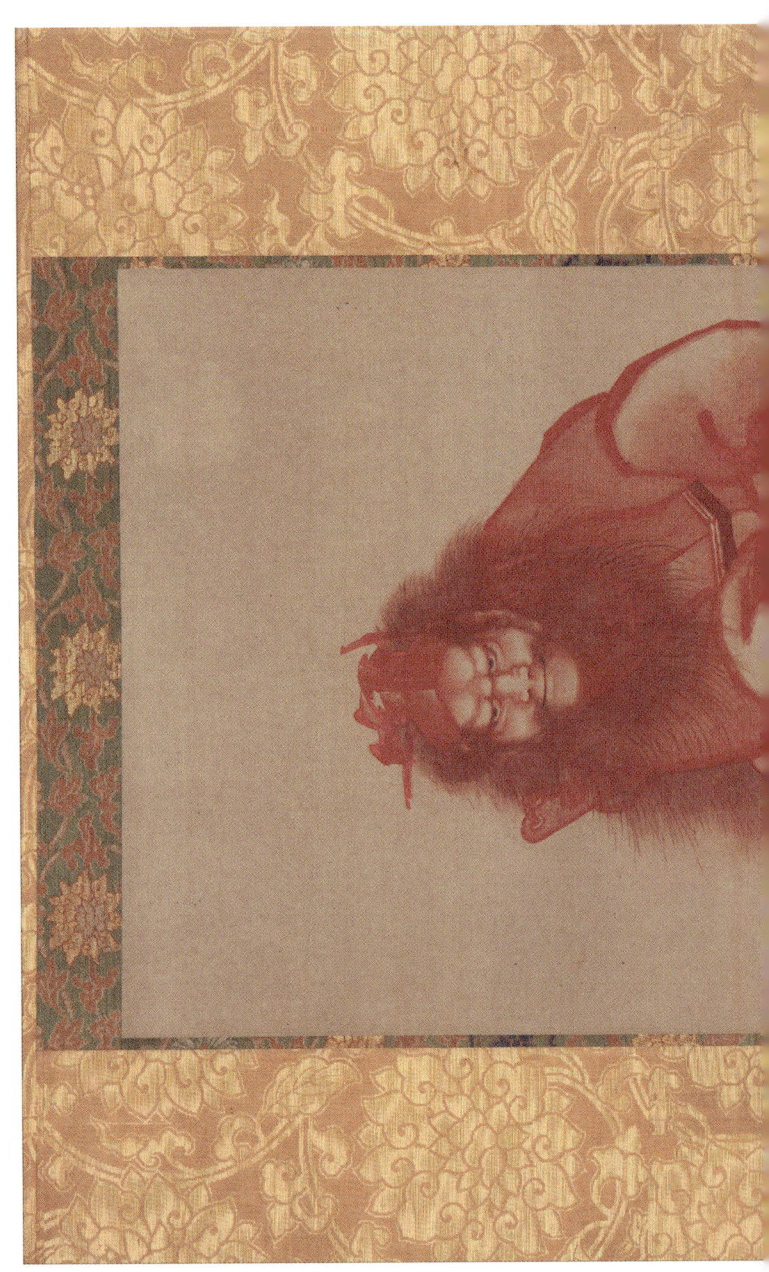

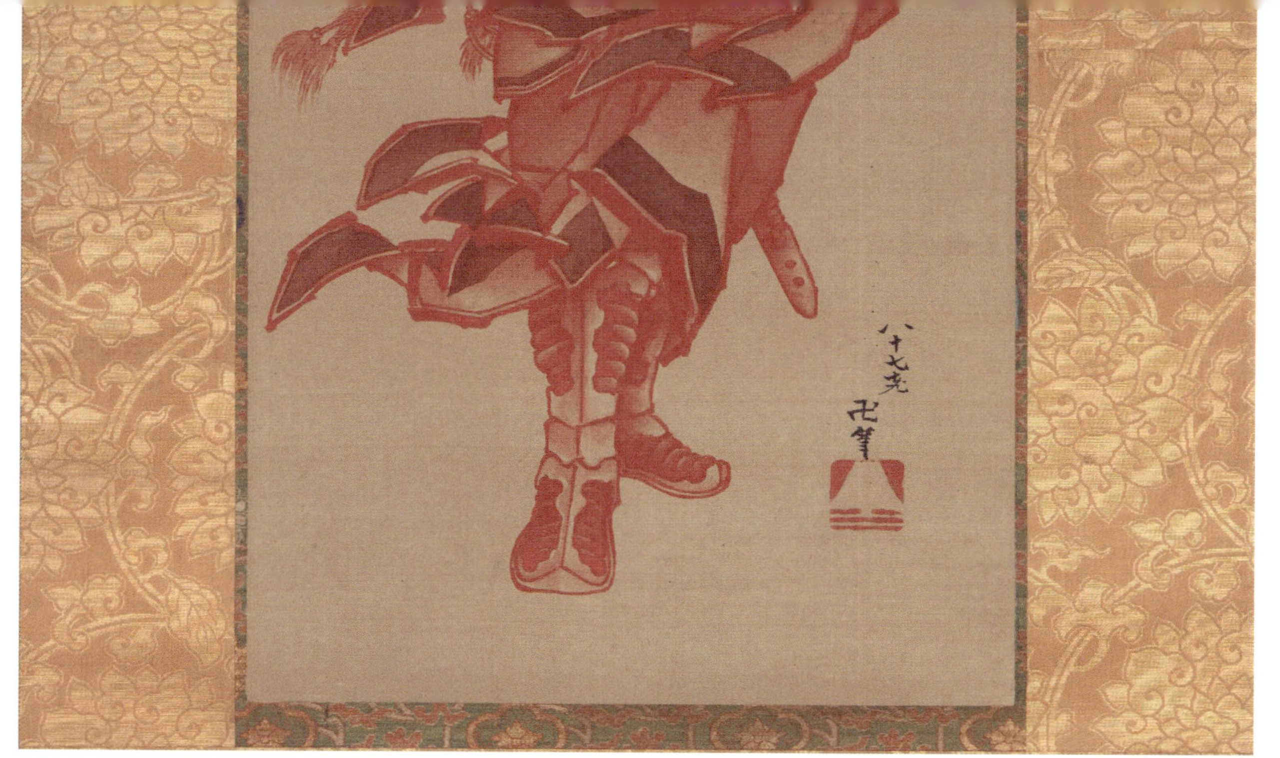
八十七老
卍筆

Li Bai Admiring a Waterfall

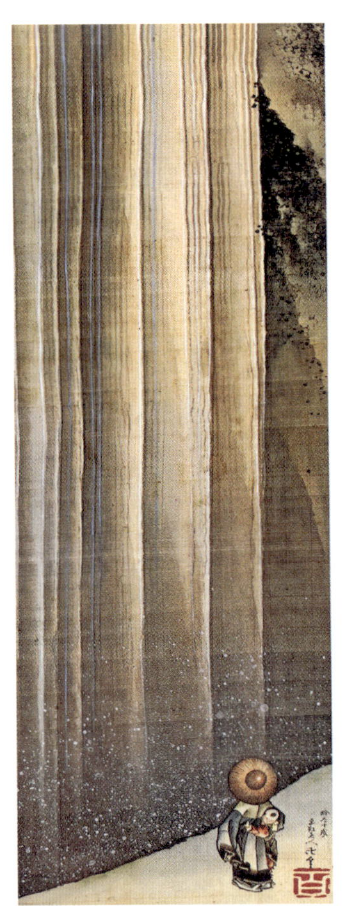

One of the prints from Hokusai's earlier series *A true mirror of Chinese and Japanese poetry* (c. 1833–1834) depicts the great Tang Dynasty poet Li Bai (701–762) contemplating a waterfall on Mount Lu. Li Bai's experience at the waterfall led to one of his most celebrated poems, in which he marvels at this wonder that seems to have descended from the heavens. Hokusai returned to the subject in the last months of his life when he created this remarkable hanging scroll painting.

Supported by a young helper, Li Bai gazes at the waterfall, its immensity made even greater by its contrast with the small figures. Hokusai's depiction of the falling water, painted in earth tones along with grey, blue and white, is visionary in its formal abstraction. Paint splatters capture the fall's spray at its base.

Throughout his work, Hokusai reveals a profound sensitivity to nature, and a keen interest in humanity's ties to the natural world. For Hokusai to have felt an affinity with Li Bai is not surprising, particularly as they were both considered rather eccentric characters. They each had a playful outlook on life that did not diminish its splendours, as Hokusai encapsulates perfectly in this late masterpiece.

*'At seventy-five I will have
learned something of the pattern
of nature, of animals, of plants,
of trees, birds, fish and insects.'*

\- Katsushika Hokusai

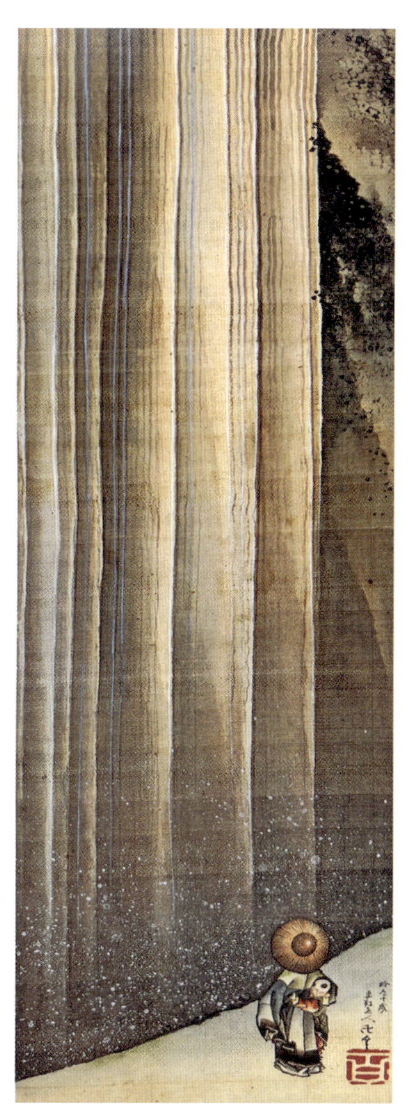

Tiger in the Snow

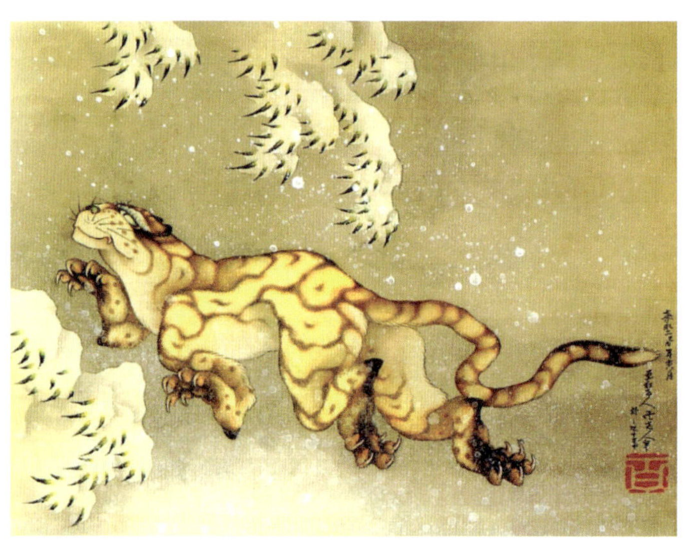

This painting is signed 'Month of the Tiger, Year of the Cock, old Manji, old man crazy to paint, aged ninety years'. Completed in the first lunar month of 1849, it was one of Hokusai's last paintings.

Hokusai was born in the Year of the Dragon, and having reached his ninetieth year (in traditional age reckoning), he was clearly conscious of death but remained defiant. It is said that on his deathbed he asked the heavens for ten more years and then, after reconsidering, for just five more, stating, 'then I could become a great artist'.

Tigers and dragons have long been paired in East Asian art as yin and yang, earth and heaven, and Hokusai also created meaningful paintings of dragons at this time. But in this work he focuses on the tiger and its tie to the earthly world. Though old – like Hokusai – the tiger leaps with joy through a snowy landscape. The striped pattern of his coat mirrors the forms of the snow-covered bamboo, just as his claws echo the pointed leaves. Splatters of flicked white paint convey the snow that still falls.

Hokusai, a consummate artist and spirited soul until the end, died on 10 May 1849.

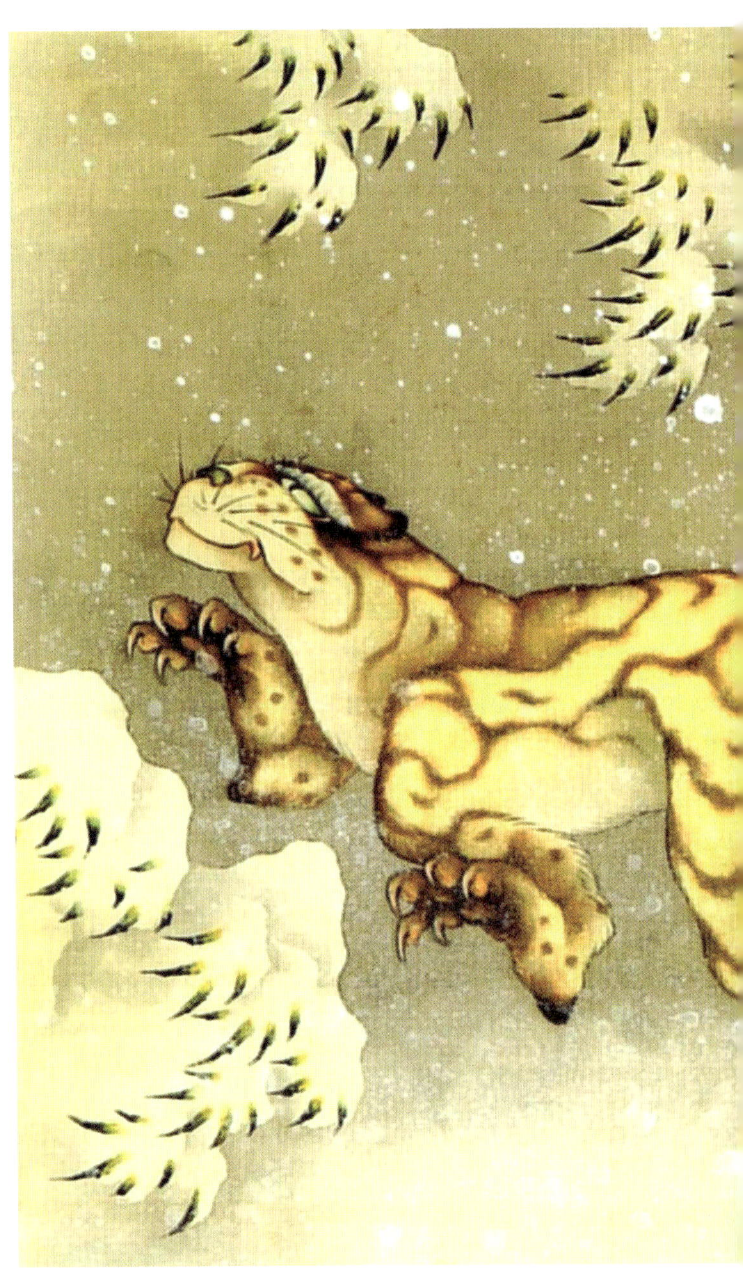

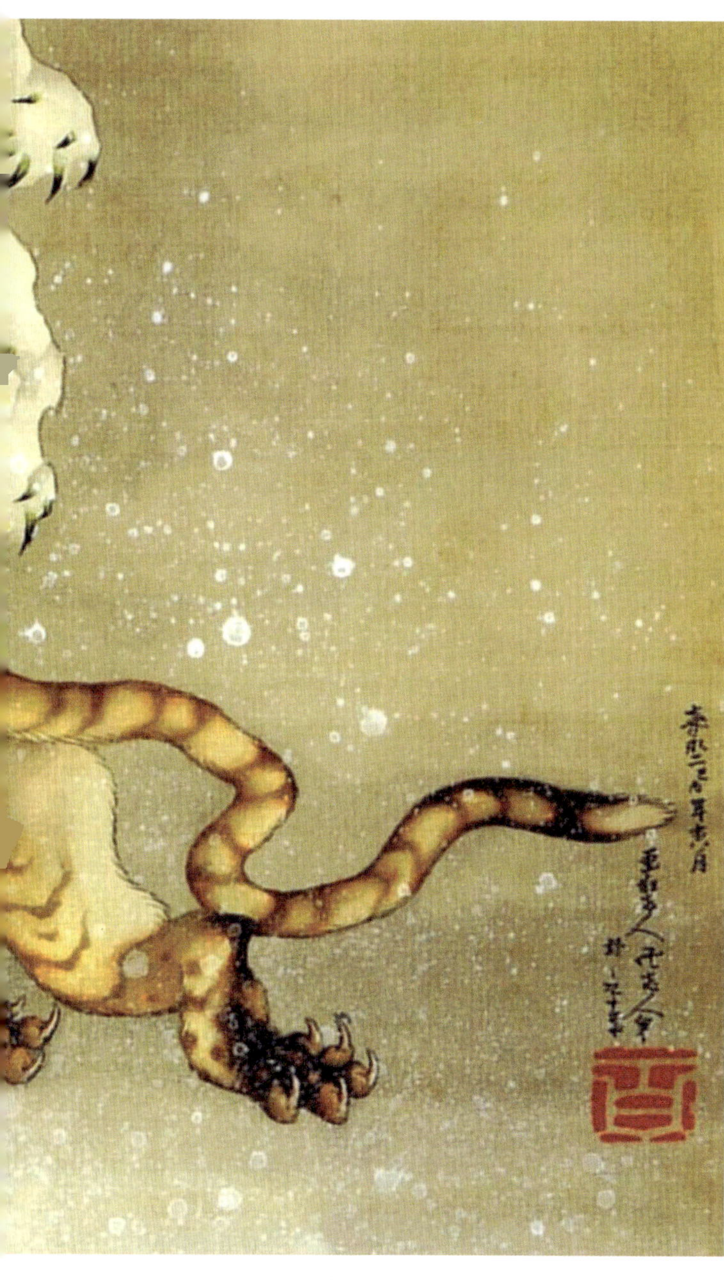

Sally Grant is an art historian, curator, and critic with a passion for the intersection of art, culture, and travel. She holds a PhD in Art History and Italian Studies from the University of Sydney, and her writing has appeared in *Artforum*, *Australian Book Review*, *Ms. Magazine*, *Hamptons Art Hub*, *Gourmet Traveller*, *BBC Culture* and *Guggenheim Articles*, among other publications. She has also contributed catalogue entries for Christie's Post-War and Contemporary Art Department in New York.

Sally's scholarly research focuses on early-modern Europe, with a particular emphasis on Venice and the Veneto. She has been a Summer Fellow at Harvard University's Dumbarton Oaks, an Honorary Research Associate of the Australasian Centre for Italian Studies, and her work has been recognised with awards and research funding, including from the Gladys Krieble Delmas Foundation.

Originally from north-east Scotland, Sally's lifelong wanderlust began at age eighteen when she travelled to Venice to work as a nanny. She has since lived and worked in Greece, Germany, Hong Kong (China), and Australia, where she earned her degrees, before eventually settling in New York with her husband.

Index of works

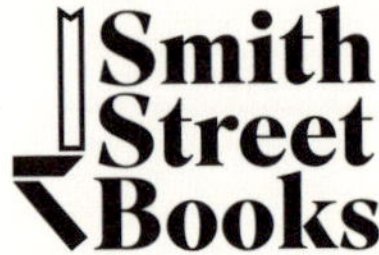

Published in 2026 by Smith Street Books
Naarm (Melbourne) | Australia
smithstreetbooks.com

Distributed outside of ANZ, North & Latin America by
Thames & Hudson Ltd., 6–24 Britannia Street, London, WC1X 9JD
thamesandhudson.com

EU Authorised Representative: Interart S.A.R.L.
19 rue Charles Auray, 93500 Pantin, Paris, France
productsafety@thameshudson.co.uk; www.interart.fr

ISBN: 978-1-9232-3974-6

Smith Street Books respectfully acknowledges the Wurundjeri People of
the Kulin Nation, who are the Traditional Owners of the land on which we
work, and we pay our respects to their Elders past and present.

Publisher: Hannah Koelmeyer
Project editor: Elena Callcott
Design concept: A Friend of Mine
Design layout: Nikola Roberts
Proofreader: Ana Jacobsen
Production manager: Aisling Coughlan

Printed & bound in China by C&C Offset Printing Co., Ltd.

Book 432
10 9 8 7 6 5 4 3 2 1

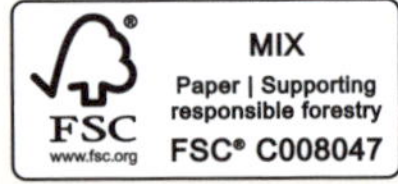

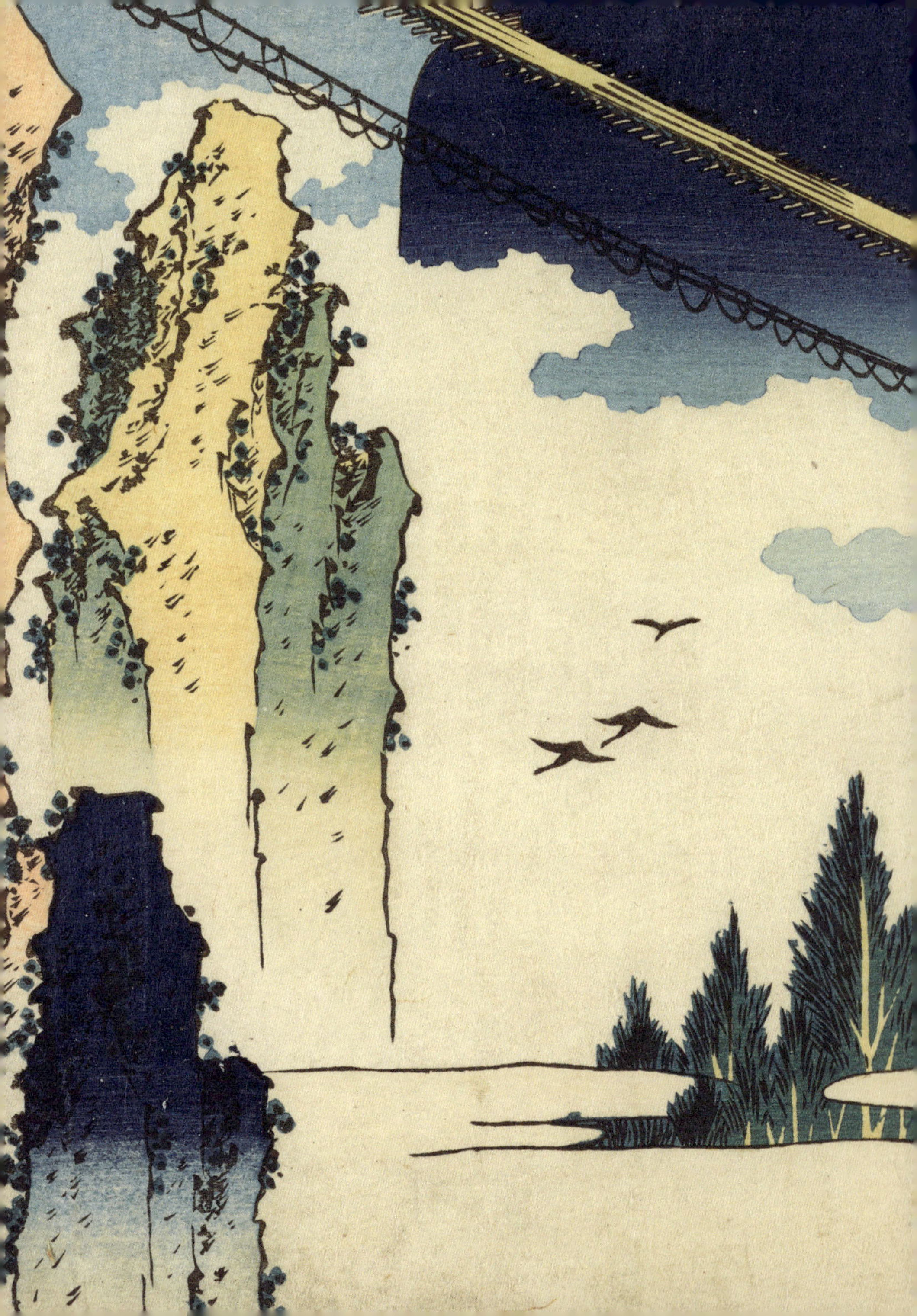